# The Stillness

## of the

# Living Forest

# The Stillness
# of the
# Living Forest

## A Year of Listening and Learning

*by*

John Harvey

Shanti Arts Publishing
Brunswick, Maine

The Stillness of the Living Forest
A Year of Listening and Learning

Published by Shanti Arts Publishing
Cover and interior design by Shanti Arts Designs
Shanti Arts LLC
Brunswick, Maine
www.shantiarts.com

Map of Prompton Lake by David Hamill
and used with his permission.
Cover image by MarinaMariya/istockphoto.com/469276176
Interior images by John Harvey.

Printed in the United States of America

ISBN: 978-1-947067-59-2 (softcovert)
ISBN: 978-1-947067-60-8 (digital)

LCCN: 2018959860

*For my wife Dawn,*
*my children Nada, Jacob, Adam, and Sarah,*
*and my grandchildren Olivia and Lovis*

# Contents

## Autumn

## Winter . . . again

# Acknowledgements

The greatest gratitude goes to nature for tolerating my presence and showing and teaching me so much during every hour I spent in the woods through the full year of my Prompton project.

I am also grateful for Jon Young's ideas expressed so simply, clearly, and elegantly in his remarkable book, *What the Robin Knows*. It was his idea of the "sit spot" method of connecting with nature that led to my many rich experiences.

On any journey friends are essential. Dave Gorman helped with brainstorming the original yearlong plan. Jerry Swendsen provided logistical and moral support throughout the process. Mike Reid, an avid outdoorsman, loyally read each chapter, provided constructive feedback, and gave encouragement. Chris Fischer, an expert birder, generously offered much needed birding information. Thanks also to the many friends who offered words of advice and encouragement.

A writer without an editor is like a missile without a guidance system. I was fortunate enough to have two outstanding editors to provide guidance. Mary Greene may have had the biggest job; she handled the initial edit, helping me to cut the fat, hone the message, and develop a consistent voice. Jennifer O'Reilly may have had the hardest job; her work came at the end when she helped me to focus, fine-tune, and prepare the manuscript for publication. Both of these wonderful editors understood the heart of this book and provided encouragement, yet were also frank, objective, effective, and kind with their guidance.

A book without a cover is really just another bunch of ideas. Christine Cote of Shanti Arts, the publisher, understood the heart and soul of this book. She used her vision, dedication, and many skills to provide my set of ideas with a design lovelier and more expressive than it may have deserved. In a way she took my nestling notions, gave them beautiful plumage, and showed them how to fly.

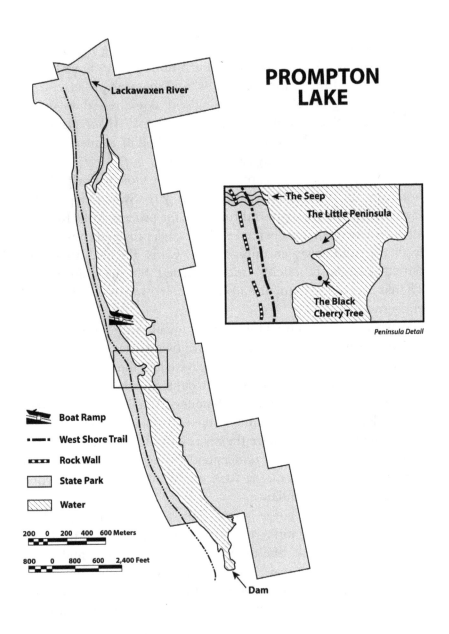

## PROMPTON LAKE

Lackawaxen River

### Peninsula Detail

The Seep

The Little Peninsula

The Black Cherry Tree

Boat Ramp

West Shore Trail

Rock Wall

State Park

Water

200  0  200  400  600 Meters

800  0  800  600  2,400 Feet

Dam

Map drawn by David Hamill

# Prologue

My journey would be through the seasons of the year, not across some long and difficult distance. The plan was straightforward. For fifty-two consecutive weeks I would go alone to the same spot in the woods, sit still, engage my senses, and observe the flow of nature through the full four seasons.

Why was I going on this journey? It seemed as if some combination of practical reasons, deep urges, and diverse motivations were converging. It felt like one of those unique times in life when needs and circumstances were bubbling and boiling together, achieving critical mass and impelling me onto this quest.

Change called out after thity-five years of work as a clinical psychologist. They had been good years, interesting and challenging years, filled with the satisfaction of understanding and helping people to take needed and important steps on their life journey. But it was also work that demanded a certain kind of rational, deductive thinking and analysis, work that occurred within a linear time structure. Now, I felt a strong need to use my mind and heart in different ways, more free flowing, process oriented, and emotionally compelling ways.

And a deep weariness, a kind of burn out, pervaded my body and mind. After years of encountering, understanding, and responding to the sufferings and setbacks of others, I needed regeneration. The subtle impressions of a sea of suffering had settled on my soul. My inner well of empathy had run dry. I needed to drink from the cool, clear, refreshing well of nature.

I also craved a different kind of learning, one based on direct experiences. I yearned to go beyond the step-by-step reasoning, conditional premises, and data-based conclusions of science. Immersion in the patterns and processes of the natural world called out to me, a world that surrounded me, that I was part of, but a world I had grown separate from.

And there was the idea of a challenge. I wanted to test myself, to find out if I could replace the enforced routine of the five-day workweek with a new schedule built on personal choices. The commitment of an hour a week in nature didn't sound like a daunting discipline, but I was to discover that it was difficult to carve out this time slot week after week through a complete year. It was a commitment that forced me to look at all the choices I was making about the days and hours of my life, a commitment that compelled me to grapple with the inner demons of doubt, inertia, and procrastination.

The motivation to spend more time outdoors and seek solace in nature had been growing during recent years. My interests had shifted more and more toward outdoor activities — hiking, kayaking, birdwatching, and gardening. As time counted down to my last day of work, I anticipated devoting more time to these activities. Then I read about a different way to experience nature, the "sit spot," described by Jon Young in *What the Robin Knows*. His idea was to go again and again to the same location, sit still for at least an hour, observe, become aware of all of the bird, animal, and plant life, listen to and understand the nuances of "bird language," and ultimately enter into to a deep connection with nature.

As I read and reread his description of the sit spot, a location for my sit spot flashed into my mind — a place on a little peninsula along the shoreline of Prompton Lake, a three-mile-long lake formed by a flood control dam on the Lackawaxen River in northeast Pennsylvania. I knew Prompton Lake well. I had kayaked on its blue-gray waters, hiked the network of trails along its wooded shores, and played disc golf on a course that overlooks the high earthen dam at the south end of the lake. I had been there often enough to notice week-to-week changes in the foliage, the seasonal cycle of the wildflowers, and the changing chorus of bird songs. I realized, at least subliminally, that every day at Prompton Lake was different, a different sky, a different wind, a different light.

The location I had in mind seemed to meet Young's guidelines by providing the desired intersection of diverse environments that attracts the greatest variety of plants and animals. The two sides of the little peninsula jut into the lake and are edged by a rocky shoreline dotted with patches of slender reeds and lily pads. Moving further on shore there is a verdant band of wildflowers, weeds, and bushes, followed by a swath of slender, moisture loving trees, and finally progressing to scattered hardwoods — tall maples, ashes, and cherries. This felt like just the right spot from where I would be able observe a full panorama of birds, plants, and animals.

Convenience was important. I could drive to Prompton Lake in ten minutes, park in the boat ramp lot, walk down a hiking trail, angle through the fern-filled forest, and arrive at the peninsula. Once situated, I could look up and down the lake, scan the shoreline, and gaze ahead into the woods. And because the peninsula juts into the narrowest part of the lake, I would be able to see and hear the fishermen and kayakers moving up and down the lake, and observe the interaction of nature and humans.

I began to picture myself following Young's suggestions to sit motionless, to remain silent, to activate my senses, to take notes on everything that occurred during ten minute intervals. I could imagine myself driving home, reviewing my notes, journaling my observations, and reflecting on what I had learned about nature, what I needed to learn, and perhaps most importantly, what I might have discovered about myself.

But I had to take that difficult first step. January came and went along with my last day of work. More days ticked by, turned into weeks, and still I hadn't started my project. I began to feel uneasy, to question my motives, to doubt my determination. What was holding me back? Was it equipment? No! I had a good back pack, bird and tree guides, binoculars, thermos, camp chair, and insulated boots.

Was timing the issue? Should I start my quest on a more logical date such as the first of January or the first day of spring? No again! Since my journey was around a circle of time, it didn't matter when I started. Late February might even be a good time with the days growing longer and the first hints of spring appearing. Should I wait until I would be at home for a full year? No! If I was traveling, I would simply have to find a good sit spot away from Prompton Lake.

Then I realized that the real obstacles were internal. I was procrastinating, assigning too much priority to tasks that truly could wait — servicing my car, organizing my home office, cleaning the garage, and on and on. I could also hear the nagging querulous voice of self-doubt. Could I stick with this commitment? Would this be another of my frivolous adventures destined to fade into the shadow lands of personal failure? Would I actually be able to develop the skills to listen and successfully see the patterns and layers of nature? Would I be able to take accurate notes, write a good journal, and transform these entries into a beneficial book? Or would this simply be another grandiose scheme that would wither like a tomato vine after the first October frost?

Beyond these doubts, I fretted about the interpersonal consequences of my commitment. The time and energy I poured into this project would decrease my availability to my family, my wife, and my grown children. This didn't seem fair. I had already been absent too much during my three-plus decades of fulltime work. And I had to acknowledge some gnawing feelings of anxiety, even fear. Once I stepped on this journey, where would it take me? How would it change my life? Was I ready to embrace those changes?

Still, everything seemed to be lining up, to be pushing me forward on this project. I felt the compelling needs, had a vivid image of the location, and for the first time in my life, had both the time and the opportunity to take action.

When I looked back on my life, I saw experiences that might have prepared me for this adventure. I grew up in southeastern Wisconsin along the shore of Lake Michigan. My view of nature had been formed by seeing vistas of prairie grasses waving in westerly winds, hearing the spring songs of meadowlarks and bobolinks, falling asleep to the sound of waves splashing and sometimes crashing against the shoreline of the lake. There was also the influence of my father — a hunter, fisherman, and proto-environmentalist. We learned about the birds, animals, and fishes we pursued. We studied their habitat, behavior, and diet. I learned to feel at home outdoors, learned to sit still and absorb the impressions of nature.

I might just have the inner resources needed for this journey. And I reminded myself that when unforeseen obstacles, interludes of discouragement, and moments of danger arose, it was likely that somehow and from somewhere encouragement, help, and support would arrive. I had to trust the process, trust that once I started this project, I would find a way to persevere.

I studied the calendar, focused on Friday the 22nd of February, wrote the number "1" in bold black ink on that date, underlined it, and circled it. This would be the day for my first observation session.

# Winter

## Obstacles and Discoveries

The day for my first observation finally arrived, the day to overcome my inertia, end my procrastination, step out the door, and launch my yearlong Prompton commitment. But my cellphone rang just as I was packing up my gear, a call from an attorney's secretary trying to schedule a deposition. Then two more phone calls chimed in followed by a volley of text messages, all from former colleagues, all with questions about former clients. I thought I was free from the old world of work, but now, at the very moment I wanted to turn the page on a new chapter in my life, it felt as if long tendrils from my past were reaching out, grabbing me, demanding my attention and energy, and holding me back.

I sighed, shifted my mind back into work mode, attended to all the questions, and addressed all the unresolved issues as quickly as possible. Finally, an hour behind schedule, I stepped out the door into a cold, cloudy February morning. Feeling the bite of the cold air, I worried if I was dressed warmly enough. Would my layers of turtleneck, wool sweater, parka, watch cap, corduroy pants, thick socks, and insulated boots keep me warm for a full hour of sitting in the cold?

Walking eagerly across the driveway, I glanced toward the street and noticed a contingent of tree trimmers cutting back branches from around the power lines. I turned, looked more closely, and to my dismay saw a huge pile of cut branches heaped across the end of the driveway next to a dump truck towing a wood chipper.

My way was blocked. Another obstacle! I had prepared myself to struggle with internal resistance, but hadn't anticipated all these external barriers. I wondered how I would ever make it through a year if I had to face these kinds of hurdles every single week.

I walked up to the truck. One worker sat comfortably inside sipping coffee while another leaned lazily against the chipper chatting on his cellphone. With the racket from the rest of the crew sawing branches, neither man heard me approach.

I spoke a loud "Hey!" to the cellphone-talker, who looked up, gave me a mildly annoyed look, and leisurely wrapped up his call. I explained that I wanted to use my driveway. He stalled for time, asking, "How long before you're going to leave?" When I answered, "Now!" he frowned, reluctantly walked over to the pile and began to slowly pull the branches aside. His coworker, apparently observing the action, set down his coffee, climbed out of the truck, and pitched in. Soon the pile of branches was cleared, the chute of the chipper folded, the warning cones set aside, and my route was free.

Ten minutes later I arrived at Prompton Lake, turned down the entrance road to the boat ramp, and spotted a small, rectangular, brown wooden sign with yellow letters reading, "West Shore Trail." At last an encouraging omen! I parked the car, stepped out, shouldered my backpack and folding chair, and set off. I was excited to start this new adventure, curious about what I might discover, but I also harbored lingering doubts, even skepticism as to whether I would actually see anything important and if I would have any type of nature encounter.

The West Shore Trail wound through the woods ahead like a pale snow-dusted ribbon. Small, neat hoof prints of a deer joined the trail, followed, then abruptly turned into the woods. Slender, straight, second-growth ash and maple trees grew along both sides of the trail. After a few minutes of walking, I came to a seep, a thin sheet of water flowing downhill, spring water squeezing out from under an old stone wall, water warm enough to nourish a bright green wedge of cress and moss that traced downhill across the snow-covered ground, a patch of vibrant life amid a moribund winter landscape, a view so verdant, so surprising, so awe-inspiring that I paused to take it in.

Stepping carefully across the wet rocks of the seep, I continued another thirty yards down the trail and then angled into the woods toward my destination at the point of the peninsula. As I walked up to my objective, I was stunned to see two orange-clad ice fishermen standing stiffly on the ice a mere fifty yards away, staring down at their tip-ups. This was not the solitude I expected! Their presence felt like one more frustrating obstacle.

I took a breath and reasoned that since I was on the peninsula, I had to find a way to start my first session. Scanning the area, I noticed a shallow swale, a spot where I could sit down and be out of the fishermen's sight, a location where I might finally begin my nature observation.

I set up my chair next to a tall ash tree, sat down, pulled out my notebook and binoculars, and checked the time. It was 10:22 AM Following Jon Young's recommendations in his book *What the Robin Knows*, I would sit, look, and listen for ten minutes, collect impressions and then write them down. Imagining that the time would go slowly, I brought Young's book along, ostensibly for reference, although I knew the real reason was to have something to read in case I was bored.

Picturing myself sitting at the center of a large circle, I now tried to hear the location and distance of all the sounds around me. I gazed at the surrounding woods, at the gray-brown tree trunks rising from the snow-covered ground. The sun burst through the clouds, and for a few moments I felt a welcome touch of February sunshine on my neck and shoulders. I inhaled a woodsy, earthy, fresh fragrance.

A glance at my watch revealed that it was 10:33, a minute over my planned ten minutes. I drew a circle on the first page of my notebook, put a dot in the middle representing my location, and began making notes. I was intrigued by how much I heard in a mere ten minutes. Behind me a big branch swayed and creaked with each gust of wind. Far away two dogs barked, big dogs with deep bellowing barks. The wind blew the distant sounds of a truck backing up, an insistent *beep, beep, beep* warning tone. Traffic whooshed by on nearby Creek Drive. I could even hear the distant hum of cars and trucks traveling along US Route 6, three miles to the south, past the big earthen dam that formed Prompton Lake.

Using the position of the sun and the direction of the wind, I concluded I was facing east. But I would need a compass to verify the direction and probably a thermometer to measure the temperature. I started to draft a mental shopping list, adding a camouflage chair, a camouflage hat, better binoculars, and . . . suddenly I realized that my busy planning mind was wandering up and down the aisles at Walmart. With a rueful smile at how easily I had been distracted, I brought my attention back to my surroundings.

A crow cawed from far across the lake. I felt fortunate to hear any bird at all given the man-made ruckus from tree trimmers working along Creek Drive, the cars and trucks driving by, and the occasional roar of a gas-powered ice auger from an ice fisherman drilling a fresh hole. Two more crows cawed, closer, louder. Behind me a black-capped chickadee called a cheery *chick-a-dee-dee-dee*. Another chickadee joined in and another, creating a chorus of cheerful calls. From the woods ahead came the insistent *kik-kik-kik-kik-kik* call of a pileated woodpecker, a crow-sized bird with a long spiky bill and a bright red topnotch. I heard another bird nearby, a clear, musical descending *peter, peter, peter*, a call I didn't recognize.

My watch now read 10:44, another eleven minutes. Time was passing quickly. I made more notes. Then the ballpoint pen seized up in the cold. Why didn't I think to bring a pencil? Luckily, I had another ballpoint in the warm chest pocket of my down jacket. I pulled it out and put the first pen in my pocket to warm up. With a smile, I added mechanical pencils to my mental shopping list.

During the third ten minutes I heard even more sounds — the whispering arc of a jetliner far above the clouds, tree branches clacking in the strengthening wind, and the resonant rattle of a woodpecker drumming on a hollow tree. The weather was changing. The interludes of sunshine came less frequently. Dark clouds rolled in, the wind grew stronger and steadier. I felt the sting of the cold wind against my face.

Seeking relief from the cold, I poured a cup of tea from my thermos, Assam tea with half-and-half and a single cube of sugar, rich tan tea, steaming generously, smelling of caramel and spice, tasting delicious. I had forgotten how good tea steeped in a thermos can taste, especially when sipped in the fresh air.

During the fourth ten minutes, my whole experience shifted as my senses seemed to open up. Directly in front of me I saw a long, maroon blackberry cane arcing gracefully over the white snow. How did I miss it? I gazed at the tree trunks around me, suddenly seeing their different textures and colors — the dark charcoal gray bark of the cherry with scaly horizontal lines, the lighter gray-brown bark of the ash interwoven with shallow ridges and furrows, the dark gray-brown bark of the maple with vertical grooves and ridges. My sight settled on a soft brown wild grapevine coiling up a tree trunk and draping across the branches.

I gazed out at the empty snow-covered lake. Roiling banks of dark clouds tumbled down from the north. Across the lake, I viewed a vivid tapestry of trees — patches of dark green hemlocks; clumps of white-barked birches; stands of gray-trunked sugar maples; and occasional tall, pale-trunked sycamores. More birds appeared — a flock of dark-eyed juncos, small slate-colored birds — calling softly as they flitted through the shoreline shrubs.

The hour passed quickly. There had been no time (nor need) to read. I became completely absorbed in the sights and sounds around me. I packed up my gear and retraced my route through the woods, across the seep and back along the trail to the parking lot.

Climbing into my car with all its modern comforts, I was struck with a pang of melancholy, a feeling of reluctance to leave behind the sense of awareness and the feelings of connection I discovered at my sit spot. I thought about how much happened, how much changed, how much I experienced during the last hour.

Suddenly, back in service, my cellphone chimed, signaling the arrival of more voicemails and texts that I chose to ignore. I started up the car and let it warm up, but lingered and looked out at the empty snow-covered lake.

The chiming phone with its demands for action felt like a summons back to my old life, a demand to use my mind in all the familiar worn out ways. But the view of the vast, open, snow white lake merging into a forest of uncountable trees looked like an invitation to a new life, a life with new ways of sensing, feeling, experiencing, learning, and knowing.

# A Stiff Breeze from the Northwest

A fresh dusting of snow coated the West Shore Trail. I looked back at my tracks — crisp, swirled imprints in the snow. It was my second week on the trail, yet already it seemed as if my feet sensed the way and anticipated the meanderings, inclines, and declines.

At the seep, I paused and listened to the thin sheet of water gurgling softly over the moss-covered rocks. This swath of slender green grasses and leafy cress, this ribbon of life flowing across the white snow-covered ground was a welcome sight on a winter day. Stepping carefully across the wet rocks, I decided the seep would serve as my symbolic gateway into the realm of the sit spot. I would pause here, tune into the forest around me, and prepare myself for nature observation.

No ice fishermen were around today, so I selected a spot near the tip of the peninsula where I could look back into the woods and up and down the frozen lake. I was still searching for the right location, still trying to combine objective analysis and intuition.

My cellphone rang, another call from the old office, another case with loose ends. I listened and responded, but standing in the woods, I was already shifting into an observing mode. I felt a peaceful distance, a lack of pressure, a willingness to contribute, yet a simultaneous inclination to let events take their course.

I checked the direction on my newly purchased compass and thermometer. I was facing northwest into a gusty wind. The temperature was twenty-three degrees. Showers of snow pellets swirled through the woods. Above, a high layer of gray clouds. To the north, clumps of low dark clouds rolled in.

Eleven minutes elapsed. Branches swayed around me, creaking and rubbing with each gust. Gazing into the woods ahead I estimated that at least a third of the standing trees were dead, their bark peeling, tops broken, and branches askew. The ground was strewn with fallen branches and downed trees. In front of me lay a large fallen ash tree, some of its skeletal branches intact, some severed like amputated limbs. The scene reminded me of a battlefield scattered with debris, a scene affording a very different view of nature than a groomed yard or park where the fallen limbs are quickly picked up and the dying trees cut down. It occurred to me that death and decay are an integral part of a healthy forest.

Two hundred yards up the lake, an ice fisherman fired up a power auger and drilled holes through the ice. I was counting the number of holes when suddenly the pungent odor of combusted gas and oil invaded my nostrils. I was stunned by how quickly the wind blew the fumes across the open lake and how dramatically the smell registered.

Three crows cawed in the distance, two more nearby. Blue jays called from the woods ahead. The sounds of the windblown branches rose to a crescendo with each gust of wind. The clicking and clacking chorus reminded me of a harbor filled with sail boats, their ropes, cables, fittings, and fasteners clattering in the wind.

Ice fishermen far up the lake began to talk, their words indistinct, but the rising and falling tone of their voices was carried clearly by the wind. An airplane whooshed high above the clouds. Over the span of ten minutes, four more planes flew over. Were there more flights today, or was I simply hearing more?

Again, after about forty minutes, my awareness dramatically shifted. I became fully aware of the wind. I heard the gusts approaching as they rattled the branches, sometimes a wave of wind to my left, sometimes a wave to my right, and sometimes the wind bore down across the open lake, the cold breeze biting at my face, causing me to hunker down. I was acutely aware of every sound and smell in the upwind vector, cars driving far up the highway and geese honking in the open water at the far end of the lake, a distance of a mile away. The wind dominated my awareness. I felt like a wild animal, a wolf or coyote sniffing the wind for prey, a prehistoric hunter listening for friend or foe.

The waves of wind reminded me of childhood episodes of body surfing in Lake Michigan after a summer Nor'easter, standing chest high in the water, feeling the tug of the turbulent surf, scanning the waves as they rolled in, waiting for a big smooth roller, jumping into it, and zooming shoreward like a torpedo. Now, many years later, I watched waves of wind roll toward me.

A snow squall blew down the lake toward me, coming closer

and closer until I was enveloped in whiteness, a white cloud of icy, sleety pellets rattling down on the forest floor. The pellets bounced around on the ground, irregular white blobs like pieces of dried pasta. Next to my foot, I spotted a perfectly formed, six-pointed snow crystal — white, symmetrical, pristine. The squall blew through. The pellets slowly melted, but the snowy star lingered, its perfect form framed against a dark brown leaf.

A flock of juncos worked across the peninsula, sparrow-sized birds, the males with a dark slate gray back and a whitish breast, the females with a lighter brownish gray back and the same pale breast. They flitted from bush to bush, from branch to branch, pausing to pick at buds and seeds, moving in a loose synchrony, communicating with soft *stip, stip, stip* calls. They appeared at ease, unaffected by the biting wind and swirling snow pellets.

On my way back through the woods, I spotted rusty cans, a green glass bottle, a plastic water bottle, and a bald tire half-buried in the ground. Should I leave this litter and just be an observer, or should I bring a trash bag, pick up the litter, and become a custodian of the peninsula? I decided to be a custodian. I rejoined the West Shore Trail, stepped back across the seep, and headed to my car, feeling fully renewed and refreshed.

Week 3 · March 7

## Wind and Snow

During the night, a Nor'easter had churned up the Atlantic coast, dropping a five-inch blanket of snow on Prompton. It then spun out over the ocean and was now back-flinging strands of thick dark gray clouds over northeast Pennsylvania. Simultaneously, a dome of high pressure was invading from the northwest, a weather system that promised clear skies, bright sunshine, and moderating temperatures. The battle line between these two armies of air seemed to run right over Prompton Lake.

Wind-whipped sprays and swirling mini twisters of snow raced across the frozen surface of Prompton Lake. My wife, home from school due to a snow day, looked surprised as I loaded my backpack and asked why I would want to run off and "sit in the woods" in this weather. I explained it was the only day I could fit in a visit to my sit spot.

The West Short Trail was covered in pristine, fresh, white snow. The gusts of wind brushed the snow from the branches, white puffs and fluffs drifted down, a kind of second snow. A brilliant red cardinal, perched high in a tree near the seep, softly called *tik, tik, tik*. I trudged through the snow out to the tip of the peninsula and set up under a tall ash tree.

Although the temperature was a relatively mild thirty-three degrees, the relentless wind knifed through my coat. The branches all around me rattled, rubbed, scrapped, tapped, and bumped. These were not the soothing harbor sounds of last week, but a chaotic, menacing cacophony that sounded more like the rigging of a ship trapped in a winter storm.

Eleven minutes passed. I tried to figure out the location of crows cawing in the distance, but the roar of the wind distorted their calls. I thought I heard juncos nearby, but the wind obscured their songs. Today I wouldn't be able to hear birds singing or animals moving in the woods; I wouldn't even hear people approaching. The wind disabled my early warning system. I felt isolated, disoriented.

I looked at the wildly swinging trees and branches. A thin ash tree about thirty feet tall had broken off a foot above the ground and fallen with its top wedged into the upper branches of a slender maple. The fallen ash angled up to the maple tree at a forty-five degree angle. When the gusts of wind swayed the living maple, the dead ash tree gently settled down and then lifted up, a movement improbable in its arrangement, but soothing in appearance. This rhythmic rising and falling of the ash tree reminded me of a chest rising and falling, of a person breathing in and out.

I gazed at the tree and felt my breath becoming deeper, slower, and fuller. I felt cool dry air flowing in and warm moist air flowing out, felt nourished by each inhalation, cleansed by each exhalation. I began to feel surrounded by rhythms of respiration — the earth rising and falling; tree branches bending and returning; gusts of wind part of a grander scheme of weather fronts advancing and retreating, of cold air moving south and warm air moving north, a kind of atmospheric respiration. The ice on the lake seemed part of another rhythm — freezing then melting, freezing then melting again and again.

Forty minutes elapsed in this soothing reverie. I reached for my thermos, opened it, and eagerly poured a cup of steaming tea, my reward for enduring the cold. But white stringy clots floated on the surface. The half-and-half must have been spoiled and curdled in the tea. It looked disgusting and tasted disagreeable, but it was hot so I drank it anyway.

The minutes ticked by. A solitary chickadee fluttered through the woods, landed on a slender branch, picked for seeds, and then flew off. The sun broke through the clouds briefly, and the moment of sunshine warmed me. But the wind and cold continued, and I had to get up and walk around to get warm, movement that seemed contradictory to the concept of the sit spot.

Near the shoreline I spotted a small circle of cement set in the ground topped by a round, faded brass plate that read "Corps of Engineers — US Army — Philadelphia, Survey Mark, Prompton, 1959," with latitude and longitude etched below. Fifty-four years ago a crew placed this stone. An image of the crew came to mind — men in work shirts on a summer day, slapping insects, checking their measurements, digging a hole, mixing cement, pouring it, and setting the plaque.

The history of the little peninsula came to life in my mind. I thought about the farmers who had worked the land before the dam was built, the settlers who explored the woods along the creek, the Native Americans who hunted and fished the land. My journey was in the present, yet I felt touched by the past. The land held visible reminders of its history and possibly even invisible impressions of all who had lived on and worked the land.

I sat down, endured the final ten minutes of my session, then packed up, walked back through the windy woods, and drove home. Later that afternoon the high pressure front won the weather battle. The clouds cleared, the wind subsided, and the March sun warmed the air, creating ideal conditions for sitting in the woods.

I realized I had gone to my sit spot according to an arbitrary schedule, squeezing my session into a day filled with office work, phone calls, emails, and errands. It occurred to me that my visits to the sit spot would work better if seen as the main event of the day and scheduled in response to and in harmony with the weather conditions. I decided to try to make that happen.

It seemed a disappointing session, yet one impression lingered — the image of the breathing tree, the slender ash rising and falling with the gusts of wind. When recalling this image hours and even months later, I always felt my breath settling into a smooth pattern, felt my respiration synchronizing with the breath of the earth and joining the rhythms of nature.

## Week 4 · March 15

# Winter Persists

The first real hints of spring appeared during the week with temperatures in the fifties on Monday and a steady soaking rain on Tuesday. But winter returned on Wednesday when a cold front with plummeting temperatures and snow squalls swept in. By daybreak on Friday, it was eighteen degrees. I waited at home and busied myself with tasks. By 11:00 AM, the temperature was up to thirty-two, the forecasted high for the day.

When I arrived at Prompton, a wintry scene met my eyes. A narrow band of open water around the perimeter of the lake had refrozen, creating white, icy fingers that reached out and grasped onto the rocks along the shoreline. Dull gray clouds hung heavily above the frozen lake. Light snow sputtered down.

Tuesday's rain had washed the leaves and debris from the West Shore Trail, leaving a narrow band of brown frozen mud curving through the woods. I saw what a hiking trail does to the forest floor. Tramping feet wear a groove in the ground. Rain flows down the groove, erodes the topsoil, exposes the roots, and digs the trail deeper. The hikers return, wear the trail down more, and the next rain digs an even deeper trough. A hiking trail brings people into the woods, awakens their enjoyment of the outdoors, and offers an opportunity to connect with nature, but it also degrades the very nature they have come to view.

I set aside these concerns, realizing that for me the sight of a trail ahead felt welcoming and created feelings of security and anticipation — security that I could see the path ahead and knew the way; anticipation that I would experience something new, would learn something previously unknown.

I found a likely sit spot halfway up the peninsula next to the gray trunk of a tall red maple. I was facing west, looking into the woods. I could turn to the right, glance through lacy birch branches, and view the north end of the lake where the Lackawaxen River flowed in, or I could turn to the left, peer through slender saplings, and see the high dam that formed the lake. I watched the snowflakes falling, studied the angle of their downward course, and registered the sensations of a light southwest breeze on the exposed skin of my face.

Water flowed down through the woods toward the lake, a soft steady murmur, continuing runoff from Tuesday's rain. Chickadees squeaked and chipped while patrolling the shoreline shrubs. Five Canada geese flew over the lake, honking steadily and loudly. A woodpecker drummed on a hollow dead tree, a male advertising his territory, proclaiming his virility. Jet planes whooshed high above me, one every five minutes, an aerial parade coursing across the sky.

It was cold sitting in the woods — another day with layers of clothing. I found myself imagining warmer weather when I could sit comfortably in the woods dressed in a T-shirt and shorts. Crows cawed all around the lake. The woodpecker drummed again. The chickadees fell silent. The branches creaked softly when a gust of wind swept through. The parade of jets marched on.

Suddenly, I realized I wasn't really listening. My mind had pushed the sounds into the background. On just my fourth visit, my brain decided that this was safe territory, that I didn't need to be vigilant, that I could think about more important matters. I had no idea what these more important matters were other than the usual list of everyday things that need to be accomplished. I took a breath and brought my attention and senses back to my surroundings with the sobering realization that I had much work to do to develop deep nature listening and watching abilities.

Three geese flew down the lake toward me, flying low, just above the tree tops, inches apart, moving in a dance-like synchrony, weaving, swerving, staying close, and honking quietly, gently, insistently, persuasively. Was this courtship behavior? They flew directly over, and I heard the soft rhythmic whistle of each wingbeat, fine feathers stroking the air. I had often seen geese flying high in formations, had heard their steady honking, but had never been close enough to hear their wingbeats and to hear such soft coos and honks.

I huddled in the cold and drank hot, strong, black coffee. More crows cawed, each with a unique voice — high, low, full, rich, raspy, hoarse, fast, and slow. A beech sapling still held a few faded spear-shaped leaves that rattled in each gust of wind. Near the dam in the distance, three ice fishermen stood like bright orange statues.

My hour was up. Glad to move in the cold, I walked around the peninsula and took pictures of a tall dead tree covered with lumps of dull white fungus, the brass survey marker, the lacy birch branches, and the new translucent ice along the shoreline.

I began to pick up the litter and was surprised to find over thirty beer cans, soda bottles, plastic bottles, and bait containers, some new, some old and rusty, some bottles with old designs. I found two worn black tires half-buried in the ground, but couldn't carry them out.

Walking back, I thought about the litter, the old tires, the survey marker, the eroded trail, the sound of traffic on the highway, and the whisper of the jets above. Human activity was all around me on this little peninsula, yet nature was also vibrant and alive on this slender wedge of forest and shoreline. Picking my way around the muddy spots on the trail, I felt the weight of my chair, my backpack, and the garbage bag filled with litter. I was glad to have left the peninsula a little cleaner than I found it, glad that even on a gray, cold wintry day there were sights and sounds of nature to enjoy and moments of beauty to appreciate.

# Spring

# Pictures at an Exhibition

Sunday arrived, the last possible day of the week to keep my commitment. I thought about giving up the whole plan. I had things to do at home, papers to grade, tax records to organize, a garage to clean. The prospect of a leisurely breakfast with a Sunday paper and relaxed conversation with my wife was very appealing. If I stopped now, it wouldn't matter to anyone. Life would go on. In fact, my life would be better with one less obligation hanging over me. Then, I reconsidered. If I gave up, I would betray myself, lose confidence, and loose inner strength. I chose to get ready.

Ten minutes later I was on the road to Prompton, listening to a dulcet-toned public radio announcer provide background information before playing Mussorgsky's *Pictures at an Exhibition.* He explained that Modest Petrovich Mussorgsky was a tragic figure who died in an asylum at age forty-two, penniless and afflicted with alcoholic seizures. His rapid decline to a premature death may have been due to a grief reaction following the death of his close friend, the artist Viktor Hartmann.

I was surprised by this information. For some reason I had formed a mental image that Mussorgsky, the composer of a memorable piece of classical music, lived a prosperous and long life, reaping financial rewards and public accolades for his masterwork. His story was a reminder that life is brief and unpredictable. I suddenly felt appreciative that I was able to go to my sit spot today and enjoy the panorama of nature.

*Pictures at an Exhibition* was inspired by a showing of over four hundred of Hartmann's watercolors held at the Academy of Fine Arts in Saint Petersburg in 1874. Mussorgsky's intention with the set of pieces for piano was to depict a person walking through the exhibition, pausing, gazing, reflecting on, and reacting to Hartmann's paintings. In a fever of creativity to commemorate his close friend, Mussorgsky composed this work in just six weeks.

Listening to the opening promenade theme, I thought how this musical journey paralleled my own journey. I walked slowly through the woods as if it were an art gallery. I looked at the portraits of nature that were affected by the continually changing light of each day and each season. I decided I would play *Pictures at an Exhibition* when I drove to Prompton. The green seep was my gateway to the peninsula, and *Pictures* would be my theme song. Both would help to prepare me, would tune me up for my hour of observation in the woods.

I headed down the West Shore Trail, paused at the seep, then angled into the woods and made my way out to the peninsula where I set up next to a tall, thick-trunked ash tree. The temperature was thirty-three degrees, the sky cloudy, the wind gusting from the northwest. Ahead in the woods, water gurgled softly downhill. The air smelled fresh and clean, air blown down from the pine forests of Canada.

I listened for the birdsongs. Juncos called softly back and forth from the nearby shrubs. Crows cawed from across the lake. A pair of jays jeered back and forth. However, the star performer was a male tufted titmouse singing a clear, whistled *here, here, here*, a song I identified. I counted the notes in his song — one-two, one-two, one-two-three, one-two-three, one-two, and on and on in an ever-varying pattern.

He flew over and landed on a nearby branch, a small gray-backed bird with pale apricot flanks, ivory breast, short black beak, and a jaunty head crest. Suddenly, he switched to a new song, a vibrant and melodic *peter, peter, peter.* After five minutes he shifted back to the *here, here, here* song. What was the change all about? Was he practicing? Was he displaying creativity and virtuosity to attract a female? Was he imitating and one-upping any nearby rivals? There had to be some reason related to survival.

The wind picked up, strong gusts that roared across the open lake, rattling the branches and drowning out all the other sounds. When the wind subsided, I welcomed the return of the soundscape — the water gurgling, the titmouse singing. I thought I heard a faint nasal *peent, peent, peent,* but the sound was so faint and seemed so unlikely that I dismissed it.

In the woods ahead, an old stone wall wound along the crest of the ridge, gray flat stones topped with a layer of fresh snow. Directly downhill from the wall, a black Labrador retriever trotted along the West Shore Trail, nose close to the ground, tail up in anticipation. Thirty feet behind the dog, a man, clad in a light brown coat, strode briskly and was in turn followed by a small brown dog. I was far enough away that I heard no sound, just watched the man and the dogs walking through the woods. I sat still. He didn't see me. The dogs were upwind and didn't catch my scent. I felt invisible, as if I blended in.

When the wind gusted, I hunkered down, zipped up my coat, and put on my gloves. When the wind let up and sunlight broke through the clouds, I sat tall and open and savored the warmth on my face, neck, and shoulders. A woodsy-earthy scent wafted up from the slowly thawing earth.

When my hour was up, I walked over to investigate the spot from where I heard water flowing. Barging through the brush, I spotted a small rivulet coursing down a narrow bed of moss-covered rocks. Suddenly, I detected movement on the snow-covered ground a few feet in front of me. I turned and saw an American woodcock, its subtle mottled camouflage pattern of brown, tan, black, and gray defeated by the white snow. It walked along on short legs, its long, brown bill bobbing up and down with each step.

I had never seen a woodcock this close before. I had stumbled on them while walking at dusk in the spring, had heard them explode into the air, had heard their nighttime nasal calls, but had never seen one close up. The complex pattern of the feathers and the delicately interlaced shades of brown, tan, black, gray, and white highlighted against the white snow was simply beautiful.

A bit of follow-up research revealed that the woodcock is a medium-sized bird, eight to twelve inches in length, with a wingspan of sixteen to eighteen inches. It prefers moist woodlands, swamps, and thickets where it uses its long flexible bill to probe the earth for worms and insects. The males arrive early in spring, claim a "singing ground," and then at nightfall engage in elaborate aerial and song routines to attract a female. It allows a close approach due to its camouflage, but then explodes into flight. I must have correctly heard its call earlier. I would have to learn to trust my senses. I also realized this woodcock was right on schedule and in its favored habitat.

During the following week the song of the titmouse and the image of the woodcock resurfaced during quiet moments. Maybe because I was sitting still, I activated a capacity to deeply absorb sensory impressions that then allowed these moments of beauty and awe to register memorably and resonate emotionally. Perhaps these encounters with beauty, these moments of awe were part of my process of connecting with nature.

Week 6 · March 29

# A Constant Chorus

As I drove to Prompton, early morning sunshine dappled the drab, brown-gray landscape. Above me, a high, clear, pale blue sky stretched beyond the limits of sight. To the west, a single thick clump of dark gray clouds rolled over the Moosic Mountains. The temperature was a chilly thirty-four degrees, but the sunshine offered the promise of coming warmth.

I reread Jon Young's statement that sunrise is the best time to learn bird language; it's the time when the birds sing to claim their territory, when they call to connect with their mate or flock, and when they sing exuberantly to celebrate the start of a new day. I had been putting off an early morning visit because of the cold temperatures, the presumed lack of migrant birds, and probably due to my own reluctance, laziness, and inertia.

Thursday night I drifted off to sleep mulling over the idea of an early morning observation session. When I awakened at dawn, looked out the window, saw hues of rose and purple layered above the eastern horizon, I knew this was the morning for an early departure. Fifteen minutes later I was on the road to Prompton.

The parking lot was empty and the West Shore Trail a stripe of dried, brown-gray mud winding through the woods. I slowed down, walked quietly, attempted to blend in, and opened my senses to take in the surroundings. At the seep, I paused as usual, gazed at the green swath of moss and grass and cress, listened to the faint gurgle of the water, and re-committed myself to fully observe all aspects of nature.

I stepped across the wet stones, turned off the trail, angled through the woods, and found a spot at the base of the peninsula next to a tall ash tree. Settling in, I began to look and listen. Puffs of wind touched my face. The sun, peaking over the hills to the east, cast long, velvety, tree trunk shadows onto the forest floor.

Immediately, I heard a variety of birdsongs, a chorus of songs that grew louder and more insistent, a much different soundscape than during previous weeks when the occasional songs seemed like separate splotches of bright paint on a large empty canvas. Today the songs were constant, like uncountable dabs of color, overlapping, blending together, and creating a color-filled portrait. The songs started and faded, came and went so quickly that I couldn't keep track of them, couldn't remember what I had heard after a ten-minute observation interval. I changed my recording procedure, noting each call as I heard it, keeping a running record. Gradually, I began to distinguish the different songs.

Two cardinals, bright red in the morning sunlight, perched in adjacent trees seemed locked in a contest, each trying to sing louder, clearer, longer, and more creatively than the other, each whistling its own version of a vibrant *cheer, cheer, cheer,* followed by a string of *purty, purty, purty, purty* calls. Along the shoreline, crows cawed back and forth as if engaged in an animated discussion. Three chickadees, busily flitting from branch to branch, sang their cheerful *chick-a-dee-dee-dee, chick-a-dee-dee-dee.* A squadron of blue jays swept through the trees calling *jay, jay, jay.* A flock of geese honked softly and steadily from the far end of the lake. Newly arrived red-winged blackbirds flew along the shoreline calling *check, check, check.* A robin, another new arrival, perched in a nearby maple, singing its cheerful *cheerily, cheer-up, cheerily, cheer-up.*

The cardinals seemed to be the lead performers in this concert, but the crows, based on numbers and volume, vied for center stage. The geese, jays, chickadees, and robins were the back-up singers, adding depth, variety, harmony, and complexity. I sat absolutely motionless, entranced by this morning chorus.

Gradually the cardinals wound down and the crows ceased. A new, quieter ensemble took over. A titmouse took the lead with its clear whistled *here, here, here.* A mourning dove added its soft melancholy coos. Jays and chickadees chimed in, each bird taking a solo for a moment, then fading into the background. This constant and ever-changing chorus of birdsongs stirred feelings of happiness, contentment, and hope. It seemed as if the birds sensed and celebrated the approach of spring.

Then, in an instant, winter returned. Gusts of north wind whipped across the frozen lake. The birds fell silent. The wind moaned through the trees, and soon the branches were creaking, clattering, rubbing, and rattling. Two ice fishermen leaned into the wind and trudged across the ice. I heard the crunching, scraping sounds of their sleds and the angry sputtering of their power augers drilling holes through thick ice.

It was five minutes past my full hour, but I lingered. I saw movement in a stand of birch trees, small birds, clinging to wispy, lacy birch branches, right side up, upside down, clutching the wind-swayed branches like a band of tiny trapeze artists. I noticed a touch of red, and my quick mind flashed "redpoll," but my slow mind reasoned "tree sparrows," birds I had seen at my feeders, birds I knew were in the area.

Once home and eager to identify these little birds, I logged onto the Cornell Laboratory of Ornithology website, *All About Birds.* Following the lead of my logical mind, I checked the American tree sparrow first. The information on their feeding behavior was all wrong. They search for seeds close to the ground and move up and down in the bushes and weeds. Then I checked the entry on common redpoll and read that they like to forage in winter flocks, hanging from the branches and fluttering through the trees. This was exactly what I had seen!

I was pleased to have solved the mystery. Habitat and behavior provided a pathway for identification, a route as valid as field marks seen and songs heard. My more holistic and intuitive impression was correct, but I discounted it. I would try to be more accepting of these quick and intuitive impressions in the future.

Week 7 · April 5

# Fitting In

A solitary crow attired in shiny, jet black plumage waddled beneath a tall pine tree at the far end of the parking lot. Unconcerned with my presence, it cawed loudly, rocking back and forth with each caw. I lingered in the car, listened to *Pictures at an Exhibition*, and watched the crow. Was it the official greeter? Were the birds expecting me? Had they accepted me as part of the weekly routine? When I opened the door, it flapped lazily into a low branch and continued to caw.

Whitish gray ice still covered the lake. The narrow band of open water that ringed the lake had refrozen during the night into thin, clear ice. The calendar said it was the first week of April, but Prompton Lake said winter persisted. The sky was a clear, high blue. The chilly, twenty-seven-degree morning air stung my nostrils with each inhalation. I was still wearing the all too familiar layers of winter clothing.

The soft flock calls of juncos and the cheerful sing-song of a robin filled the air alongside the West Shore Trail. Pausing at the seep, I noticed that in spite of the persisting cold, the grasses and cress had grown greener and more lush, growth most likely spurred by the lengthening daylight and the rising angle of the sun. Here, at least, was a glimpse of spring.

I found a spot under a tall red maple tree and sat down to listen and look. The April sunshine cast pleasant warmth on my neck and shoulders. A light breeze puffed down from the northwest. Jetliners whooshed high overhead. Morning traffic whined along the highway, people heading to work and school.

Three blue jays glided through the branches, loudly crying *jay*,

*jay, jay.* They pulled up and landed in the bare branches of an ash tree where the bright sunshine illuminated their blue, white, black, and gray plumage. Hopping from branch to branch, they sang a hollow *queedle, queedle, queedle,* then switched to a musical, bell-like *toolol, toolol, toolol* song. They alternated between these songs, mixing in occasional clicks and gurgles. Suddenly, they took off in unison and flew across the lake.

I heard the aria of a song sparrow, two clear tones, a jumble of musical chirps ending with a string of clear whistles, a song represented as *maids, maids, maids put on your tea kettle-lettle-lettle.* Ahead, a cardinal sang a different song, a resonant *right here, right here.* Red-winged blackbirds called *check, check, check* as they flew along the shoreline.

This wasn't the constant chorus of last week, but more of a progression of performers. The image of an expansive forest pavilion with musicians scattered around it sprang to mind. One musician in one spot would perform a solo, improvise, and create variations. Another might join in, and then still others would add more tones and patterns, all of it interspersed with intervals of silence. Yet behind the many songs, variations, and repetitions I sensed some greater coherence, some jazzy jam of life and energy.

I listened to the individual voices of the jays — some high, some low. I heard the similarly unique caws of each crow. I listened to the song sparrow, knowing that in Ohio or Oregon its song would be slightly different, sung in a local accent. I heard two cardinals, each with a slightly different song, each seemingly tweaking, changing, and improving its offering.

Variation, variation, and more variation. Sitting under the towering maple, ash, and cherry trees, it seemed that variation was an essential element, a core dynamic, an inherent principle of nature. What was this drive to diversity? Was it an evolutionary principle to keep spinning off new songs and novel behaviors to seize a selective advantage? This might be true for the cardinals as females are known to choose a mate with the best song and the brightest plumage, seeing these as indicators of health, virility, and protective capability. But was there some dynamic of diversity beyond evolution? Was there some resonance between this diversity in song and plumage and the idea of an infinitely expanding universe?

I was pulled from my reverie by the realization that the birds were flying and perching nearby, going about their business, undisturbed by my presence. Were they becoming used to my weekly visits? Were they realizing I wasn't a threat? It seemed unlikely that they could remember such a brief event occurring at an irregular weekly interval. Maybe they were so busy with the urgent business of establishing a territory, finding a mate, building a nest, and foraging for food that they just couldn't spare much attention for some harmless human sitting in a blue camp chair.

Then another possibility came to mind. Perhaps my demeanor changed. I was entering *their* world, listening to *their* songs, watching *their* flights, sensing the wind and sun as *they* did. Perhaps I was breaking through the barrier of being a stranger in the forest. Perhaps I was beginning to fit in. Maybe changes in my awareness, attitude, and attention changed something about my presence, something the birds perceived and led them to respond in a more relaxed manner. This seemed hard to believe. Yet there was clearly a change. There was an effect, and I reasoned there had to be a cause.

My hour was up. Thoughts of breakfast — scrambled eggs, jam-slathered toast, and a steaming cup of coffee — filled my mind as I ambled back along the trail. Approaching my car I spotted a crow perched in a pine tree. Was this the same crow I saw when I arrived? Was it checking on me to see how I had done with my observation? Or was it simply saying farewell until next week?

Week 8 · April 11

# Changes

The ice had vanished. A few warm, sunshine-filled days, a few nights with temperatures holding above freezing, and the ice melted away. Now the water, imprisoned since November, seemed to delight in its newfound freedom. Tiny wavelets danced across the blue surface of Prompton Lake and splashed softly against the concrete boat ramp. An overnight thunderstorm scoured the debris and driftwood from the ramp, leaving it fresh, clean, and ready for use.

Along the West Shore Trail, welcome hints of green poked through the faded brown leaf litter — slender blades of grass; lacy fern tendrils; and clusters of yellow trout lilies, short woodland flowers with two dull green, lobe-shaped leaves flecked with light brown spots, each leaf looking like the flank of a brook trout. Soon their butter yellow flowers would appear. For these diminutive lilies, the clock was ticking. They needed to flower, pollinate, and produce seeds quickly to grab their share of sunshine before the canopy of leaves shaded their home on the forest floor.

Trout lilies, always one my favorite early spring woodland wildflowers, intrigued me. I later read that the yellow flowers bloom at the tip of a leafless stem, and each blossom has three petals and three sepals. On the warmest spring days, the petals curve backward displaying six yellow and purple stamens that attract ants to perform pollination. After the seeds form, the ants assist again by dispersing them. By late May the leaves wither and die, leaving the bulb nourished and ready to grow anew next spring.

Trout lily is ubiquitous over a wide swath of northeastern woodlands and has many lovely and evocative names such as dogtooth violet, adder's tongue, yellow snowdrop, and yellow fawn lily. The bulbs can be boiled and eaten, a useful survival tip. Native Americans used trout lily leaves and bulbs for medicinal purposes.

I continued past these patches of spring lilies and made my way to the peninsula. Having forgotten to bring a chair, I had no choice but to sit on the ground. With the temperature approaching fifty degrees and spring in the air, it felt right to sit on the ground, to lean back against the thick trunk of a black cherry tree, to be in direct contact with the earth, to feel the solid, timeless earth.

The wind was light. Birdsongs and calls sounded all around me, familiar songs and calls — the *tik* calls of cardinals, the nasal *yank* of a white-breasted nuthatch, the lilting aria of a song sparrow, the whinnying of a robin, the hollow *queedle* of a blue jay, and in the distance, the steady soft honking of a flock of Canada geese.

Suddenly, a volley of splashes on the lake nearby, sounds I

wouldn't have heard a week ago. I turned cautiously, peered through the bushes, and spotted five ducks swimming on the water — two males with distinctive bright white bodies, dark green heads, and long, thin, bright orange bills; and three females with grayish bodies, white breasts, chestnut-colored heads, and the same long, fish-snatching orange bill. These were common mergansers pausing at Prompton on their journey north to Canada where the females would build a nest in a tree cavity alongside a forest lake and line it with feathers and down from their breasts. I watched them glide through the water, dive down with a little jump, disappear underwater to snatch small fish with their serrated bills, and pop back to the surface.

In the distance, a shrill siren wailed, a volunteer fire company sounding its alarm. Off to the west, someone was target shooting, a staccato burst of shots, a few minutes of silence to reload, then another volley.

Nearby, where water flowed down to the lake, I heard spring peepers, little tree frogs calling out high-pitched mating calls, the combined sound like a chorus of chiming sleigh bells. The singing of peepers was a true and welcome harbinger of spring. Yet I tempered my enthusiasm, remembering the old saying that once the peepers start calling, they will stop three times due to frost.

Peepers are adapted to survive spring cold snaps because they can tolerate their body fluids freezing. They simply hide under logs or beneath tree bark and wait for the warmth to return. Early spring is mating time. The males inflate and deflate a small sac at the side of their throats to create the brief, clear peep that when caroled in a chorus can be heard up to two miles away. The loudest and fastest singers have the best chance to attract a female who will then lay between 750 and 1000 eggs. These eggs are immediately fertilized by the male, eggs that soon hatch into tiny tadpoles. Six to twelve weeks later the young frogs leave the water to begin their life in the woods.

As loud as these little frogs are, they are almost impossible to spot due to their diminutive size and their camouflaging colors of tan, brown, olive green, and gray, colors that can change, chameleon-like, to blend into their surroundings. The peeper carries a dark "X" across its back, the reason for its Latin name of *Psuedacris crucifer*, crucifer referring to cross-bearer. Tree frogs are nocturnal feeders, and with their large toe pads they move easily through the leaf litter and climb shrubs and bushes where they feed on beetles, ants, flies, and spiders; in turn they are fed upon by snakes, skunks, and bull frogs.

The clouds were breaking up. The sky was clearing. A puff of wind caressed my face. The air smelled loamy and earthy as if the ground was opening up and yielding its scented secrets. The April sunshine warmed my skin. The sounds and sensations blended together, pulling me into a reverie, into a web of singing, growing, calling, migrating, mating life.

I glanced at my watch. Fifty minutes had passed, and I realized I would need to cut ten minutes from my hour. I promised to meet a friend for kayaking to celebrate the newly ice-free lake. I thought I would try to continue my observation on the water instead of alongside it. Still, I felt guilty about leaving early. When I stood up, the mergansers that had been feeding peacefully just thirty feet away jumped up, skittered across the water, and took flight.

We enjoyed that first kayaking trip of the spring, sitting low and close to the water, moving freely, gazing down at the rocky bottom, listening to the water lap against the hull, and watching foamy circles swirl away with each push of the paddle. As we slid through the water, we talked about our kayaks, the weather, wine, and our families. We paddled up into the Lackawaxen River, the stream that feeds Prompton Lake, past black mud flats tinged with pale green, sprouting grasses and weeds.

Part of my attention remained with the birds on the water, in the air, and along the shoreline. I saw more common mergansers, mallards, a pair of blue-winged teal, and a flock of Canada geese. I spotted a belted kingfisher perched at the tip of a branch, chattering as it flew off. A pair of tree swallows swooped and twittered above. Two spotted sandpipers, small brown shorebirds with short orange legs and a white brown-freckled breast, walked gracefully along the rocky shoreline picking for food with their long bill. A pair of wood ducks flew over the tan marsh grass, and I heard the high lonely *oo-eek, oo-eek* call of the female. It was spring and Prompton Lake was open for business.

Week 9 · April 19

# Red Maple Flowers

Along the West Shore Trail, wildflowers dotted the forest floor — delicate, lacy-leafed wild geraniums; vigorous, spear-leafed dandelions; pale green arrowhead trillium leaves. Higher up, blackberry, honeysuckle, and Russian olive leaves were unfurled, each displaying a different shade of spring green, that transient, delicate, minty, yellow-green.

As I walked down the trail I heard the birds — juncos softly calling, a song sparrow singing, and the clear descending *fee-bee* of a male chickadee advertising for a mate. Deeply pressed tracks of mountain bike tires traced along the trail. Further on, the fresh hoof marks of a deer joined then departed the trail. Stepping over the wet rocks of the seep, I noticed that the dull, brown dirt of the trail was strewn with tiny, bright red flowers.

I picked one up and studied it — a delicate, luminous, fringed flower fallen from a red maple that grew alongside the trail. I looked out across the lake and spotted a stand of red maples, reddish-tinged trees that are always doing something red — red hued branches in the summer; blazing red leaves in the fall; red tipped twigs in the winter; and now in spring, a mantle of brilliant red flowers.

I later discovered that a red maple tree with a twelve-inch-thick trunk may hold as many as a million of these flowers, some male and some female. The male flowers are fringed with an orange tinge; the female flowers, waiting to be pollinated, are more compact, more opulent, more intensely red. This profusion of flowers provides both an early pollen source for insects and a favorite food for squirrels. By mid-summer the female flowers produce a seed with a thin propeller blade attached, seeds that in a breeze whirligig down to the ground by the thousands.

This abundance of red flowers strewn across the trail brought to mind the image of a wedding in India where the celebrants throw rose petals along the path to grace the beginning of a couple's marital journey. Here at Prompton, it was just me treading along the flower-laden way.

I set up near the breathing tree. Gray clouds blanketed the sky. The wind blew from the southeast, and the temperature was a mild sixty-five degrees. Waves lapped along the shoreline. Gusts of wind swayed the branches, lifted dry leaves from the ground, and skittered them across the forest floor.

In spite of the bountiful bouquet of red maple flowers, the increasing number of wildflowers, and the multitude of green unfolding leaves, I sensed a mood of melancholy. The weather seemed off, the wind huffing up the lake from the southeast, the air balmy, almost sticky, roaming rain showers spritzing down. According to the forecast, a long band of thunderstorms embedded in a cold front was advancing from the west. The air pressure was dropping, always an ingredient for a blue mood.

But the melancholy I felt wasn't only linked to the weather. I was sick and tired of the burden of my commitment, of the daily pressure to sit down and write up the last week's observations, of the weekly struggle to carve out an hour of observation time. As usual, this morning, while I prepared to depart, a flurry of distracting calls jangled my phone. On the drive to Prompton, even Mussorgsky's normally triumphant music sounded harsh and atonal.

I gazed at the breathing tree still perched precariously at a forty-five-degree angle, still moving up and down, breath-like with each gust of wind. I wondered how much longer it could cling to this unique position, how long before the slender tree would take its last breath and crash to the earth to rot and decay along with all the other fallen trees.

A kingfisher rattled along the shoreline. Swallows swooped and trilled overhead. A flock of tree sparrows softly called *tseet, tseet* back and forth. And a crow flew silently over me at tree-top height and didn't flare when I looked up. I wasn't camouflaged. In fact, I was sitting on a bright blue chair wearing a green jacket and dark red ball cap. But it seemed like the birds didn't see me or didn't care.

Something about the sound of the waves lapping onto the rocks sounded familiar. I searched my memory, and the first association that surfaced was the waves on Lake Michigan that I heard from the bedroom window of my childhood home in Wisconsin. But those waves were bigger, deeper, and more rhythmic. Frustrated, I listened again and searched deeper in my memory.

Another association emerged — an inland lake, a rocky shoreline, small splashy waves, Lake Koshkonong, the wide, shallow lake in southeastern Wisconsin where I spent many hours during my childhood and adolescence fishing from the shoreline, crouched in a duck blind in the fall, scanning the sky, always hearing the waves splash against the rocky, muddy, marshy shoreline.

My dad was a member of the Carcajou Hunting Club on Lake Koshkonong, a lake created by a dam on the Rock River that flooded a vast marsh where in earlier days Native Americans camped, hunted, fished, and harvested the abundant wild rice. I remembered crouching behind the reeds and branches of a duck blind, sometimes on a sunny day, sometimes on a cold, gray, windy day. We would scan the sky for flying ducks, stare hopefully at the decoys bobbing in the water, and strain to hear the sound of whistling wings and calling ducks.

Sometimes my dad would head off by himself to hunt along the river, in the forest ponds, or the marsh potholes. Then, I sat by myself, listening and watching as I was now. But our hunting was goal oriented. We scanned selectively for our quarry — the ducks, geese, rails, and coots — and disregarded the other birds and animals. I liked what I was doing now better, open-ended listening and looking at all of nature.

Another crow flew over. A lone jay looped from tree to tree across the peninsula. A second jay called from the woods and a third from across the lake; each jay seemingly on its own. I heard juncos hidden in the brush calling softly. A hen mallard quacked loudly. A pair of kingfishers chattered. Insects appeared, a moth fluttering in front of me, mosquitoes whining in my ear.

The feelings of melancholy lingered in the woods and in the air, but inside me something had shifted. When I arrived I felt a sharp, acute melancholy that cried out for resolution. Now, after an hour of sitting still with open senses, the melancholy had evolved into more of a light presence, a background motif to be accepted, lived with, even embraced. I thought how nature has its moods, its moments of melancholy, but even in the midst of these moods everything continues — the wildflowers grow, the birds sing, and the red maple flowers flutter down to the ground.

# Skunk Cabbage

Another busy week, another scheduling struggle. The last possible slot to meet my commitment would be Friday after dinner, a time likely to cause disappointment on the home front. I chilled a bottle of New Zealand Sauvignon Blanc, my wife's favorite, set two glasses out, prepared an appetizer of crackers spread with cream cheese topped with thinly sliced radishes and sprinkled with slivers of garden parsley. Then I made an early dinner of grilled salmon and sautéed kale.

It felt good to sit in the early spring warmth and sunshine sipping, eating, and talking. It was difficult to break the mood, pack up my gear, and head to Prompton. I felt weary from the weekly scheduling battle, felt the awkwardness of my departure, and sensed my wife's disappointment. I thought about giving up and returning to the sun-dappled table for another glass of wine and more conversation.

Somehow I managed to break away, climb in the car, and drive off. On the way, I listened to the orchestral arrangement of Mussorgsky's *Pictures*, music that sounded rich, melodious, and triumphant; music that resonated with the surrounding panorama of bright sunshine, blue skies, and green lawns; music that strengthened my resolve.

A crow was perched in a pine tree at the end of the parking lot. Perhaps the same one I had seen before. Perhaps it had claimed the boat ramp area as its home territory, a shrewd decision given the combination of natural food available on the mowed grass and the supplementary tidbits of bread and chips and snacks left by the boaters and fishermen. I was a guest on the crow's turf, and it watched me warily the way a homeowner might stand on his porch and eye a stranger walking through the neighborhood.

Walking along the West Shore Trail, I made an effort to attend to all the sounds and sights. The time of approach to the sit spot, a time that Jon Young and his associates call the zero interval, is rich with hints regarding the state of nature. I heard the clear whistled *here, here, here* of a tufted titmouse, the lilting aria of a song sparrow, and the cawing of a crow, songs that sounded relaxed and communicated all was safe — the birds could carry on with the life-building activities of feeding, mating, and nesting. This restorative state of nature resonated within me. I felt myself settle and relax.

I set up again by the large black cherry tree beneath a branch that corkscrewed up at a forty-five degree angle. This spot felt right today, closer to the tip of the peninsula with an open view of the lake. I faced west into the warm late day sunshine. A light breeze blew down the lake.

In the angled sunlight, I noticed filaments of a spider web stretched between two trees, shiny, silvery threads that moved up and down and back and forth with each puff of wind. Tiny fluffy white insects filled the air. With each breath of wind the insects drifted horizontally like snowflakes in a storm. When the air calmed, they hovered like myriad white stars in a midnight sky. The air grew still, and the tiny white insects organized into two funnels, each about four feet tall, each a living vortex of white insects swirling, rising, and falling in the soft sunlight. Here was the protein smorgasbord the birds flew north to feast on.

I expected to hear a full chorus of birdsongs at dusk, but all was quiet except for a robin whinnying. In the distance I heard the angry droning of a weed whacker. A truck and a car whined noisily along the road. Waves lapped upon the rocks.

I heard voices and saw two mountain bikers cycling down the West Shore Trail. I heard a loud *thunk* as each rolled over a large loose rock. More bikers pedaled down the trail, each *thunking* over the big loose rock.

The bikers never saw me. I imagined they thought they were connecting with nature while riding through the woods, but to me they seemed like outsiders passing all too quickly through the trees. I was glad to be sitting still and to witness nature's story unfold.

A trio of crows cawed, mourning doves cooed, a cardinal sang. A lone jet flew high overhead, tracking west to east. A motor boat putted toward the landing.

Looking down I saw that the trout lilies were now in full bloom, pale yellow bell-shaped flowers attached to slender stalks. Another wildflower with green arrow-shaped leaves poked through the brown and tan layer of dead leaves. The sun slipped below the hill ahead, and suddenly the air felt chilly. I zipped up my fleece. Without the sunlight, the cloud of insects and the thin spider web vanished from sight.

Quiet enveloped the peninsula. The day's story seemed to be over. I stood up, strolled over to the shoreline to take pictures of the trees across the lake still bathed by the last rays of sunshine. As I crunched through the dry leaves, a chipmunk chattered a warning call and dove for cover. Five mallards jumped up from a patch of brown reeds, quacking, veeping, wings whistling, heading up the lake. Five mergansers skittered across the water and took flight. A pair of kingfishers lifted up from a dead tree limb, chattering as they flew off. I had misread the silence.

On the walk back, I paused and gazed at the seep, now a swath of vibrant, dark green cress, weeds, and grasses. Downhill I noticed a cluster of large green-leafed plants that I recognized as skunk cabbage, a plant I knew from childhood that grew in profusion in a ravine behind a friend's house, a plant that we avoided given its stinky name.

I cast away my childhood prejudices, moved in for a closer look, and viewed loose clusters of delicately veined, wide, spear-shaped, green leaves. There was no bad smell, just a vigorous colony of plants, some taller, some shorter, some bunched together, some on their own.

Curious about these plants I later searched online and found an informative article by Craig Holdrege, PhD, the founder of The Nature Institute in Ghent, New York, and an "unabashed admirer" of skunk cabbage, a plant he has studied for years

Holdrege provided a detailed history of the life cycle of *Symplocarpus foetidus*. The broad green leaves I saw actually represented the middle of the story, a story that began in early March when this plant claimed the title of the first flower of the spring. From still-frozen ground the skunk cabbage sends up four-to-six-inch-tall hood-like leaves that can vary from wine red to yellow-green in color, from twisted to pointed in shape, and from round to squat in stature. This hood is a specially adapted leaf called a spathe that wraps around itself to form a protective cover for the spherical, straw-colored flower composed of four plain spongy sepals. During the flowering period, the skunk cabbage has the extraordinary capacity to generate and regulate heat over a period of twelve to fourteen days so that the flower temperature hovers near thirty-six degrees no matter how cold the outside temperature. During this warmed blooming phase, the flower releases pollen and, according to Craig Holdrege, generates a "lightly pungent, somewhat skunk-like odor," an odor that attracts flies and insects to perform pollination.

On sunny days in March, I had noticed insects flying around and thought it incongruous; either the insects had emerged by mistake or had lost their seasonal bearings. I now realized my error. Every insect, plant, animal, and bird in the forest knows precisely what it is doing, knows its time niche, and takes full advantage of its opportunity to propagate.

By the end of April, when temperatures rise, the spathe wilts and a firm bud at the base of the plant rapidly unfolds into large, light green, oblong leaves. By mid-May the leaves grow to three feet long and if crushed exude a skunk-like odor, and if eaten cause inflammation, a protection from being grazed upon by deer.

By mid-June the leaves, which are mostly water without fibrous material, begin to break down. A few holes appear, the leaves droop, turn black and slimy, and slowly dissolve, but not before the flower forms a ball shaped fruit head that drops to the ground where its many berry-covered seeds can germinate.

Each skunk cabbage plant has an extensive root system branching out in a dense maze from a central rootstock. Holdrege, an advocate of "delicate empiricism," a perspective based on the writings of Johan Wolfgang von Goethe, views plants and animals as dynamic organisms integrated into "the larger web of life," and representing unified and coherent themes. Holdrege notes that the roots grow in the spring and contract in the summer, a movement that pulls the rootstock deeper so that the plant "becomes more deeply anchored in the ground."

Skunk cabbage embodies a "bud-like quality." It flowers within a bud, its leaves unfold from a bud, and it even contains within its subterranean stem a series of embryonic buds that will grow in future years. Skunk cabbage is also characterized by "a fluid-like quality." It lives in wet woodlands and manifests the water-like qualities of fluidity, movement, and continuity, qualities seen in the upward flow of sugary sap to power the warming of the flower head, the pulling of water from the ground to create the structure of the wide green leaves, and even the watery dissolution of the leaves.

I was glad I had found this article by Holdrege and read his perspectives on this unfortunately named plant. I now had a better understanding of this plant and a new appreciation for the themes in nature that it represents. My perception of beauty and complexity when I paused and gazed at the broad green leaves was confirmed. My childhood prejudice had been overcome. My curiosity was piqued. I hoped I would encounter more of these nature themes, themes that were simultaneously clear, organized, and scientific in a way that satisfied my mind, yet were awe-inspiring and emotive in a way that filled my heart.

Week 11 · May 3

# New Arrivals

Why didn't I tell him what I was doing? The assistant dam tender was a good man. I had known him for years and was glad to see him when he pulled up in his government-issue white pickup. We exchanged greetings and caught up on the Prompton news. I saw his eyes angle up and take stock of my loaded backpack and camp chair slung over my shoulder. With a curious smile he asked me what I was doing and if I was going into the woods to take a nap.

I made up a bogus story about going for a hike. Was I so unsure of my project? Did I think he would find it weird or think less of me? At least we parted in agreement that it was a truly beautiful spring day, the first warm one of the season.

Continuing across the parking lot, I spotted the "boat ramp crow" near the shoreline, its plumage a shimmering, iridescent, purple-black in the morning sunshine. It waddled through the deep green, dew-covered grass, glanced up and down, snatched morsels of food, and radiated full self-acceptance and comfort with its mission.

I wished I could be as accepting and comfortable with my mission. And I reflected ruefully — if I couldn't embrace my project fully, how could I ever expect others to understand and accept it?

Along the West Shore Trail, the weeds and wildflowers had grown taller and fuller and were now a dense, green band of burgeoning vegetation crowding both sides of the brown, dirt path. Delicate, minty, spring-green leaves were unfurling on the bushes and shrubs, the forest understory. Just as I angled off the trail, I spotted a large yellow and black bee cruising inches above the ground, then another one, then two more — he first bees I saw this year. They darted busily from one wildflower to the next, feeding on yellow trout lilies, white wood anemone, and dark blue violets.

Setting up my chair beneath a tall ash tree, I sat quietly, settled in, and in a few minutes heard the familiar, melodious whistles of a northern cardinal and the raspy *check, check, check* calls of a red-winged blackbird. Then a new song, a distinctive, loud, accelerating *teetcha, teetcha, teetcha* rang through the morning air. This was an ovenbird, a small brown denizen of the deep woods, a secretive bird that high-steps across the forest floor picking insects and caterpillars from the leaves and debris. Then another new song, the *sweet, sweet, sweet, I'm so sweet* of a yellow warbler, another newly arrived migrant from the Neotropic, a region that includes Central America, the Caribbean, and southern Florida and Texas. These birds are butter yellow with delicate streaks of rusty red across their breasts, and their arrival in the mid-Atlantic was right on schedule.

I had acquired a sense for the timely arrival of songbirds when I lived in a hilltop house surrounded by open hay fields. Every year during the first week of May, I would wake up one morning and hear the exuberant bubbling song of the bobolink, a long-distance flyer freshly arrived from the pampas of Argentina. And last week, while working in the yard, I heard the feisty chattering of a male house wren, another early May arrival, claiming a birdhouse, building a nest of sticks, hoping to attract a female.

I reflected on each bird's sense of timing. Cued by increasing daylight and a higher angle of the sun, the birds departed from their wintering grounds in the Caribbean, Central America, and South America, often flying at night to take advantage of the cool still air and to use darkness to hide from the hawks. They winged north, navigating by stars and magnetic fields, riding southerly breezes, arriving on their breeding grounds as early as possible to claim the best nesting sites, to feast on the emerging smorgasbord of protein insects, the plentiful food that would be needed to nourish their nestlings. Perfect timing — without a calendar, clock, or watch.

I wondered if vestiges of this nature-based timekeeping persisted in modern humans. Or had a lifestyle linked to linear time and blurred by artificial light overridden any such sensitivities? Mosts years I notice that the progressively earlier sunrise prompts me to wake up earlier. Sadly, though, my response is usually to pull down the shades and drift back to sleep. I have also observed that I have more energy this time of year to work outside into the lingering last light of the day. And on a morning like this, with the sun climbing to an angle that some caveman part of my brain must have interpreted as a harbinger of warmth and abundance, it was easy to feel energetic and upbeat.

I gazed at the trees around me. The leaves on the black cherries and maples were opening up, but the ash trees remained gray and bare and leafless, running on their own unique schedule. What advantage, I wonder, came from leafing in later? Perhaps the ash trees wanted their own time with the pollinating insects. Whatever their strategy, it seemed to be working for I had noticed hundreds of ash seedlings sprouting in my garden beds at home.

Suddenly, a crow, flying silently above the trees, cast a sharp shadow across the forest floor. I flinched reflexively, immediately vigilant, stared at the swift black shadow tracing across the ground, muscles braced, feeling the wariness of a predator that could quickly become prey.

The wind picked up. The waves splashed against the shoreline, creating a deep, loud galumphing sound. I studied the maze of dead trees and fallen limbs littering the woods. A slender tree had broken off halfway up the trunk, fallen and wedged against another tree to form a perfect ninety-degree angle. Another fallen tree formed a neat forty-five-degree angle while its many limbs traced a plethora of acute and obtuse angles.

Gazing at these angles, I was reminded of my high school geometry teacher, an enthusiastic, ever-cheerful young woman who put so much effort into making that abstract subject understandable to our class. But I was an indifferent student and muddled through the course. Perhaps if she had been allowed to take us out of the box of the classroom and into the woods to show us the myriad angles of nature, I might have done better, might have grasped the importance and relevance of geometry, might have felt a real enthusiasm for the subject.

A yellow warbler sang, a second joined in, their songs ringing like dueling dulcimers. A song sparrow chimed in with its lilting aria. The tree branches swayed in the wind, making soft sounds, not the frozen clacking and knocking sounds of winter. The air smelled fresh and clean. As I left the peninsula, I heard another bird call, a loud, husky descending *veer, veer, veer,* yet another new arrival. I hoped it would stick around so I could identify it the next week.

## Week 12 · May 10

# Fire Throat

Two kingbirds perched on a white rectangular "No Parking" sign — slender, medium-sized, gray-backed, white-breasted birds. They appeared agitated, heads bobbing, tails flicking up and down. One fluttered over to another sign, the other followed. The first flitted to a third sign, the second followed. The first flew over and landed on a slender willow branch that swayed up and down with the weight of the bird. The second bird followed. The first bird took off across the lake, the second followed.

My impression was that they were having a domestic spat; she was upset, and he kept trying to placate her, to make amends. It was consoling to imagine these kingbirds might be having a relational tiff, a common human experience. But I was projecting, guilty of anthropomorphism, attributing human characteristics to birds. Their behavior was much more likely linked to a crucial life issue, finding a partner, establishing a territory, building a nest, or preparing to mate.

Perching on the sign, however, was typical behavior for kingbirds.

David Sibley, in his classic *The Sibley Field Guide to Birds of Eastern North America,* notes that kingbirds are common in open habitats near water and favor a perch where they can dart out and snatch insects out of the air. This was another reminder that each bird has its specific habitat and behaviors, its unique niche, its precise fit into the web of life.

Walking along the West Shore Trail, I was relieved that mild weather had arrived, weather I had been hoping for since February. The sky was a clear blue, the sun was shining, the wind calm, and the temperature in the mid-sixties. I inhaled the scent of earth and fresh growth. Washed by two days of gentle rain, the trail appeared clean, soft, and fresh.

The plants had grown dramatically over the last week. Stalks of invasive prolific garlic mustard topped with clusters of tiny, off-white flowers now stood a foot tall. Long, slender blades of grass reached up toward the sun. Red-tinged leaves of poison ivy sprouted menacingly from vines that slithered along the ground and wound around the tree trunks.

I walked slowly, naturally, fully aware, all senses open, trying to pick up on the mood of nature. I remembered what Jon Young wrote about the folly of attempting to sneak through the woods, a maneuver so forced and unnatural that it creates a disturbance greater than walking normally. My sense was that today the woods were happy and busy. An ovenbird chattered, a gray catbird trilled through a rollicking stream of songs. Frogs droned in a steady hum from the weeds along the shoreline.

I settled in beneath a large ash tree. The maple, cherry, and birch leaves had unfurled more fully and now wove a lacy, spring-green canopy above. I listened to the morning birdsongs — two ovenbirds singing their insistent *teetcha, teetcha, teetcha*; another catbird rolling through a series of song snippets and concluding with a whiny mew. Above, hidden in the emerging canopy of leaves, I heard a distinctive, high-pitched, ascending *zip, zip, zip, zip, titititi, tseeee,* a song that I didn't recognize. The frogs continued their steady drone.

The word symphony sprang to mind, a word derived from the Greek *symphonia,* meaning "agreement or concord of sound" or a "concert of vocal or instrumental music." The main players — the ovenbirds, the catbird, the unknown warbler, and the frogs — created a soothing, steady body of this nature symphony. Then a soloist would appear — a sing-song robin, a chattering chickadee, a checking red-winged blackbird. The voices of two women, conversing while kayaking, blended in, distant at first, gradually closer and clearer, accompanied by the steady *plash, plash, plash* of their paddles.

Now there were two birds above me singing the same unknown *zip, zip* song, probably spring warblers, always a challenge to identify. I listened carefully, attempted again and again to convert their song into syllables or words, tried to count the repetitions, to note the length of the song, to catch any changes in pitch. I paged frantically through Sibley, reading and rereading song descriptions, trying to lock in information on plumage and field marks, scanning maps of migration pathways and breeding areas, noting details on habitat. I began to experience information overload. I doubted I would ever identify these birds.

As if they sensed my struggle and took pity on the meager efforts of a novice birder, the two warblers swooped down, dodged and weaved through the branches, and darted past me just three feet away. I had a brief glance, but it was enough. The flash of a bright orange throat, a butter yellow belly, and a black and white back told me these were Blackburnian warblers, nicknamed "fire throat," the only warbler with a fiery orange throat. Their display of aerial acrobatics was no fluke. They are streamlined, long-winged warblers, long-distance flyers that winter in Central and South America. They live high in the trees, flashing out, gleaning insects and spiders. They are strongly territorial birds during the breeding season. I probably had seen two males engaged in a turf war.

I was pleased with this identification. For me, identifying a bird, a wildflower, a tree, or a shrub adds richness to the experience. Once seen, heard, and named, the bird becomes a friend to be appreciated and enjoyed during all subsequent encounters. And these new friends can be a focal point for further research and learning, for understanding a new array of adaptive characteristics, for appreciating another graceful fit into the symphony of nature.

My gaze drifted to the forest floor, to a patch of flowering wild lily of the valley. Compared to the domestic variety, these leaves are shorter, rounder, and more pale. I reached down and picked a cluster of the white flowers — tiny, star-shaped blossoms — sniffed, and inhaled a fragrance strikingly more subtle and wild than that of the lilies in my yard.

A bumble bee cruised over the ground in front of me. I expected to see it search out and feed on the wildflowers. Instead, it landed in an area covered with old, brown leaves and quickly burrowed under the litter. I kept my eyes focused on the spot where it disappeared, expecting it to emerge at any moment. Nothing happened. It stayed under the leaves. I watched for ten minutes; it never reappeared.

I found this extraordinary. What kind of bee was this? What was it doing under the leaves? Here was another creature, another pattern of behavior, another environmental niche that I knew nothing about. More researching and reading, more connecting the dots lay ahead of me. I was finding more questions than answers in the woods along the shore of Prompton Lake.

Week 13 · May 19 and 20

# Am Finkenmoor In den Duhner Heide

So much seemed familiar — the pines and deciduous trees, the scatter of fallen branches, the litter of tree trunks, the blanket of brown needles and fallen leaves, the background chorus of birdsongs, the earthy smells. Yet so much was different. The birdsongs were unfamiliar, and the pines grew in long straight rows.

I was sitting in the Wernerwald, a 375-hectare patch of wind-buffeted coastal moor planted with black pine trees in 1880 under the direction of a conservation-minded Hamburg official, Dr. Charles Werner. The tough black pines survived, flourished, and over the years covered the ground with needles, enriched the soil, provided partial shade, and created favorable conditions for flowers, weeds, bushes, and a variety of native trees to prosper. Now, the Wernerwald, located next to the northern German resort town of Sahlenburg, stands as the only patch of forest along the

Wadden Sea, a vast expanse of muddy tidal flats stretching from Holland to Denmark, a unique coastal environment, a designated world nature site.

It was another day of typically chilly, wet weather in northern Germany. A trough of low pressure drifted down from Iceland, dropped temperatures into the fifties, and brought a thick layer of gray clouds, sprinkles of rain, and a raw, gusty wind. My daughter, her husband, and their two children were staying in their trailer at a campground, a German-style campground with neat rows of closely ordered trailers and RVs. After two days of cold and rain that deflated all hopes of a fun family vacation, they were packing up. My daughter, a psychologist in training, understood my Prompton project and wished me a "good encounter" with nature.

Soon I sat on the ground looking at the still surface of the Finkenmoor, or Finch Swamp Pond, a freshwater pond with a thick patch of reeds on the far end and clusters of lily pads along the shoreline. I saw familiar ducks — mallards — and also an unfamiliar waterfowl the size of a small goose with an iridescent green head, a long green shoulder patch, a rusty stripe on the side of the breast, large side patches of bright white, and a striking orange bill. This was a *brandgans*, a goose that breeds along the coast of the North Sea.

The Wernerwald, bisected by a grid of trails, was filled with industrious vacationers undeterred by the less than favorable weather. Walkers, hikers, joggers, bikers, and parents with little children, all appropriately dressed and equipped, strode and rode through the woods and around the pond. At the south end of the pond, next to a stone memorial to Herr Doctor Werner, a teacher lectured to a group of teenagers. His purposeful voice carried across the water, as did the muffled voices of his students who appeared more interested in chatting with each other than listening to their teacher.

I sat thirty feet into the woods, my back resting against a black pine trunk, gazing toward the pond. I was by intention unprepared to identify the birds and had no local bird guide. I wanted to listen and look without the structure of bird names to see if birds similar to those at home filled similar environmental niches. Far across the pond toward the Wadden Sea, I heard crows cawing, a familiar cadence but a deeper tone. A pair of *brandgans* flew over, honking a high-pitched *eh, eh, eh*. I heard the cooing of a pigeon, a coo similar to that of a mourning dove, but louder, longer, and more insistent.

Wind-kicked wavelets splashed softly against the shore of the pond. A father and his three-year-old son strolled along the path, the boy holding a net, possibly on the hunt for frogs. Two walkers, shiny poles in each hand, strode by, their poles *tap, tap, tapping* with each step. No one noticed me, although I sat in plain sight. I was rendered invisible; no one expected a person to be simply sitting in the woods.

A jetliner whispered across the sky, reminding me that some of the first sounds of the jet age reverberated through this forest, when, during the last year of World War II, at a site hidden beneath the thick pines, the Nazis launched V2 rockets toward England. The birds and animals must have been shocked by the roar of a jet-powered rocket. Now the sound of a jetliner barely affected them.

Missing the solitude of Prompton, I moved further into the woods to hopefully spot the woodland birds that seemed to busily go about their life within the neat rectangular patches of forest between the paths. It felt better deeper in the woods with the fragrance of the black pines and the sound of an occasional pine cone dropping through the branches and landing with a soft thump on the bed of needles and leaves.

I spotted a medium-sized black bird perched halfway up a nearby tree, an *amsel,* the European cousin of the American robin. Its song is complex and melodious. I saw a junco-sized bird chirping as it hopped along a branch. A small wren-like bird flitted among the shrubs, warbling a beautiful and complex song. I heard more birdsongs, all sounding more complex, varied, and musical than their American cousins. Comparing American and European birdsongs seemed like comparing a domestic Riesling to a dry, minerally, aromatic, complex Riesling from the slate-covered hills slanting steeply down to the Mosel River.

When I returned to the campground, my daughter and her family were packed and ready to go. We agreed I would stay another day since I had already booked a warm, dry room in a nearby guest house. They departed. I rented a bike, put on a newly purchased, warm stocking cap, zipped up my fleece and parka, and rode north on a trail atop a tall dike. I looked across the tidal mudflats at clusters of horseback riders trotting through the mud. Further out I spotted a line of horse-drawn coaches making the six mile, low-tide trek to the distant island of Neuwerk. I saw groups, couples, and families with children walking on the dark muddy flats, some wearing rubber boots, others stepping barefoot. Later, over a beer, a frequent visitor to the area assured me that walking barefoot is the true way to experience the mud flats, a way that feels good and that confers important health benefits.

The bike trail traversed nature preserves, farm fields, campgrounds, and cottages and wound through small resort towns with hotels and shops. Even though the day was gray, raw, and chilly, the trail was filled with bikers and walkers. Germans don't wait for sunny weather to hike or bike. If they have a day off, they dress warmly and hit the trail. Even small children were bundled up and riding small pedal or push bikes. I saw cafés and restaurants where one could pause for a tall glass of foam-topped beer or a cup of dark aromatic coffee accompanied by a slice of apple strudel or a piece of poppy seed pastry. I stopped at a kiosk and bought a refreshing elderberry soda.

In Cuxhaven I found the Ritzebuttel Cemetery, searched through the rows of stones, and found the resting spot of my first wife, Antoinette, a much too young victim of cancer. I pinched a purple zinnia from an arrangement on a nearby grave and laid it on her tombstone. Looking down I felt regret for all the silly and inconsequential, lingering, post-divorce arguments and hostilities. I felt a great sadness that she missed knowing our two grandchildren. I felt grateful that among the crazy circumstances of our time together and in the stressful context of an American-German marriage, we created such a wonderful daughter.

I biked over to the fish harbor where an annual seafood festival was taking place. Inside a vast hall, where normally pallets and trays of fish were bought and sold and packed and shipped, stood long rows of stands selling beer and schnapps and North German specialties like raw or grilled herring, tiny North Sea shrimp, and fish burgers. I bought a serving of grilled herring smothered with freshly cut onions accompanied by a thick slice of black bread. At another stand I bought a big cup of beer and sat down at a long table to eat and listen to three accordion players singing traditional sea shanties. Many in the crowd, their emotions freed and fired by beer and schnapps, sang along loudly and enthusiastically. I could feel the swells of sentiment sweeping through the hall.

On my journey back, I stopped to walk a discovery path in the Duhner Heide, a preserved plot of coastal moor. I found this open landscape of low rolling dunes, purple-green heather, and clumps of cross-weaved heath dotted with clusters of small birches and bushes appealing. In contrast to the sculpted dike, the manicured bike path, and the neat and tidy inns, houses, and hotels, this land seemed primeval and natural. Something about this moor resonated with me. I decided to come back in the morning.

Early the next morning, under a gray sky, I found a spot thirty yards into the moor, near woods, and within eyesight and earshot of the North Sea. I leaned against a young tree and heard the shore birds and seagulls crying as they walked along the mud at the edge of the receding tide. From the woods came a symphony of birdsongs. Over the moor, swallows swooped down to snatch insects, swallows that were dark gray on top and white underneath and had long, bifurcated tails, swallows that seemed more delicate than those at home, though their musical trills sounded familiar.

Two light brown, cardinal-sized birds landed in a small tree twenty feet in front of me and worked their way down the branches to the ground to feed. Two large black and white birds — magpies — flew in front of me and landed in the grass to the left. Ahead, a small, brown finch-like bird perched in a tree and sang a complex and musical song. I was reminded that if you sit quietly, the birds will appear.

Far to my left, in the nearby village, I heard the insistent siren of a German emergency vehicle, a *whoo-hee, whoo-hee, whoo-hee*. As the siren faded, church bells began to peal announcing the celebration of Ascension. Suddenly, the two tan birds bolted from the grass and darted away on a low line. The two magpies took off low and fast. I wondered what spooked the birds. Fifteen seconds later I heard the loud *clump, clump, clump* of a jogger coming down the discovery path. This was an illustration of what Jon Young calls the plow, the scattering of wildlife before the intrusion of a walking or running person. The birds fled long before I heard anything.

I sat for a half hour. The path along the ocean edge of the moor was getting busy with morning walkers, so I decided to stroll through the moor. I stepped up a rise and kicked up a flock of *brandgans* that had been feeding in the moor. I listened to their strange honking sound as they flew away. I saw a pair of small, yellow-headed birds in a clump of bushes communicating back and forth with soft *tisk, tisk, tisk* calls. A small, brown bird sang a song similar to that of a song sparrow. At the top of a dune, I looked back and saw that the shorebirds had followed the receding tide further out onto the mud flats.

I came to the end of the path, mounted my bike, and rode back to my rented room. It was time to pack up and journey back to Bremen to rejoin my daughter, son-in-law, and grandchildren. I thought I might like to come back when the weather was warm and sunny to walk barefoot in the dark, moist mud and then sit in a seaside café and sip a tall beer, watch the shorebirds, seagulls, and people, and gaze out at the cold, blue sea beyond the tidal flats.

Week 14 · May 25

# A Cold Day in May

It was Saturday of Memorial Day weekend, the unofficial beginning of summer, a time for planting tomatoes and peppers, for filling flower pots and window boxes with geraniums and petunias, a time to grill hot dogs, hamburgers, and steak. But all of this had to be put on hold. The temperature was forty-four degrees, a gusty wind whipped down from the northwest, the wind chill hovered at a miserable thirty-five degrees, gray clouds covered the mid-morning sky, and the ground was soaked from an overnight rain. It was another day for layers of clothes — sweatshirt, jacket, jeans, boots, and hat. Cold, wet, windy weather seemed to be following me.

On the drive to Prompton, I gazed at the distant Moosic Mountains, a line of softly rounded forested peaks stretching south to north studded with bright white windmills churning steadily in the stiff breeze. I swerved around a windblown limb on the road. A red-tailed hawk flew high over the highway, clutching a snake in its talons. Bursts of sunlight broke through gaps in the clouds, traced across the dark green mountains, and offered a promise of better weather. In spite of the cold, I sensed a mood of resilience in the air as if the plants and birds and animals were not to be deterred by a brief spell of nasty weather.

A single car was parked in the lot, unusual for a holiday weekend. Swallows swooped and skimmed over the lake, hunting for insects. I stepped onto the West Shore Trail and felt as if I entered a rainforest. Bushes and shrubs were tall and lush and green. Leaf-draped branches drooped over the trail. Drops of water from last night's rain plopped to the ground. Patches of ferns — tall, low, light green, dark green, lacy-leafed, and large-leafed — spread across the forest floor. The wet and exuberant mass of growth created an acoustic amphitheater that softened and held the morning birdsongs. The seep, once an isolated green swath across a brown forest floor, was now buried beneath a riotous patch of weeds and grasses and only recognizable by the soft murmur of water over mossy rocks.

Hesitantly and without the clear intuitive sense I was hoping to cultivate, I selected a sit spot at the base of the peninsula under a big red maple tree. I settled in, relaxed, and tried to embrace the chilly spring day. But I didn't feel comfortable and the voice of intuition nagged at me, telling me again and again that this wasn't the right spot. After a few minutes of this unease, I gave in, picked up my chair and wandered around until I found another location near the tip of the peninsula under a tall black cherry tree, a spot with a good view of the lake, a spot that felt better.

At my feet, a colony of wild lily of the valley was in full bloom, tiny sprays of delicate white flowers reaching above rounded, green leaves. Ahead, deep in the woods, I heard the haunting, ethereal, flute-like song of a veery, a descending *vrdi, vrreed, vreer, vreer, vreer.* I listened to this song, one of my favorites, and pictured the veery — a cinnamon-brown bird, smaller than a robin with a delicately spotted chest — hopping along the ground, flipping over the leaf litter, searching for beetles, ants, grasshoppers, and caterpillars.

I saw movement along the shoreline to my left, brought up my binoculars and was stunned to spot a big black bear rambling down the shoreline, stepping over rocks, wading around fallen trees, drops of water glistening on its dark black fur. It looked as powerful and determined as a tank, yet moved as smoothly and gracefully as a sumo wrestler. I watched, transfixed, until I realized the bear was heading my way. I wondered if it would cut across the base of the peninsula, which meant I might see it ahead of me in the woods, or if it would continue to follow the shoreline, which meant it would come close to me. I wondered if it was a mother bear with cubs trailing along, in which case I might be in danger.

I anxiously ran these possibilities through my mind and looked and listened intently. But after a few minutes, I didn't see the bear, didn't hear anything that sounded like a bear crashing through the underbrush, and began to relax, look around, and listen to the birdsongs. Suddenly, I sensed a presence, glanced up, and saw the bear thirty feet in front of me, standing tall and still, head tilted, gazing at me quizzically. Alarm and fear flashed through my mind and body. I had just read an article about encountering black bears that advised one to stand tall, look large, wave your arms, and yell loudly, which I did. The bear looked at me, flinched in surprise, turned, and ambled off into the woods.

Heart pounding, adrenalin surging, and limbs shaking, I slowly sat down and looked at the spot where the bear had been standing, which was right at the base of the maple tree, right where I had been sitting a few minutes earlier. If I hadn't moved I never would have seen the bear along the shoreline, never would have known it was around. If I had stayed in that spot I might have had a very close, uncomfortably close, encounter with a bear. I thanked my intuition for guiding me to safety and reflected that there must be a protective dimension to intuition, a dimension I hoped to cultivate in the future.

As my nervous system slowly settled back to baseline, I wondered, with a tinge of regret, if I reacted in the best way. Was my immediate fear of the bear based on what I knew or based on what I recently read? Part of me wished I had sat still, watched the bear, taken pictures. Maybe I needed to overcome my learned fears and become more comfortable with all aspects of nature.

The sky was clearing, but the wind grew stronger, ripped down the lake, wildly swayed the branches, and whooshed loudly through the leaves. My attention drifted to the sheltered bay to my left where I noticed swallows dipping, dodging, chirping, and twittering. I watched them swooping, lifting, banking left and right, tree swallows with iridescent blue-green backs and smaller northern rough-winged swallows with brownish backs and whitish breasts. Altogether there were thirty or forty or fifty swallows swooping over the bay, flitting in and out of the trees. It was a hypnotic scene, a swarm of swallows swirling through the air — acrobats, winged dancers, whirling mystics above the wind-rippled water.

How quickly the swallows had congregated in the sheltered bay. Most likely finding the wind over the lake too strong for good insect hunting, they quickly moved to plan B, the quieter air in the lee of the little peninsula. It seemed as if swallows from all over the lake must be connected by some communication network, had simultaneously received the update on plan B, and quickly congregated above the waters of the little bay.

A rabbit dashed across the peninsula, likely spooked by a predator I never saw, maybe a weasel or a fox. An eastern phoebe perched in a bush along the shoreline, dark gray head, light gray body, long tail flicking up and down. A yellow warbler darted through the bushes, its bright plumage illuminated by a burst of sunshine.

Even with the sunshine it was cold. I glanced at my watch. Two minutes remained. Nobody was watching. I could leave. Then I reminded myself that a commitment is a commitment, an hour is an hour. I settled back into my chair, turned my face into the wind, inhaled and savored the sweet smell of fresh open water. I looked at my watch again. My hour was up.

Week 15 · May 31

# A Warm Day in May

What a difference a week can make! The unseasonably cold weather departed and summer warmth arrived. When I left home at 9:15 in the morning, the temperature had already risen to a balmy seventy-four degrees. On the drive, I sensed a festive mood in the air, as if all of nature was celebrating the softly angled morning sunshine and the new green growth in the fields and forests. A brilliant orange and black Baltimore oriole darted across the highway. Robins patrolled the freshly mowed, dark green, dew-covered yards. A pair of sun yellow goldfinches looped above a field of grasses where buttercups were tall enough to sway rhythmically in the breeze, like yellow-tipped waves in an ocean of green.

The scent of pine needles and the fragrance of the forest floor filled my nostrils as I walked down the West Shore Trail. Canes of blackberries festooned with delicate white blossoms offered the promise of dark, sweet, seedy berries that could be made into jam. Spread on hot buttered toast on a dark winter morning, blackberry jam might bring back the sensations and memories of this summery day.

A whitish squirt of bird poop lay upon the dark dirt of the trail. What were the odds of this poop landing right in the middle of this slender trail? It struck me that the earth, which was now giving so much to support the life of the forest, was already receiving bits of nourishment in return.

I sat down under the tall black cherry tree at the tip of the peninsula, the spot I found last week. Dappled sunlight filtered through the dense green canopy of leaves. An opening in the shrubs allowed a view of the little bay. Thickly leafed bushes and saplings obscured the view into the woods ahead. The still surface of the lake shimmered like a vast blue mirror.

Summer seemed in full swing. Frogs croaked along the shore line. A rich rollicking chorus of birdsongs rang through the morning air. I recognized a few — a robin, an ovenbird, and the warbled mimic fragments and whiny mews of a catbird. But there were so many songs, a jumbled chorus of trills, whistles, and buzzes, rising and falling in myriad patterns too complex for me to sort and identify.

Occasionally, I spotted a winged shape flitting from one leafy tree to the next. Maybe I would discern the shape and size of the bird. Maybe I would even get a glance at the plumage and detect a flash of color. In this dense summer foliage, I realized I had to rely more on my hearing than my vision to inform me which birds were around. I needed to listen to the birdsongs to understand the story of nature.

A light breeze arose, just enough to move the leaves, a south wind wafting across the little bay, bringing the smell of fresh water.

Suddenly, I inhaled a sweet fragrance, like the heady, lush fragrance of a woman's perfume. Surprised, I scanned for the source. Near the shoreline, I noticed a Russian olive bush draped in tiny ivory flowers. I walked over, sniffed the little flowers, and inhaled a fragrance that was floral and delicate, yet rich, sensual, earthy, and spicy. I had never heard of a perfume called Essence of Russian Olive. A great pity, I thought.

Perhaps this thorny shrub's lack of romantic reputation stems from its origin as an invader from central Asia. Also known as silverberry or wild olive, the Russian olive is a hardy, drought-resistant shrub that grows seven or more feet tall. The aromatic flowers produce clusters of small orange-red fruit readily consumed by a variety of birds that then spread the seeds and effectively propagate the plant. The fruits, described as having a sweet taste, are eaten in Iran. The dried powder when mixed with milk is reputed to be an effective remedy for arthritis and joint pain.

I looked down and saw a small, pale green inchworm, as slender as a segment of a dry spaghetti noodle, crawling across my hand. It reared up, waved the front part of its body around, picked a direction, stretched forward, front feet landing on my skin, pulled its rear section up, and then repeated the maneuver. I watched it move steadily across the back of my hand, probably wondering what kind of strange surface it had found. I reached my hand down and let it inch its way onto a large leaf where it immediately worked its way to the underside, a safer location in a woods filled with hungry birds. A minute later I peeked under the leaf, but the little green worm was gone.

A motorboat putted through the narrows off the tip of the peninsula, the loud motor disturbing the morning quiet. A few seconds later, I inhaled the sharp smell of combusted gasoline. Slowly, the sound of the motor and the smell of gasoline faded away. Quiet returned. A different soundscape emerged. A cardinal whistled. A song sparrow chanted. I focused and strained and listened to these songs—loud and quiet, near and far—and had the strange sensation that my ears were opening up, growing physically larger to take in more and more of the soundscape, making a needed adaptation.

A chipmunk crawled out of a hole at the base of a tree about twenty away, carefully stepped across the forest floor, stopping, sniffing, scanning. A minute later it came to a big maple tree, paused, looked around, and disappeared down another hole, the purpose of this brief foray known only to the chipmunk.

Small black flies hovered and whined yet didn't land or bite. A yellow swallowtail butterfly fluttered by in front of me. A small black spider scuttled down my pants leg. Bees buzzed. High above in the leafy canopy, a Baltimore oriole sang in familiar sweet, clear tones — *pidoo, tewdi, tewdi, yew*. Two drake mallards winged up the lake, calling a low raspy *kreep, kreep, kreep*. In the distance a black-billed cuckoo sang a melancholy *cu, cu, cu*.

It was 10:30. My hour was up. The morning freshness was morphing into mid-day heat. The day would turn hot and humid. I packed up, walked back to my car, happily wearing a T-shirt, enjoying the sensation of the warm air on my bare arms.

Week 16 · June 8

# The Colorado Hummingbird

I leaned back against the thickly grooved, sun-warmed bark of a ponderosa pine and looked down into a narrow ravine filled with thickly leafed shrubs and scrubby deciduous trees. Across from me stretched an open meadow of pale green grasses speckled with blue, violet, pink, and white wildflowers. Beyond the meadow, a dark green blanket of pines spread a thousand feet up the flank of Flagstaff Mountain. Outcroppings of gray-brown rock poked through the pines. Above the long horizontal line of the mountain crest, a deep azure-blue sky extended up into space, the kind of endless blue sky one sees in the mountains of Colorado.

A quarter of a mile downhill, the snow-melt waters of South Boulder Creek rushed across the rocky stream bed, creating a steady sloughing sound that blended in with the whoosh of early morning traffic. The air was dry and fresh and warm and smelled of earth and pine. Gusts of wind sighed softly through the pine boughs above me. The ground was littered with squat, small-lobed cacti and wild yucca plants festooned with thin, spiky leaves surrounding upright, asparagus-like stalks loaded with ripe buds.

Today, on my second try, I thought I might have found a good sit spot. Yesterday's attempt had gone poorly. The owner of the motel where I was staying while accompanying my daughter on a visit to a friend had told me about a deer trail that started at the far end of the parking lot, wound up the mountain, traversed meadows, and led to the top of Flagstaff Mountain where, he assured me, I would have a spectacular view of the distant snow-capped Rockies.

Following his advice, I awoke early, sipped a quick cup of tea, packed my gear, and was out the door by six. At first the meandering deer trail was easy to follow. Then it vanished. I continued to walk uphill, weaving left and right, searching for traces of the trail, trusting my eyes and feet to find it, discovering it, losing it, finding it again, and realizing that all of this disappearing and reappearing was just the nature of a deer trail.

After twenty minutes of climbing, I came to a likely location for a sit spot, a small meadow edged by a wooded ravine. I sat down and started my observations. But I soon realized I was facing east, looking directly into the rising sun, and the bright, angled light made it hard to see. The wind blew the traffic noise toward me, making it hard it to hear. After twenty minutes, I had only seen one robin in a tree and two blackbirds flying overhead, and had only heard the cooing of a single mourning dove.

I decided to climb higher to search for a better spot, and after ten minutes I came to another meadow where three mule deer grazed peacefully, their light-brown, dew-covered coats shimmering in the morning sunshine. They stepped slowly, nibbled at the grass, glanced up, eyed me for an instant, and resumed grazing, unconcerned with my presence.

I kept climbing, and soon some strange and strong compulsion took over. I had to reach the top of the mountain. I followed the deer path when I could, wandered through grass and scrambled up rocks when I couldn't. Several times I was sure I was close to the summit only to discover that I had just reached another narrow plateau. I pushed on and on and after an hour of increasingly arduous climbing, finally reached the top. The view of the Rockies was as spectacular as advertised, a long distant line of high, jagged, triangular, snow-capped summits piercing the bright blue sky, white peaks illuminated by the bright morning sunlight.

I rested. I was tired, sweaty, and thirsty. The temperature was rising. I had neglected to bring along a water bottle, a stupid mistake. I looked far down the mountain and spotted the distant roof of the motel where cool tap water, plentiful breakfast fixings, and freshly ground coffee awaited. But the motel looked to be a long distance down the steep slope, the path unknown. I hesitated, paralyzed by the prospect of a daunting descent.

If I wanted a drink of water, breakfast, and coffee, I better get started, I thought. I located the deer trail, followed it, and even recognized a few spots from my ascent. Then I lost the trail, found it, lost it again, and ended up barging through thick brush and scrambling over rocks. I paused to check my bearings and realized that somehow I had wound up on the wrong side of a deep, impassible ravine. I no longer had a direct route back to the motel. Starting to feel desperate, I pushed my way down through the bushes and eventually came to a steep, rocky bank covered with blackberry brambles that dropped forty yards down to a gravel parking spot behind a small wood-framed house. I was stuck. I couldn't go back up. Deep ravines hemmed me in on both sides. The only way out was to slide down through the thorny bushes and hope for the best.

I plopped down on my butt, launched myself downhill, but slid too fast and felt brambles ripping my shirt and scraping my skin. I thudded to a stop and stood up cautiously, checked for serious injuries and fortunately found none. Brushing off the dust, I stepped briskly across the parking spot, squeezed through the gate barring the driveway, and strode quickly over to the nearby highway. I breathed a sigh of relief, paused, glanced back, and read bold black letters on a wooden sign on the gate:

PRIVATE PROPERTY
NO TRESPASSING
VIOLATORS WILL BE SHOT FIRST AND QUESTIONED LATER

But, that was the previous day's adventure. Now, with the sun rising behind me, I settled in to my new sit spot, one I had noticed on an earlier walk but dismissed as too easily found and too close to the motel and traffic. I looked over to the middle of the meadow and spotted a shiny, purple-black common grackle perched at the top of a tall solitary pine. The grackle squawked a series of harsh calls and then took off to continue its flight up the mountain. A robin, flitting from tree to tree, worked its way up the ravine below me. I smiled at the sight and sound of this common bird that lives in yards and wild areas across the country, always singing its sweet, cheerful song. Maybe the robin should be the national bird, and we could all emulate its qualities of adaptability and tunefulness.

A hummingbird buzzed down the ravine, helicoptered up, and perched at the tip of a dead branch in a cluster of three little pines directly across the ravine. I brought up my binoculars to focus on the tiny bird, but in the bright angled sunlight, I couldn't discern its colors. Still I was struck by its "birdiness." At home, hummingbirds buzzed by, hovered, sipped nectar, appearing more like large insects than birds. But this hummingbird's tiny feathers were ruffled by the breeze, its black needle-like beak stood out clearly, and its miniature claws clutched the branch.

It buzzed away but reappeared a few minutes later to perch on the same branch. I watched its movements, a dip of its head, a bob of its longish tail. But I still couldn't distinguish its colors. Then two more hummingbirds appeared in the ravine below, and the first flew in to attack, chattering while chasing the intruders away.

A pair of crows flew lazily over the meadow toward me, long black wings touching at times, weaving back and forth, dropping down, rising up, flying in tandem in a kind of sensual, aerial dance. Was this a courtship flight, or were they just playing around, pulling aeronautic maneuvers simply because they could?

The hummingbird returned to the pine branch, rested, lifted off, darted down through branches, swooped to the edge of the meadow near me, hovered, and began to feed on a stem of bright blue flowers just ten feet away. The light was exactly right, and I could clearly see its rosy red throat, shiny green back, and a long broad tail. A quick check in my Sibley revealed that this was a male broad-tailed hummingbird, a western species, a little larger than the ruby-throated hummingbirds I knew from home. He worked his way up and down the full length of the flower stem, pausing to feed at each blossom, then zipping back to his favorite perch.

The blue flower he fed upon was a penstemon, a native of the Southwest that blooms in shades of blue, violet, pink, and lavender, colors I could see dotting the field around me. Penstemon prefers sandy, loamy soil, tolerates dry conditions, and attracts butterflies and hummingbirds. Spread by tiny seeds, it is one of the first flowers to sprout in burned out areas, a fact I verified later that week when I hiked through a recent burn in Rocky Mountain National Park and saw clusters of slender green stems topped with blue and lavender, growing with apparent hope in desolate tracts of black charred earth.

A robin landed in the little pine tree across the ravine, seemingly a favorite landing spot for all birds moving up and down the ravine. It sang a few bars and moved on. A few minutes later, a tiny bird, dark gray above, light gray below, hopped through the branches of the same pine and flew off, possibly a bushtit, a western bird. Another small bird worked up the ravine, a bird with the familiar black, white, and gray coloration of a chickadee, but this was a mountain chickadee.

The hummingbird returned to his perch at the end of the branch. Based on his possessive behavior, I was pretty sure it was the same bird. After a minute, he flew out to the meadow to feed on flowers then returned to his perch to rest and survey his domain. This must be his home territory, so he knew the flowers, the cover, and the perch with the best view. Perhaps he had selected this territory to attract a mate. Maybe there was a little nest nearby hidden in the thick cover of the ravine, a nest tended by his mate, containing a clutch of miniature eggs.

A harsh call echoed from the meadow, another western bird, a black-billed magpie perched in a tall solitary pine. Through my binoculars, I observed its jet black head, bright white belly, and long blue-black tail. It flew toward the ravine and called out a harsh *jeeeek, jeeeek, jeeeek*. A few seconds later another magpie flew in and landed in the same pine tree. I read later that magpies are social birds, members of the corvid family, cousins of the crow and the blue jay, clever omnivorous birds that eat seeds, steal eggs, and snatch nestlings.

I glanced across the ravine at the hummingbird resting on his branch, calmly surveying his kingdom. It was 7:30. The sun was climbing higher, and the morning's freshness was fading. It was time for me to leave the hummingbird's realm. On my walk back to the motel, I reflected that the rich drama of life I had just seen would continue to play out through the rest of the day, through tomorrow, and hopefully forever in the deep, wooded ravine, in the pine tree, and on the green, grassy meadow where the bright blue penstemon flowers bloomed.

Week 17 · June 15

# The Warbler's Woods

Through sleepy eyes I peered out my bedroom window at the first slivers of predawn light edging into the night sky. Tentative beginning notes of the morning chorus sounded, a robin sing-songing, a cardinal caroling. I checked my watch, 4:54 — way too early to get up. I dropped my head back down into the welcoming softness of the pillow, fully intending to let the birdsongs carry me back to sleep when suddenly a voice from some unknown area of my brain told me to get up and go to Prompton. I ignored the voice, hoping it would fade away. Instead, it grew more insistent, repeating its message in louder and more directive tones. Finally, I gave in, got up, and minutes later was on the way to Prompton.

The highway ran along the top of a miles-long north-south ridge. Off to the right I saw the sun slowly push above the horizon, a huge, brilliant yellow orb spreading illumination over the dew-covered hayfields and the dark green woodlots. On either side of the ridge, down in the valleys, pale gray-white mist wafted above the creeks and ponds. On three occasions, solitary deer, now attired in their summer tan coats, walked peacefully, even regally, across the road in front of me.

At Prompton three pickup trucks with boat trailers attached stood in the parking lot, no doubt belonging to fishermen eager to get out on the lake after a string of rainy days. The West Shore Trail was muddy and dotted with tiny puddles. A fresh set of raccoon paw prints were perfectly imprinted into the soft mud. Runoff from the rain rushed down rocky channels to the lake.

I reminded myself again to walk naturally and slowly, to look and listen, to try to blend in. The birds sang all around me. Maybe I was blending in. But as soon as I turned off the trail and headed into the woods, the songs ceased and the tentative warning calls began. Perhaps the birds had come to accept people on the trail but became watchful when someone veered into their territory.

By 6:00 AM I had set up under the angled branch of the thick-trunked, dark-barked black cherry tree. From behind me sunlight filtered through the leaves and branches, dappling the dense, green forest understory ahead. The air was motionless, the temperature a comfortable fifty-five degrees. The fragrance of earth, water, grass, and leaves flooded my nostrils.

A blue heron, standing sentinel-like near the shoreline, seemed to grow uneasy with my presence, flapped into the air, squawked, set its long wings into a smooth rhythm, and flew down the lake. Slowly, the morning chorus resumed. I counted the songs I knew, six of them — American robin, gray catbird, ovenbird, song sparrow, yellow warbler, and one I had just mastered — the common yellowthroat's enchanting *witchety-witchety-witchety*. Then I tallied the unknown songs, listening carefully to different trills, whistles, buzzes, chips, and chirps, and discerned at least eight distinct songs, many of them probably the songs of warblers. Altogether, fourteen different birds sung on this tiny wooded peninsula, a treasure of evolved diversity in song, plumage, behavior, and habitat preference.

Suddenly, the songs fell silent. Instantly alert, I strained to listen, and finally detected the whipping sound of a fishing rod, the zing of line running off a reel, and the splash of a lure hitting the water. Partially obscured by bushes, a mere twenty-five yards away, two fishermen cast their lures and talked quietly. Although I saw them, they didn't notice me. The sudden silence of the birds had been a clear communication, as articulate and expressive as a bold print newspaper headline announcing strangers in the area.

The fishermen's boat, propelled by a tiny trolling motor, slowly putted away. Gradually, the birdsongs resumed. I felt myself relax. Life on the peninsula returned to normal.

A medium-sized bird landed on a slender branch twenty yards ahead. I brought up my binoculars, focused, and gazed at a vision of beauty that took my breath away. It was a male cedar waxwing. I had seen photographs, paintings, and drawings of cedar waxwings, seen flocks from a distance feasting on berries, seen families fluttering above a stream, darting out, and snatching insects from the air. But this view was totally different, absolutely mesmerizing. I stared through my binoculars, absorbing every detail of the bird's plumage, the tan back shading into the dark gray-brown of the wings, the perfect bright red band at the tip of the wing, the bright yellow band at the end of the tail, and the white-edged black eye mask.

I spotted two more waxwings perched on a Russian olive branch, a male and a female next to each other. The male plucked a green berry, held it in his bill, and offered it to the female. She took it, held it briefly in her beak, and then returned it. He offered it again. She accepted and this time lifted her head and swallowed the berry. They hopped in tandem along the branch and then flew off wing to wing.

I later read that such back and forth berry exchanges are common courtship behaviors for waxwings. Perhaps some rituals of courtship extend across species. The male brings a gift. The female coyly rejects it, testing his commitment, his persistence. The male offers the gift again, and reassured of his devotion and commitment, she accepts. The bonds of relationship are built. The couple moves off in synchrony and works together to build a nest and raise a family.

Cedar waxwings are highly social birds that fly, feed, and even nest in groups. They consume a wide range of wild fruit and in the summer hover and dart acrobatically in the air to capture insects. Waxwings benefit when people plant fruiting trees such as mountain ash and serviceberry. Their population is slowly increasing.

I spotted a small plain brownish bird hopping along the ground beneath a bush. I trained the binoculars on it, watched as it stepped closer — a small stocky bird with a streaked chest and a short thick beak, a very subdued beauty compared to the waxwing. It snatched a caterpillar from a leaf and swallowed it. When it flew away, I pulled out my bird guide.

Based on the shape and coloring, I figured it was a sparrow. As I leafed through the pages, I read Sibley's description of the song sparrow: a solitary bird that hops along the ground in bushy areas. The habitat and behavior were a perfect fit. The picture and the description of the streaky chest clinched the deal. I had heard song sparrows singing, had learned its lilting song, and now could fuse image and song in my mind and memory.

My hour was up, but I was reluctant to leave. It seemed as if the birds were putting on a show with songs, plumage displays, and even an inside look at a courtship ritual. I turned my eyes away from my watch and settled back in the chair. Crows cawed in the distance. A catbird mewed and then sang a stunningly accurate imitation of a robin and a blue jay.

Some minutes later, when I finally stood up to leave, a male redstart, a bright orange and black warbler, darted out of the bushes, landed on a branch six feet away, fanned his tail, and flashed his bright black and orange plumage. Ah, I thought, the performance in the warblers' woods is never over!

# Summer

# Fulfillment

The routine of a nature observer was growing easier, taking on a momentum of its own as once again I managed to pull off an early morning departure to Prompton. I lingered in the parking lot and watched the sunrise, saw the great golden life-giving orb edge slowly above the long line of dark wooded hills that stretched above the far side of the lake. Feathery strands of mist rose, drifted, and intermingled above the glass-smooth lake. A lone fisherman in a simple aluminum rowboat cast along the far shoreline.

Down near the boat ramp, two crows suddenly took off from the stony shoreline, flew away low and silent like black specters vanishing into the thin gray mist. A third crow, luminescent and shiny in the angled sunlight, waddled peacefully across the shoreline pebbles, eyes down, picking for bits of food. It turned its head and threw me a brief glance, seemed satisfied that I was going about my business, and turned back to its business.

The word "fulfillment" rolled around in my brain, a word that had sprung into awareness during the drive to Prompton. The word surprised me. I decided not to doubt or question it, but to remain open and observe what might unfold during the hour ahead.

Along the West Shore Trail, two favorite birdsongs welcomed me — the insistent *teetcha* chant of an ovenbird; and the rich, mysterious, multi-toned, flute-like song of a veery. I made my way to the big black cherry tree, set up, and settled in. The temperature was a fresh fifty-five degrees. A light, intermittent, soft southwest wind arose, a breeze that touched my cheek, rippled the surface of the lake, and moved the morning mist.

A chipmunk raised its head from a tiny hole at the base of a large maple, paused, looked around carefully, and then slowly stepped across the leaf-littered forest floor. I trained my binoculars on the little chipmunk and saw its shiny black eyes and striped tan fur, its cheeks bulging with nuts and seeds. It was good to see a mammal, a creature moving on the ground.

I kept track of the chipmunk's time on the surface. A minute and thirty-three seconds later it slipped back beneath the ground, emerged sixty-six seconds later, and then after a brief thirty-two-second foray, disappeared back down its hole. These seemed like brief intervals of activity, but the chipmunk's behavior, honed by centuries of evolution, must represent a balance between the search for food, the efficient use of energy, and the avoidance of predators.

Gazing down I saw that the leaves and flowers of the wild lily of the valley, an early spring wildflower, had faded and shriveled. But inches away, the next wildflower in the seasonal progression, the lacy-leafed, pink-flowered wild geranium, was now in full bloom.

I listened to the familiar birdsongs — the robin, catbird, yellow warbler, ovenbird, chickadee; and five or more unfamiliar and unknown songs. I noticed that the songs were less frequent and less insistent than last week, a scattering of songs instead of a constant chorus.

What had changed? Was there something about today's weather that suppressed the birdsongs? No, that couldn't be the answer. It was a perfect spring day. Then it occurred to me. It was no longer spring. Yesterday was the summer solstice. Today was already a few seconds shorter. Summer had arrived. The birds no longer needed to sing to attract a mate or to claim territory. They had paired off weeks ago, built nests, laid eggs, and now were feeding their rapidly growing nestlings. They sang just enough now to maintain their territory.

The word "fulfillment" returned to mind. The promise of spring, the promise that began in February when the days grew longer and the skunk cabbage unfurled its protective shroud, the promise of March with hints of warmth and the return of the blackbirds, the promise of April with sprouting weeds and budding leaves, the promise of May with the rising chorus of birdsongs — all of these promises had been fulfilled.

I listened with a changed sensibility, an acceptance, a celebration of fulfillment. Curious on the origin of the word, I later read that fulfill comes from the old English *fulfyllan,* which means to fill up, to make full. Certainly, the woods were made full with new life.

My hour was drawing to an end. I felt the welcome warmth of sunlight on my shoulders, and saw the ascending sunlight illuminating the grasses, trees, and leaves. I heard the distant mournful *cu-cu-cu* song of a black-billed cuckoo. A catbird hopped along the ground. A flicker called. A flock of red-winged blackbirds, already augmented by a new generation, called *check, check, check* as they flew down the shoreline.

On the walk back, I spotted a small bird with an olive back and a yellowish throat, a plumage pattern that describes at least twenty or more spring warblers. I brought up my binoculars, but the bird darted into a thick bush. A second bird appeared. I focused on it and saw a vivid yellow throat and a dramatic black eye mask edged with a fine white line — a male common yellowthroat, another view of beauty that no drawing, painting, or photograph could ever capture.

The first bird reappeared, the female, and the pair flitted from branch to branch, flicking their tails, calling out their scolding *tchep* calls, appearing agitated, but holding their ground. They must have had a nest nearby with hungry nestlings. I lingered for a moment, transfixed by the close-up view of these perfectly plumaged, busy little birds, then continued on my way, leaving the yellowthroats to fulfill their purpose.

Week 19 · June 29

# Power

Heavy, steady rain fell through the night Thursday. On Friday I waited patiently for the water to recede and the woods to dry out.

Early Saturday, as I drove to Prompton, conditions looked as if they had returned to normal. The sun pushed above the horizon into a vast, pale blue sky. Morning dew glistened on the grass, on the freshly mowed hayfields, and on the dark green leaves of the trees. A momma black bear ambled across the road leading three cubs, their dewy wet coats shining in the sunlight, their movements loose, fluid, and powerful. The landscape looked cleansed, refreshed, and renewed by the recent rainfall.

But as I descended the long hill down into the valley of the Lackawaxen River, the stream that feeds Prompton Lake, a very different picture began to emerge. Jagged lines of rain-washed gravel stretched across the road. A section of ditch had washed away, leaving a ragged, menacing two-foot-deep trench right next to the road. Suddenly, I encountered a wedge of brown rocks and reddish mud that extended across the road and blocked my way. I slammed on the brakes, paused, surveyed the scene, and finally spotted a route through the debris. Edging over to the other lane, I cautiously worked my through the mud, gravel, and rocks. I came upon four more of these wedges of mud and rocks wrought by the flood, and fortunately, each time I was able to find a way through. At the bottom of the hill, a tiny unnamed creek, normally a barely visible silver of water, was now a boiling, frothing torrent rushing through the culvert and flooding the adjacent fields.

At the junction with Creek Drive, I looked north and saw that the road was flooded by the muddy waters of the Lackawaxen River. Three orange cones set in a haphazard row proclaimed the road closed. Tree swallows swooped over the newly formed open water foraging for insects. I turned and headed toward the boat ramp only to encounter two even bigger wedges of brown clay-mud and huge rocks covering the highway. Again, I had to slow to a crawl and work my way through the debris.

Feeling very relieved to have finally arrived at Prompton, I found the concrete boat ramp was underwater and blocked across the top by a thirty-foot-tall, flood-born, dead tree with bare branches and a snarl of dark roots. Looking out at the lake I saw a vast mat of debris floating in the middle — uprooted trees, broken branches, clumps of reeds and grasses, abandoned boards and bottles — all of it bobbing in the wind and waves.

The West Shore Trail had been transformed into a narrow trench of squishy, tan mud. I had to jump over a small water course that normally was bridged by a few flat rocks, but the rocks had been swept away by the flood, and now the water rushed and roiled downhill toward the muddy lake. Arriving at the peninsula, I managed to find a solid spot of dry solid ground near the black cherry tree. I set up, sat down, and settled in to listen and look. The woods seemed quiet, but not silent. A few familiar songs and calls carried through the morning air — an ovenbird, a yellow warbler, a song sparrow, and a robin.

Looking at the ground I saw small green berries clinging to the wilted stems of wild lily of the valley. Vigorous vines of poison ivy with their distinctive three-lobed, burgundy-tinged leaves coiled serpent-like up the trees. Virginia creeper vines with friendlier five-lobed, green leaves spread across the ground, crawled over the rocks, and wound around tree trunks. Drops of dew dripped down from the leaves and branches. Morning mist hung over the lake. Once again I felt like I was in a rainforest.

A small bird flitted by and perched on a nearby branch. I trained my binoculars on it and began to mentally check off identifying features — thick sparrow beak, light brown plumage, pale legs, short tail. It was too small for a sparrow; it was possibly an uncommon species. Trying to contain my rising excitement, I held the field marks in my mind and quickly scanned through my *Sibley Field Guide*, hoping to identify this bird. Then another bird, similar in appearance but bigger, landed on the same branch, holding a fat caterpillar in its beak. The birds edged closer, and the bigger one offered the caterpillar to the smaller one. The bigger bird was a mother song sparrow. My hoped-for rare species had simply been an immature bird. Laughing at myself, I watched the momma bird fly off and reappear a minute later with another caterpillar in her beak. From a bush near the shoreline, I heard a male song sparrow singing his lilting *maids, maids, maids put on your tea kettle-lettle-lettle*. I counted the repetitions — one, two, three, four, five, and six. Using the sound of his call, I located the bird, trained my binoculars on him, and watched him sing, his beak opening and closing for the emphatic *maids, maids, maids*. Then, as he rolled into the accelerating trill, his whole body shook, and his wings, tail, and head quivered while tiny droplets of dew sprayed into the air. He looked like an opera singer belting out an aria. I felt admiration, even a tinge of jealousy. How good it must feel, how exhilarating, how cathartic, and how satisfying it must be to sing a song so beautifully and with such full body engagement.

More birds — a cardinal, a robin, and a catbird — landed one after the other in the bush where I had seen the song sparrow, a bush that seemed to be a "hot spot" today for the birds, a place where they all landed, where they all must have felt comfortable and safe.

The next morning, curious about the effects of the flood, I kayaked around the lake. Apparently, the area around Prompton had received "a locally heavy downpour!" When I arrived, the water had receded part way down the boat ramp, but the tree remained beached across the top. The debris field had drifted toward the far shore. I paddled up to the shoreline and saw a gray-brown mud line on the leaves that marked the high water level. Holding one edge of my seven-foot paddle at the current water level I determined that the other end barely reached this mud line. Performing a quick mental calculation on the surface area of the lake times the seven-foot-plus height of the paddle, I was stunned by the amount of water that must have poured into the lake.

Suddenly, I understood the vital importance of Prompton Dam and its sister Jadwin Dam on the Dyberry Creek north of Honesdale. Without these two dams, the little town of Honesdale, nestled in a valley below the confluence of these two streams, would have been flooded just as it was many times in the past prior to the construction of the dams in the 1960s.

Paddling up the lake, I noticed a large cylindrical hay bale half-submerged in the brown muddy water. Curious, I later researched the weight of such a hay bale. Based on the dimensions, the density, and the type of grass, weight estimates ranged from eight hundred to twenty-two hundred pounds. I tried to visualize how much raw power it would take to lift one of these heavy hay bales out of a field, sweep it downhill, and float it like a cork onto the lake. Continuing on, I counted six more of these flood-floated, half-submerged hay bales scattered around the lake, a dramatic testimony to the power of the flood.

I pushed my kayak into the middle of the debris field where I saw brown, dead stalks of Japanese knotweed, dense tangles of dead branches, uprooted trees, Styrofoam cups and containers, new plastic bottles, old glass bottles, and old aerosol cans with faded paint and streaks of rust. The flood waters must have reached far up in the woods and fields and cleansed out discarded cans and bottles from long ago.

Proceeding up through the flooded grasses and reeds into the mouth of the Lackawaxen River, I noticed that a flock of tree swallows followed me, swooping, twittering, and chirping. I thought I might be disturbing their nesting area, but they continued to glide along behind me as I paddled further upstream. Then I realized that I was carving a V of disturbance through the water, kicking up insects, and the swallows were following me to reap the benefits, much like a flock of seagulls trailing a fishing trawler.

On my return I guided the kayak over to the peninsula to view yesterday's "hot bush" from the lake side. I immediately spotted a catbird perched in the bush. A small brown bird flew down, landed on a patch of debris floating in the lee of the peninsula and stepped skillfully along the floating tree trunks searching for food, its head bobbing, its tail up. I thought it might be a song sparrow, but it was more olive than brown, and the black stripes on its chest were more pronounced. It was an ovenbird, a bird that I had often heard but never seen.

I thought how adaptable this little bird was, how quickly it took advantage of the newly created debris field, how rapidly it seized a new feeding opportunity. I recalled the swallows swooping over the flooded road and following me up the river. For humans this powerful flood had wreaked havoc with the road, blocked the boat ramp, and caused general damage and inconvenience. The cleanup and repair would require time, effort, and considerable expense. On the other hand, the birds simply adapted, quickly, opportunistically, the way they probably have for eons. They knew how to "go with the flow."

# Easy Living

The flood-ravaged roads to Prompton had been cleared of debris. A few deft scrapes with the township road grader had pushed aside the wedges of dirt and rocks. Now, only faint smears of dried mud served as a reminder. The water level at Prompton had receded to normal, and the lake looked calm, blue, and pristine. On the boat ramp, thin rows of sawdust marked where the beached tree had been sawed into pieces. Three pickup trucks with boat trailers stood in the parking lot; the fishermen were back on the lake.

On the West Shore Trail the dried brown mud held the neatly imprinted tracks of mountain bike tires, raccoon paws, and deer hooves. A lush band of three-foot-tall jewelweed festooned with small, tubular, pale orange flowers grew in profusion along both sides of the trail.

During the week, in an effort to improve my knowledge of birdsongs, I listened to a newly purchased CD, *Birding by Ear: A Guide to Birdsong Identification.* This guide presented song samples from common eastern birds along with classification categories and memorization tips. An immediate reward for my effort arose when I recognized the thin, high-pitched song of a black and white warbler, a song compared to a squeaky wheel barrow and phonetically transcribed as *wee-sa, wee-sa, wee-sa.*

I was gratified to recognize this song and reflected on the process of learning a new song, a developmental sequence requiring the formation of new neural pathways, pathways that transformed unfamiliar sounds to vaguely familiar patterns, then to readily recognizable strings of sound, and finally, to tonal patterns that were as locked-in as the voice of a friend or family member. This warbler, with its distinctive song and vivid squeaky wheelbarrow mnemonic, was easy to learn. But other songs, less distinctive, more complex, and more similar to other birds, would be more of a challenge to learn.

A bird fluttered across the trail and landed in a bush. I stopped, scanned, and after a minute spotted a medium-sized bird with an olive brown back, subtle rufous crown, white eye ring, and a cream-colored breast with delicate black streaks. It dipped its head, flicked its tail, and flitted to another branch. It was an ovenbird. After years of hearing its distinctive *teetcha, teetcha, teetcha* call, I was seeing my second one up-close in less than a week. Maybe I was making progress. Maybe I was being accepted by the birds. Maybe through my weekly practice of stillness and attention I was blending into their world.

I set up under the big black cherry tree again, and a few minutes later heard the voices of a man and two boys nearby. It sounded like a father and his sons. The boys were excited and talkative and peppered the man with questions that he answered patiently and quietly. Slowly the sound of their voices and the putting of their trolling motor faded into the distance.

Quiet held for a few minutes, and then gradually the morning chorus resumed with occasional songs — a catbird, a robin, a chickadee, a titmouse, tree swallows, a song sparrow, and another vaguely familiar song. Had I heard it before in the woods? Had I heard it on the CD? The mystery gnawed at me, yet served as a humbling reminder that as many songs as I knew, there were still more to learn.

I glanced at my watch. Twelve minutes had passed, an extra two minutes on my first ten-minute period. I checked the temperature — already seventy-four degrees, a warm morning. Puffs of wind swayed the stems of grass and rustled the leaves. The air smelled richly of earth and growing plants. Water gurgled down a nearby stream bed.

The wind picked up, light gusts swaying the branches and softly whooshing the dense canopy of leaves. I wondered if native people had their own system for describing the strength of the wind. Perhaps they used gradations such as wind moving grass, moving leaves, moving thin branches, moving thick branches, moving trees. Such categories seemed more natural and vivid, more directly linked to sensory experience, and more richly informative than the objective miles per hour.

The morning birdsong chorus seemed to wind down, and for a few minutes all was quiet. Then I heard a nearby chickadee and from across the lake a solitary blue jay, both birds year-round residents. The Neotropical migrants that had journeyed so far north to Prompton to claim territory, to nest, to breed, to raise and fledge their chicks were singing less frequently.

A blue jay flew in, landed in a tree above me, and began to sing, at first with a harsh *jay, jay, jay,* then a pipe-like *toolol, toolol, toolol,* and finally a musical *queedle, queedle, queedle.* I had listened to the surprising variety of blue jay songs on the CD. I remembered the narrator saying that the jay's singing abilities are often underestimated and that they can even imitate the high-pitched call of a broad-winged hawk, presumably a ploy to scare other birds away from food sources.

I thought about the blue jay perching above me and singing its lovely repertoire of songs. Was this a coincidence? Did the jay just happen to fly to this little peninsula, just happen to perch in a tree above me, and just happen to sing its various songs the very day after I had learned about its unique singing abilities? Or was there some type of connection in play, some form of quantum entanglement, some aspect of what Albert Einstein famously described as "spooky action at a distance." After all, knowledge of the blue jay's songs was fresh in my mind, was physical in terms of neural connections, and was energetic in terms of the flow of electro-chemical impulses. Did these newly formed physical and energetic entities somehow interact with similar properties in the blue jay? Or was it nothing more than a simple coincidence?

The blue jay flew away, and I heard the spring birds again — a catbird mewing, a tree swallow twittering, and the familiar melodious *sweet, sweet, sweet, I'm so sweet* of a yellow warbler. The warm morning air felt soft and relaxing against my face. The water lapped softly against the shoreline. The leaves swayed in the wind. The insects hummed.

Enveloped in soft warm air, surrounded by sweet sonorous sounds, gazing at dark green leaves, and sitting under a vast blue sky, I felt myself descending into drowsiness, into a kind of nature-induced trance. Thoughts and images about being a grasshopper, about surrendering completely to the sensual delights of summer drifted through my mind. High above, in the thick green canopy of leaves, a Baltimore oriole, sounding like a shepherd with a flute, piped its rich and melodic *pidoo, tewdi, tewdi, yew*, a song that drew me deeper into my forest reverie. On this summer day I lost track of time.

Week 21 · ~~June~~ *July* 12

# High Summer

Steamy mist rose from the dark green, dew-covered grass of my yard. Another hot, humid, summer day was on the way. Driving to Prompton, I saw a man and a woman loading a trailer, both deeply tanned, both dressed in worn blue jeans and t-shirts, loading mowers, weed whackers, and gas cans, stepping through a well-practiced routine, preparing for another day of mowing and trimming the ever-growing lawns.

I gazed at the lawns along my route — the short, even, light green, freshly mowed grass; the dark green, ragged, unmowed grass. In the fields, the grasses were waist high, the tips of the stems already tinged a faint yellow-brown, already going to seed.

Piano tones of Mussorgsky's *Pictures* resonated softly through the car. I opened my mind for a word that might capture the mood of the day. "Eternal" and "illusion" instantly popped into awareness. This time I thought I understood. Summer seemed eternal, seemed as if it would go on forever, one sunny day after another.

Yet it was an illusion. The plants were racing to grow, to flower, to disperse their seeds, to strengthen their roots, to store nourishment. The birds had fledged their chicks, and now both the new and old generations were feasting on the richness of summer, readying themselves for their next challenging chapter, the great migration south. The fawns were losing their spots, the bear cubs growing bigger, the baby woodchucks fatter, all the animals packing on pounds for the privation of the upcoming cold, dark months. It looked like eternal summer, but nature was busily and urgently preparing for winter.

More signs of summer surrounded me along the West Shore

Trail. The blackberries were growing bigger and showing the first hints of color. Dense coveys of tiny, tan, double-winged insects scattered before me as I stepped through a patch of tall, pale green, lacy-leafed ferns, a thick cloud of swirling insects, unknown and uncountable.

I settled in under a slender ash tree in the middle of the peninsula. A few minutes later a slate gray catbird flew in and perched in front of me. Nearby, two more catbirds sang jumbled strings of song snippets ending with a whiny *mew* call. A blue jay flew onto the peninsula, landed above me in the ash tree, and sang a series of *queedle, queedle* calls that were answered immediately by a jay across the lake and by a third jay down the shoreline. This trio of jays was singing in synchrony across a distance improbable for a human chorus, but natural for the jays with their different sense of space and proximity.

I heard more birdsongs — a robin, a song sparrow, and a yellow warbler. I made myself listen more carefully and detected the less pleasant, sharp, metallic, and somewhat agitated *tik, tik, tik* call of a cardinal. I had been filtering out this less melodious call, suppressing my attention to the harsh tones and focusing on the pleasant songs. I realized how quickly and how unconsciously my hearing had grown selective and subjective.

I forced myself to listen carefully to the robin's song, a song so familiar that I initially paid it scant attention. On the birding CD, I learned there are a number of similar songs in what is called the "sing-songer" category, including the songs of tanagers, vireos, and the rose-breasted grosbeak, songs with slightly different characteristics — a hoarse tone, a different cadence, or a distinctive ending note. How easy it is to listen and automatically classify, to quickly foreclose on a decision. This time I determined that the song I heard was indeed a robin.

After sitting absolutely motionless for forty-five minutes, I felt a sharp cramp in my left calf and decided I had to stand up to stretch the muscle and ease the pain. The instant I stood, two deer, only thirty yards away in the woods, whose approach I never heard, jumped in surprise, snorted alarms, and bounded away, their white flag tails flashing in the shaded light.

I sat back down. A light breeze rustled the leaves. Two more blue jays sang, a crow cawed, a song sparrow trilled. Above in the dense canopy of leaves, a bird sang a lovely complex song, vaguely familiar. Perhaps I had heard it on my birdsong CD; perhaps I had heard it online. A cardinal whistled a distinctive *all right, all right, purty, purty, purty, purty*, a familiar song, one that I clearly remembered hearing in March. I wished I could sing back *Hey, good to hear you again. Glad you're back on the peninsula.*

I glanced at my watch. It was five minutes past my allotted hour. Absorbed in listening, I had once again lost track of time. I packed up and walked slowly back along the West Shore Trail, noticing the sounds, the sighing of the leaves in the wind, the birdsongs, and the steady *tamp, tamp, tamp* of my feet on the ground.

The next morning over breakfast at a local café, I spoke with a young professor, a composer of contemporary music who draws inspiration from the sounds of nature. He explained how he has gone to a variety of nature locations and recorded the sounds. Then he runs the recordings through a computer program that provides a visual representation of all the sounds, a representation that shows their frequencies, their rising, falling, overlapping, and even interaction. He said, "You will be stunned by how much you miss. But once you've seen the graph, you will hear a lot more the next time out. You'll have a better idea of what to listen for."

I told him about my progress in learning birdsongs through listening each week in the woods and studying the CD over and over again. This made sense to him. He believed we all have considerable untapped potential to develop our listening abilities and said, "We have become a culture of visual learners, but sounds are all around us. Listening is the sense that early humans relied on most of all."

The next day we continued our conversation while kayaking around a small lake surrounded by forest. A mysterious flute-like *eee-oh-lay* rang out. He noticed it immediately, smiled appreciatively and asked, "What bird was that? That song is amazing!"

It was the song of a wood thrush, one of the most beautiful birdsongs created by the thrush's unique ability to sing two notes simultaneously, to literally harmonize with itself. I realized that a portion of this young musician's attention, a part of his mind, was always attuned to the sounds of nature around him. I hoped that I was developing a similar listening capacity. I also hoped that I might someday join him to record a session of nature sounds, to view the graph, to see all the sounds I was missing.

I wondered if what I heard while sitting in the woods was another kind of illusion, a partial sample of a full reality, limited by the sounds I missed, truncated by the sounds I ignored, molded by unconscious preferences, and diminished by a faltering focus. But perhaps with repeated visits to the woods, my hearing might improve, open up, and gradually reveal a fuller reality. I hoped so.

*JULY 20 ?*

Week 22 · ~~June 10~~

# Cherokee Marsh

"Why not find a place that you feel an emotional connection to?" said my wife as we drove across northern Illinois on I-90, taking in the view of the gently undulating landscape; the fields of dark green, head-high corn; the vast acreage of soybeans; the blue and white and yellow wildflowers blooming in profusion along the shoulder; a scene punctuated with trim white farmhouses, large red barns, and towering, dark blue Harvestore silos. I was considering the challenge of finding a good sit spot during our visit to Madison, Wisconsin. I remembered only too well my difficulties in Germany and Colorado where it had taken a second try in both places.

The idea of an emotional connection made immediate sense. I had been thinking in more objective terms about locations with the right mix of terrain, such as the University of Wisconsin Arboretum, a 1,260-acre urban park of restored tall grass prairies, savannas, forests, and wetlands, or my sister-in-law's farm that straddled marshland along the Crawfish River. A third possibility was Cherokee Marsh, a conservation park just northeast of Madison where, during my graduate school years, I had hiked with friends and searched out wildflowers. This was the location to which I felt the strongest emotional connection.

By 6:45 the next morning I was on my way to Cherokee Marsh under a clear, high blue sky. A string of fluffy white clouds floated above the far northern horizon. Opening my mind for a word that might capture the mood of the day, I heard "clarity." Was this merely a reaction to the view of the sky ahead, or a forecast of something I might discover?

By the time I reached the gravel entry road to the park, the temperature already registered seventy-two degrees, and the air was heavy and humid. In spite of the heat, I wore blue jeans and a light flannel shirt, and had smeared natural bug repellent over every inch of exposed skin. Hoping I was adequately mosquito-proofed, I climbed out of the car, walked along a path through the woods, and found a trail I remembered that led to a tree-covered hill surrounded by a marsh on three sides and at the far end slanted down to Lake Cherokee.

I walked out to the middle of the hill, which upon closer inspection turned out to be a conical earthen structure, a mound constructed by Native Americans. At the base of the mound, a metal plaque mounted on a large granite rock noted that starting about two thousand years ago and continuing for a few centuries, people of a hunting and gathering culture met at sites such as these to participate in unknown ceremonies and possibly to bury their dead. I wasn't the first person to favor this location. Perhaps the early Native Americans appreciated the same harmonious confluence of water, earth, sky, field, marsh, and forest that I now viewed and enjoyed.

I considered sitting on top of the mound, but rejected the idea as disrespectful, even sacrilegious. I looked back along the trail, noticed a spot where the meadow ended and the trees began, walked over, and set up my camp chair. I was facing southeast with an open view of trees, marsh, and field. A fresh breeze from the southwest blew across the lake and the open marsh, chased most of the mosquitoes away and carried the smells of water, marsh, and field to my nostrils.

I studied the trees growing around me. Ahead to the left stood a half-dozen tall hickory trees with gray, shaggy bark and feathered compound leaves; to my right was a stand of tall, thick-trunked oak trees draped in sharply lobed, dark green leaves. Further to my right, a trio of huge cottonwoods rose high into the sky, their long gray branches covered with light green, rounded leaves. Behind me, where the back of the mound sloped to the water, grew willows densely covered with thin, pale green leaves that swayed and shimmied in even the slightest breeze.

Soon I began to see birds — a pair of goldfinches looping over the tall green marsh grass, and a catbird perched in an oak rolling through its rollicking mimicry of songs. A robin, on my left, upset about something, called out a scolding *tut-tut-tut*. A song sparrow, a bird well known for its regional song variations, trilled its aria with different notes in a different sequence.

Two sparrow-sized birds landed on a thin, dead branch of a tall hickory tree forty yards in front of me. I brought up my binoculars, but was looking into the morning sunlight and couldn't discern the colors of their plumage or identify any distinct field marks. They flew over the field and disappeared. Soon one returned to the branch and a minute later the other. They perched side by side for a few minutes, motionless, peaceful, seemingly reflective, then simultaneously received a prompt invisible to me and flew off together. A minute later a catbird landed on the same dead branch, launched into a litany of jumbled song snippets, sat still, and then flew away.

An eastern wood peewee, a medium-sized gray bird, landed on the same hickory branch, surveyed the territory, and began to preen, running its beak through the feathers on both shoulders, grooming each wing, bending around to comb through its tail feathers, and then seemingly satisfied with its efforts, flew off. After a minute one of the little sparrow-sized birds returned to the branch and was joined by the second. They perched for several minutes and then flew off again.

This dead hickory branch in front of me seemed to be an avian hot spot, a perch that all the birds favored. Something about that branch must feel right to the birds. Maybe it was in the open and an easy place to land and take flight. Maybe it provided a good view, a spot where a bird could keep an eye out for predators while simultaneously searching for prey. Maybe it was the location at the edge of the trees but near a field with thick bushes, places to quickly hide from a hunting hawk. Maybe there were other favorable factors that I was unable to perceive but were obvious to the birds.

I heard a tapping, turned and spotted a male hairy woodpecker, black and white with a patch of bright red on the back of his head. Longer and larger than a robin, it climbed up a tall dying hickory, holding a few stubby remaining branches, tapped again, dug its sharp beak into the wood to snatch insects, sang its high-pitched even rattle, climbed higher, and tapped and drilled again.

I looked out over the marsh and noticed a solitary tree — long dead, bark gone, gray bleached wood, only a skeletal trunk and two arm-like branches. I watched the tree for a while and noticed that almost every red-winged blackbird, cowbird, grackle, or tree swallow that flew over the marsh landed in that tree, rested, looked around, and flew on.

As I gazed at the ghostly tree and the birds coming and going, I experienced a moment of clarity. The birds liked and used dead trees and dead branches. The branches were ideal spots for perching and pausing. The birds hunted for insects in the dead wood. They chiseled out holes and built nests in the hollows and cavities of dead trees.

Unfortunately, landowners, myself included, routinely cut off dead branches and remove dead trees to rid their property of dead wood. I realized this practice was not natural. The birds lived their life on dead branches and in dead trees. The belief that an attractive yard and garden was one cleansed and purged of all dead wood suddenly seemed short-sighted. I resolved that in my one-acre yard, I would leave the dead branches, maybe even a few dead trees. I would begin to see these branches and trees as having their own type of beauty, as playing their own unique role in the matrix of life.

My hour was up. I walked away from the wooded mound on the edge of the lake, following a path through a meadow, gazing at the wildflowers — the curled, bright orange Turk's cap lilies; the pale lavender wild bergamot; the slender-stemmed, white sprays of yarrow; the butter yellow petals and chocolate brown eyes of black-eyed Susans. My emotional connection to Cherokee marsh had been renewed.

Week 23 · July 26

# Wild Cherries

I started up the car, paused, and gazed at the yard ahead, at the dark green grass covered with dew drops that caught, reflected, and refracted the morning sunshine, creating the appearance of a field of sparkly diamonds. Selecting the orchestral version of Mussorgsky's *Pictures at an Exhibit*, I lingered and listened to the opening stanzas, the musical march through the art exhibit. The word "richness" popped into my mind. Surprised by the word's sudden and definitive appearance, I once again decided not to mull it over, but to set it aside and see what might be revealed about "richness" during my upcoming hour in the woods.

I was eager to return to my home sit spot and curious to see what might have changed during my two week absence. I felt as if I was returning to my office after a vacation. Thankfully, I now had an outdoor office where I could view subtle changes in nature and track the progression of the seasons instead of walking into a stuffy, windowless room facing a desk piled high with letters, reports, memos, phone messages, and a computer laden with an interminable list of emails.

The flood damage on the road to Prompton had been repaired, the ditches reshaped and lined with protective riprap — big fist-sized, whitish gray, earth-holding stones. The last traces of mud had been cleansed from the roads by gentler summer rains. Driving down the long hill toward the Lackawaxen River, I looked out at the recently mowed, pale green hayfields on the right, the dense dark green woodlots on the left, and far ahead the long verdant line of the Moosic Mountains festooned with bright white windmills. The hill I was descending was called Bowens Hill, named after the family that built their homestead on the crest many years ago, information a longtime county resident has recently shared with me. Somehow, it seemed fitting that a hill with such lovely views should have a name.

In the parking lot, two bright yellow and black goldfinches flew over, lifting, dipping, and singing their lilting *per-chik-o-ree* flight song. Goldfinches are active in mid-summer. They breed later than other birds because they wait for the thistles to go to seed and then use the silky white down to line their nests. They also wait for wildflowers to go to seed to provide an abundant food supply for their nestlings. Timing, timing, timing, I thought. Every creature has a unique niche timed to take full advantage of nature's bounty.

Walking down the West Shore Trail, I spotted a slender tree draped with clusters of bright red fruit — choke cherries — much enjoyed by the birds and black bears. Proceeding further along the path, I entered what felt like a gallery of sound with cardinals chipping and blue jays calling all around, a small flock of Canada geese honking overhead, and further away a kind of hoarse *yeck, yeck, yeck* call I didn't recognize.

I set up at my home sit spot under the big black cherry tree, then looked up and down the placid surface of the lake and ahead into the dense green canopy of the summer woods. More birdsongs sounded around me — a song sparrow trilling, a pair of chickadees chanting, a flock of tree swallows twittering, the hoarse *kuk, kuk, kuk* of a solitary green heron and the *tap, tap, tap* of a hairy woodpecker. Blue jays, silent in spring while nesting, now called continuously, seemingly making up for lost time, and possibly practicing the communication skills they would need to function as a group and survive the upcoming winter.

A catbird flew in and landed on a branch to my right. I trained my binoculars on it. The official name is gray catbird, and at a distance and in the bird guides, it looks like a drab, gray, medium-sized bird. But up close, viewed through binoculars, I saw a lovely bird with a slate gray back, a light gray breast, a black cap, and a streak of orange-chestnut-colored feathers underneath the tail, an understated but classy beauty. More catbirds sang and mewed all around the little peninsula, maybe a family of several generations, feeding, foraging, and flitting from branch to branch.

Nearby I heard an unknown birdsong, a series of short sweet notes with an emphatic ending. I listened intently, counted the notes, the pitch, and the progression. The song sounded familiar from the audio CD, and I scanned the guide only to realize there were a number of possibilities, all woodland warblers, including the chestnut-sided, magnolia, redstart, hooded, or even an atypical yellow warbler. I peered intently into the tree where the bird sang, but the foliage was dense and it either fell silent or flew away. There would be no identification of this bird.

Then I heard the *yeck, yeck* song again, the simple song I couldn't identify. There is such a wealth of birdsongs, and it seemed that as many songs as I learned, there were always more to learn. I feared I would always remain a novice birder. I wanted this annoying *yeck, yeck* bird to fly away and leave me alone.

Then I reconsidered. This was a mystery to unravel, a puzzle to solve, and it would only happen if I calmed down and took a systematic approach. I took a deep breath and made myself think systematically. First, I considered habitat. This bird was up in the trees, leafy deciduous trees, with a full layer of leaves. Then, I considered what it might be eating. The lush green canopy is inhabited by an abundance of insects so this bird must be an insect eater, hovering, flitting, gleaning, and feasting on the abundant insects. I thought about its song, a simple song, repeated over and over. I began to sort through categories of woodland birds and then a flash of intuition came — it might be a flycatcher.

I blocked out all the other songs, listened intently, and slowly realized I had mistakenly heard one long sound, when in fact it was two sounds slurred together with an emphasis on the second sound. I grabbed my *Sibley Field Guide* and scanned the section on flycatchers, a family of drab, similar-looking, insect-eating woodland birds seldom seen and usually identified by their song. I found a good possibility for my bird. It might be a least flycatcher. The range and habitat fit. Its call was represented as *chebek, chebek* with emphasis on the second note, a more accurate label than the *yeck* I had perceived.

I reflected on the rich variety of birdsongs around me that I was slowly beginning to hear, to learn, to appreciate. Much the way a tea taster, a wine critic, or chef trains his or her palate to detect nuances of taste, I needed to train my ear to hear subtle tonal differences, to discriminate between songs, and to eventually fully enjoy the world of birdsongs. And there were no short cuts. I needed to put in time and effort in the woods listening and learning.

The birds lapsed into silence. My attention drifted to the insects flying around in the soft morning sunlight. I closed my eyes, opened them, looked ahead, and counted until I spotted an insect. I only made it to three before a slender winged insect fluttered by. I repeated this experiment five times with results of two, seven, four, three, and nine seconds, an uncountable number of insects, a massive web of life, a richly laid table for the birds, their reward for taking on the risks of migration.

On my walk back, I paused by the choke cherry tree. The sun was higher and brighter and the colors of the tiny currant-sized chokecherries ranged from the deep red-purple of a Bing cherry to the brilliant bright red of a pie cherry.

Curious about their taste, I reached up, picked a few of the darkest and ripest cherries, and put them in my mouth. Each cherry had a thin layer of soft ripe fruit surrounding a large seed. I sucked the fruit away from the pit and found the taste mildly tart and faintly sweet. Then a rich, earthy, cherry aftertaste flooded my mouth and lingered and lingered, a taste that reminded me of a fine French Burgundy, a taste of cherry fruit and earth and minerals, a taste of the richness of life.

## Week 24 · August 2

# Calm and Still

The parking lot was empty, the pavement wet, dark, and shiny from a steady overnight rain. Wisps of mist floated over the lake, shrouding the tree-covered hills above the far shoreline. Lumpy gray clouds rolled across the sky. The water was calm, the woods still.

At first all was quiet along the West Shore Trail. A mourning dove's melancholy *ooaah, cooo, coo, coo* broke the silence, was followed by the metallic *tik, tik, tik* calls of a cardinal and the insistent whinnying of a robin. A doe, tan with wet fur, long alert ears, and soft brown eyes, stepped into the middle of the trail ahead and looked cautiously around. A few seconds later a big fawn, its white spots already fading, joined her. They gazed directly at me, then stepped into the woods, and disappeared without a sound.

I settled in under the big black cherry tree, looked down, and noticed a single blade of grass swaying so slightly as to be almost imperceptible, pushed by a breeze so soft that I couldn't feel it against my cheek, a breeze so light that it didn't move the leaves or ripple the surface of the lake. Was the air ever completely still? It didn't seem so at Prompton where the long, north-south lake funneled the slightest breeze, where the temperature differences between lake and land stirred the air, and where the force of gravity pushed air down from the surrounding hills.

I had grown much more aware of the wind over the last months, and now, upon arriving at my sit spot, immediately registered its direction, strength, and consistency, all factors that would profoundly shape my experience, that would determine how much and from what direction I would hear and smell. Today, I would be able to hear all around me and would be able to inhale the smells of the earth, vegetation, and water from all around the peninsula.

Lingering raindrops from last night's downpour slipped off the leaves and pattered softly onto the ground, a subtle and subdued second rain. A gust of wind swayed the leaves, and the second rain fell harder, louder. A few drops splashed onto my open notebook page leaving tiny wet smears, the page itself now joined to my experience. The wind abated, the sounds of the second rain diminished, and quiet returned.

After a few minutes the birdsongs started up again — catbirds singing jumbled song snippets and whiny mews, a song sparrow launching into its lilting aria, blue jays jeering and jaying — all familiar songs, all as well known to me as the voices of friends and family. I also heard a less familiar song, a series of rich, clear, melodious notes floating down from the leafy canopy. I closed my eyes and listened carefully, but the mystery bird was an indifferent singer with long pauses that made it difficult to classify, categorize, phonetically transcribe, or notate with dashes and lines. The song also varied, sometimes a series of three notes, sometimes six, sometimes steady, and sometimes dropping off at the end, and then it stopped. I opened my eyes, gazed up at the thickly leafed tree where the mystery bird sang, and realized I wouldn't be able to see it amid the leaves.

Turning my gaze down to the ground, I thought about a book I had recently been reading — *The Forest Unseen: A Year's Watch in Nature* by David George Haskell, a book I had fortuitously discovered while absentmindedly surfing the internet. Immediately, I recognized that his project was similar to mine; his focus a square yard of forest floor in the hills of eastern Tennessee. He called his patch of ground a mandala, a nature drawing that revealed the web of life, a microcosm that illuminated the macrocosm. He drew on his background as a biology professor to illuminate the richness, the complexities, the finely tuned adaptability, the interconnections of life within the mandala, and all the changes that occurred over the course of a year.

Now, I studied a generous square yard in front of me and noticed the plants — a few shade-dwarfed goldenrods with flower plumes poised to bloom; some reddish tinged, three-leaved poison ivy vines; several wilted leaves of wild lily of the valley; three small scattered clumps of grass, brown at the edges and green at the center; and in the middle a slender, solitary, two-foot tall ash sapling. The square of ground was covered with last year's leaves, brown and partially decayed. Twigs and branches of varying length and thickness and in varying stages of decomposition lay scattered on top of the blanket of leaves. A clump of white fungus grew on the side of a dead branch. Dark green moss spread at the base of the cherry tree. Plenty to see and even more to understand, I thought.

The birdsongs resumed, the staccato *wicka, wicka, wicka* of a northern flicker, the loud *skeew* of a green heron, and the mystery bird again with a song that now sounded like *do, do, do, doodle doot*. People noises impinged on the soundscape as well — jetliners whisper-whooshing high above; car and truck tires whining along the highway; dogs barking far in the distance; and a truck backing up, its warning horn droning a high-pitched *beep, beep, beep.* Plenty to hear, I realized.

Patches of blue appeared in the sky, the first hints of a sunny day, the promise of the coming transition from cloudy and wet to clear and dry. A burst of sunshine broke through a gap in the clouds, shone upon the back of my neck and shoulders, bringing sensations of warmth and comfort. A gust of wind touched my cheek and carried the smells of fertile earth and fresh water. Plenty for my skin to feel and my nose to smell, I thought.

The mystery bird flew to the top of a nearby tree, continuing its variable and intermittent song punctuated with occasional *chuck, chuck* calls. My hour was drawing to an end. I had to acknowledge with increasing feelings of frustration that I probably wouldn't be able to identify this melodious singer. I attempted to fix the song in my mind so I could go home, listen to birdsongs, and try to figure it out.

I folded up my chair, put my bird guide into my backpack, but kept my binoculars around my neck. The mystery bird flew closer, its song growing louder, clearer. Then it darted down to a nearby bush, perched on a slender branch. I saw its form, a medium-sized bird with a longish tail; but it was in the shade, and I couldn't discern its colors. Standing still, I slowly lifted my binoculars for a better look, but it took off and flew back up into the dense foliage.

There was no way to see it now. I was ready to give up once again and move on, but for some reason decided to persist, set down my chair and backpack, stepped over to the tree where it sang and stared up. It continued to sing as it moved from branch to branch and tree to tree but was hidden from view by the impenetrable stratum of thick, dark green leaves. Then I noticed that as it moved, it brushed against the leaves, dislodging the lingering rain drops and creating a localized second rain. I trained my binoculars on the source of the falling drops and tracked the bird's movement through the green canopy. Suddenly, it darted out into the bright sunshine and perched at the tip of a dead branch — a robin-sized bird with a rich orange breast and a jet black head, the colors radiant in the sunlight.

It was a male Baltimore oriole clad in the hues of the family crest of Lord Baltimore, the founder of Maryland. My persistence paid off. But then I thought again — was it really my effort or was it more nature's plan to reveal itself to a novice birder? When the song wasn't enough, the bird flew nearby. When that didn't work, it showered me with a soft second rain until I finally looked in the right spot. Then it revealed itself in a spotlight of sunshine.

Inspired by the vision of this luminously colored Baltimore oriole, I later read that they are often more easily heard than seen because they feed on insects high in the dense leafy canopy. Their preferred habitat is deciduous trees in open woodlands and forest edges, and along rivers and lakes. When feeding, they prefer ripe fruit and carefully select the deepest colored mulberries, cherries, and grapes while ignoring the unripe fruit.

Baltimore orioles sing a variety of songs. I knew the standard song but had to listen to five song samples online before I found one that sounded exactly like "my bird." The female oriole also sings, somewhat shorter songs, but with similar flute-like tones. Sometimes the male and female sing a duet. The female is a master nest builder, weaving a hanging bower high in a tree with grass, strips of grapevine, wool, horsehair, cellophane, twine, even fishing line to build the outer supportive bowl while lining the inside with soft, downy fibers and feathers.

Baltimore orioles eat a variety of insects, including beetles, crickets, grasshoppers, moths, and flies. They also gobble up pests like tent caterpillars. Sometimes their love of ripe fruit brings them into conflict with orchardists. They breed across eastern North America up to Canada and winter on Caribbean islands and in Central and South America where they frequent coffee and cacao plantations. They migrate at night and can be disoriented by tall buildings, windmills, transmission towers, and even rainstorms. They have adapted to human habitation and their population is stable.

There was much to admire in this bird, I thought. They build magnificent houses, sing beautiful duets with their spouses, eat ripe summer fruit, and spend their winters hanging around coffee plantations and cacao farms.

I packed up and walked back along the West Shore Trail. Looking through the trees, I saw that the wind had picked up and now rippled the surface of the lake and stirred the leaves. My initial parking lot impression of calm and still had been a monumental error. Along the shoreline of Prompton Lake, it was seldom calm and never still. The rich complex pulse of life beat steadily and persistently in this patch of woods by the water.

Week 25 · August 9

# The Laughing Gull

The motel owner, a tall, hard-edged man, leaned in, lowered his voice, and in a gravely conspiratorial tone told me to head over to the nearby bayside park at low tide, climb down the bulwark, duck under a private pier, and walk right onto the Holgate National Wildlife Refuge. He added, "It's beautiful out there, man. You'll have the whole damn place to yourself. You can walk along the bay beach for miles and see all the nature and birds you want."

He paused, fixed me in a knowing gaze and added, "Oh yeah, and if you're lucky, you might see them piping plovers. They're out there, but they're damn hard to spot."

When low tide approached, I followed his advice, shouldered my backpack and camp chair, strolled over to the park, scrambled down the bulwark of beams, stepped over the slippery, seaweed-coated rocks, ducked under the pier, and with a sense of satisfaction walked onto the sandy beach of the refuge. My satisfaction was short-lived. Only the first hundred yards of the refuge was open. The remaining three and a half miles, the southern tip of Long Beach Island, New Jersey, was roped off from April to August to provide protected breeding habitat for the endangered piping plover.

That morning my wife and I had visited the ocean side of the refuge where a spacious parking lot stood at the terminus of the main road that traversed Long Beach Island, New Jersey. Visitors could park their cars, walk to a viewing area, gaze out at the deep blue ocean, listen to the surf rolling in, and watch the wet-suited surfers bobbing in the water while waiting for a wave.

At the far corner of the parking lot stood an information stand staffed by a park ranger and several volunteers. We signed up for a guided nature walk, and a few minutes later we entered the refuge with a small group of fellow visitors and trooped down the beach, across the dunes, and through the grasses and shrubs while the ranger told us all about the plants and shells and birds. We paused at the top of a low hill, a vantage point from where we could see both the ocean and the bay as the island is only a quarter mile wide at that point. The ranger related that during Super Storm Sandy, the storm surge flowed over the island. She pointed out remaining debris and explained that the plant life was slowly recovering and nature was gradually restoring this crucial and ever-changing barrier island habitat.

Our group was diverse and included a family with two young boys who mostly wanted to run around and grab everything. There were several retirees and a power birding couple — he with a slouch hat, multi-pocketed, khaki vest and a fine set of expensive binoculars around his neck; she attired in high fashion hiking shorts and shirt, an REI ball cap, and an impressive Nikon camera around her neck. He quickly named every sanderling, sandpiper, shorebird, and gull that we saw while she busily snapped pictures of the birds, the shells, the occasional fish or bird skeleton, the dune grasses, the wildflowers.

I edged near him and expressed admiration for his knowledge. He related that he was a longtime birder, that his wife was an avid nature photographer, and that they traveled together to birding "hot spots." They were hoping to see the rare and protected piping plover, a bird that had eluded them through the years. He was certain that today would be the day he would place a check mark next to piping plover on his life list. His wife, who joined us, patted her telephoto lens as if it were a gun barrel and said, "And I want to get some good shots of that little bird."

The birder and his wife scanned the ocean beach and bay shoreline as we walked. The guide said she had seen piping plovers all week, but this morning none were spotted. At the end of the tour, the birding couple walked slowly back to their car, frustration etched across their faces.

Now it was afternoon. I was on my own at the edge of the refuge. I set up my chair next to a patch of tall marsh reeds where I had a view of a small beach, a tidal mudflat, and the mainland a mile away across the bay. A brisk wind blew steadily out of the southeast, rustling the reeds and carrying the distant sounds of the ocean surf. The sky was blue, the sun bright, the temperature a summery eighty-five degrees.

A line of dead brown weeds and scraps of aquatic plants marked the reach of the last high tide. Bits of red, green, and brown seaweed dotted the beach. Sea shells — white, tan, and brown, oval, round, and angular, some complete, some fragments — peppered the beach. This was a natural beach; no sand added, no trucks and tractors grooming it.

Shorebirds appeared on the mud flat, scurrying on tall slender legs, pausing, probing the mud with long sensitive bills. I saw a trio of black-legged, gray and white sanderlings and a pair of ruddy turnstones with orange legs and calico plumage — birds that had already bred in the high Arctic and were now recuperating from their long southward journey to Long Beach Island. A small flock of semipalmated plovers with brown backs and black neck rings, also just returned from the Arctic, flew along the beach, set their long slender wings, and landed amid the other birds. All the birds scuttled along the beach, wandered away, flew off and reappeared — active feeders, moving quickly, grabbing food, leaving, returning.

A snowy egret landed near a patch of marsh grass, stalked regally along the shoreline on long, slender yellow legs, white plumage glistening in the afternoon sunlight, lacy feathers ruffled by the breeze. It stared down at the water to scan for fish and frogs, its sharp spear-like bill poised to strike.

A laughing gull landed at the water's edge right in front of me. I studied its jet black head, reddish beak, folded gray wings, and white body. It walked across the sand toward me and stopped fifteen feet away, angled its body into the wind, settled down on its legs, and looked at me. Two more laughing gulls flew in, calling out their loud, distinctive *ha-ha-ha-ha-ha*. They landed near the grassy point and waded through the shallow water, picking and searching for food. The first gull remained in front of me, watching me while I watched it.

Laughing gulls are common now along the east coast, having recovered from the legions of egg hunters and plume gatherers that decimated their numbers in the last half of the nineteenth century. Now, their laughing call, their crisp white body, trim black head, and wheeling flights are part of the sights and sounds of summer at the beach. Like most gulls they are opportunistic feeders and have learned to frequent public beaches, docks, and even parking lots where they pick through garbage, sift through litter, and readily accept handouts.

Maybe the gull in front of me was experienced with humans and thought I might provide a treat. It continued to watch me. When I pulled my camera out, it edged away toward the beach. When I put my camera down, it walked back to its spot and resumed watching me. Eventually, it walked down to the water and flew away.

The beach was empty, and I gazed at the tufts of grass, the shells, the stones, and the water lapping rhythmically onto the sand. Suddenly, the beach was filled again with sandpipers, plovers, and turnstones, a variety of birds requiring quick visual identification. I used my binoculars to note significant field marks — size, leg color, plumage, and beak length and form; whether the bird fed on the beach, at the water line, or in the water. I referred to my bird guide to make a tentative identification and then looked again at the bird to verify all of this while the birds moved and mixed and came and went.

The laughing gull returned, flying lazily into the wind, setting its wings, landing at water's edge. It waddled across the sand, returned to its sit spot, faced into the wind, and trained a shiny, black eye on me. Who was observing whom? Who was the observed? It felt like role reversal.

Later that evening, after a sudden heavy downpour and a dinner of fresh bay scallops paired with a tasty Pinot Grigio, we strolled to a small bayside beach park where families with children and couples young and old gathered to watch the sunset. Across the shimmering waters of the bay, the huge orange glowing orb of the sun slowly sank below a horizon crowned with shifting and changing bands of brilliant pink and purple. I sneaked a peek at the beach to see a group of shorebirds walking along the sand. There, amid the sanderlings and sandpipers, I spotted several small, pale, sand-colored birds with orange legs and short, thick bills. I realized instantly they were piping plovers. They had flown out of the protected reserve and were hanging out here on the family beach.

I felt a wave of excitement. I wanted to shout out. "There they are!" But I kept silent and watched the ghost-like birds scuttle and shift along the sandy shore. The children played, the adults talked, we all walked barefoot. The piping plovers picked through the wet sand searching for morsels of food.

Week 26 · August 16

# Affinity

Delicate fingers of soft predawn light filtered under the window shades and slowly lifted the darkness from my bedroom. Fresh morning air wafted in through the screens. It felt warm and comfortable under the covers. Half-listening to two crows cawing back and forth, I thought happily about drifting back asleep. Then I suddenly remembered—this was week twenty-six! Today's observation would mark the halfway point of my yearlong commitment. I sprang out of bed and ten minutes later was ready to go.

On the drive to Prompton, sunlight sparkled on the dew-covered lawns, creating myriad pinpoints of luminous light. A doe crossed the road followed by a big fawn, spots gone, almost full-grown. Further along, another doe crossed the road with a younger, much smaller fawn, white spots present and prominent. I wondered if the two fawns born weeks apart were an example of nature seeking a natural selection advantage while also pursuing a cautious course.

The first fawn was probably born in late April, a risky time if there was a late cold snap or a chilly, wet spring. The second fawn was most likely born in early June, a safer time with moderate weather and abundant food. This year, with a mild spring, a warm summer, and generous rainfall, the fields were filled with tall, green, juicy grass. The advantage went to the earlier born fawn that would be big, strong, well fed, and ready for the test of its first winter.

Driving down Bowen's Hill, I noticed the pale green hayfields fresh from a second cutting, the dark green woodlots, and the newly emerged clusters of wildflowers along the road — sky blue chicory and pale pink Joe Pye weed. Once again, everything looked green and growing and blooming, and it seemed as if summer would last forever. Yet during the week, I had looked at historic photographs of Bethany with scenes from winter, scenes that showed bare trees and deep piles of frozen snow, scenes that looked unreal, like landscapes from a different planet, hard to imagine on this summer morning.

Pulling into the parking lot, I saw swallows swooping over the lake, and as I stepped out of the car, a flock of goldfinches lifted and dipped and sang sweetly overhead. Two crows waddled through the thick, green grass near the shoreline. Along the West Shore Trail, a sequence of songs sounded — a robin, a black and white warbler, a chickadee, and a pair of cardinals chipping back and forth.

The birdsong serenade continued as I set up under the big black cherry tree. I heard the *yank, yank, yank* of a white-breasted nuthatch, the jeering of blue jays, the cawing of crows, the insistent chant of a flicker, the whiny mews of catbirds, and as usual, one unknown song, a complex *da, wat, da, da do* repeated three times from high in a tree, and then it was gone.

I savored the information that the birdsongs offered, the affirmation that all was well, that the woods were safe for the everyday bird business of feeding, perching, and preening. And again, it seemed as if the birds were totally ignoring me, as if my presence no longer caused a disturbance, as if my visits had become part of some greater routine. I felt wonderfully invisible.

A short, slender ash sapling about three feet tall stood in front of me. Some of its leaves had spots of yellow, some had tiny holes, and some were partially gnawed away. This little tree, struggling for light under the forest canopy, driving its roots into the soil, searching for water and nutrients was, as its leaves testified, already providing food for the host of insects and caterpillars that lived in the forest.

I gazed at the trees around me, the ashes, maples, and black cherries with their tall, dark, thick trunks. At the base of each trunk, bark-covered roots spread across the ground and burrowed into the earth. As I continued to gaze at the trees, it seemed as if they were in motion, no longer static and still, but vibrant and moving. Their sunlight-searching leaves swayed in the morning breeze. Their trunks appeared as four-lane highways pumping vast amounts of water up and piping sugars and nutrients to the leaves, branches, and roots. The vast webs of roots busily mined the dark, rocky, clay soil for water and minerals.

Each leaf in the canopy above me was a tiny busy factory where the chemical reaction of photosynthesis used the radiant energy of the sun to convert inorganic matter — water and carbon dioxide — into organic matter — glucose — which in turn was pumped and distributed to the branches, roots, and leaves where growth and repair took place. Oxygen, a byproduct of photosynthesis, streamed into the atmosphere. All of this complex, dynamic activity occurred slowly, silently, and steadily.

A tufted titmouse landed in a branch just ten feet away. It seemed upset — scolding, calling, chatting, flouncing its tail, bobbing its head. I studied it through my binoculars — the short, strong, black, seed-cracking beak; the large, black shiny eyes; the light gray eye rings; the buff-colored feathers along its flanks; the gray squared-off tail. Gradually, it calmed down and whistled a few bars of its clear *peter, peter, peter* song.

I thought about what had brought the titmouse so close, so easy to view and study. Sometimes it seemed as if nature actively revealed herself. During the preceding weeks when such events occurred, I figured that my intention to observe caused the observed to appear. But now, I was reconsidering. Recent reading on Jung's notion of synchronicity led me to question this cause and effect thinking. Jung wrote that certain types of events like to cluster together. Drawing on his understanding of classical Chinese philosophy and medicine, he explained that the ancient texts did not ask, "What causes what"? Rather, "What likes to occur with what"?

Perhaps this principle of affinity was at work and not the mechanism of cause and effect. Perhaps the observed likes to cluster with the observer, the discovered with the discoverer. I had carried the cause and effect model into the woods, a model absorbed during my years as a scientifically trained psychologist, a model based on the premise that discrete events cause specific symptoms, traumatic events cause mental illness, brain insults cause cognitive disorders. But now, after six months of separation from the practice of psychology, I felt like I was taking off the heavy coat of cause and effect thinking and trying on the light, finely-woven mantle of affinity.

I considered other changes that might have occurred during the first six months of my Prompton project. Perhaps I was letting go of my professional identity with its responsibilities and authority, its written and spoken findings and conclusions, its knowing and deciding. But as I shed my professional identity, a certain vulnerability emerged. I thought about past shortcomings, failures, and inadequacies. Feelings of self-reproach and guilt floated to the surface. The armor of my professional identity must have covered and contained these thoughts and feelings.

Surprisingly, I didn't feel distressed about it. Physically, I felt more relaxed, noticed a loosening of the muscles in my neck and shoulders. It was good to simply be "John" and not "Doctor Harvey." Every week when I sat in the woods I felt happy, tuned in, connected. Life seemed simpler. Perhaps I was undergoing some personal alchemy, experiencing the *solvae*, dissolution of the old, before the *coagulae*, formation of the new.

On my walk back I noticed a bright red cardinal perched directly above me. Two chickadees perched in a bush next to the trail and called *chick-a-dee-dee-dee* as I walked by. Further along, a brownish bird with a softly spotted breast edged out on an open branch, a hermit thrush, a bird with the exotic flute-like song.

I saw more birds on my walk back than I had seen on the way in. Was I treading differently after an hour in the woods? Was I projecting a more harmonious image? Perhaps this was affinity in operation, the observer and the observed clustering together.

# The Sounds Around

At the end of August the first signs of fall could already be seen. A solitary maple by the road, its leaves a brilliant red-orange, stood as a flag bearer leading the legions of green trees on the march into autumn. Along the West Shore Trail, a thin layer of dry, brown, fallen leaves crunched under my feet. Two windblown trees lay across the trail. One was thick trunked, ripped out of the ground, with dirt-clogged roots sticking in the air; the other was thin, snapped off two feet above the ground. Both carried a heavy mantle of leaves; both had been pummeled by the swirling gusts of a late summer thunderstorm.

I set up under the big black cherry tree. It was quiet — no wind, no leaves moving, the only sound a bee buzzing around a lush spray of goldenrod. In the stillness, I had to send my hearing out in wider and wider circles to search for sounds. Finally, I detected a rooster crowing from a distant farm; a jetliner whispering high across the sky; and two fishermen conversing far down the lake, their words indistinct, but the tones of their voices carrying across the open water. I listened for bird sounds and eventually heard two blue jays calling from across the lake, a pair of crows cawing far across the highway, and from deep in the woods, the faint whistled *here, here, here* of a tufted titmouse.

A flock of Canada geese at the far end of the lake began to honk, sporadically at first, then louder and more consistently, as if they were rousing themselves, readying themselves to take flight and begin their day. The honking reached a crescendo. They lifted in unison from the water and flew toward me at tree-top height, their honking growing louder and louder as they flew closer. I heard the blended interplay, the seamless duet between the deeper *a-honk* of the ganders and the higher-pitched *a-hink* of the females. Directly over me they flew, their honking and pulsing wingbeats filling the soundscape. They winged down the lake, gained altitude, formed a loose V, and flew off to forage in nearby fields. I listened to their calls slowly fade away.

Quiet returned. Again I scanned for sounds around the lake and in the woods. Once again, I discerned the distant calls of blue jays and crows, and then suddenly much closer, the insistent whinny of a robin, the mew of a catbird, and from the lake behind me, a few seconds of a strange deep quacking, oinking sound, a sound so unusual, so surprising that I wondered if it was actually a bird. Maybe it was a frog or some other animal. I waited and listened for the call to come again, but heard only silence. What was it?

I hoped I would hear this strange call again and be able to identify it. After all, it was a very good morning for listening, a late summer Saturday with few cars and trucks on the highway, few boaters on the lake, and few bikers and hikers in the woods. The air was so still that even the slightest sounds carried well. And maybe my hearing had improved over the twenty-seven weeks of my Prompton project.

I had learned a number of new birdsongs. Practice and repetition had helped, listening over and over to *The Birding by Ear* CDs, listening to calls on websites, and perhaps most important of all, listening to the birds in the field. Perhaps Jung's notion of circular learning was right. Each orbit around a topic revealed new information. Each loop solidified the learning. Each hearing of a birdsong added new levels of understanding, created more associations, and anchored it more deeply in memory.

These improving listening abilities made me feel more at home in nature and more in tune with and connected to the rich palate of sounds around me. This connection in turn felt like a link to the history of the human species, a bond with those ancient ancestors who survived because they listened to the sounds around them, and because they had learned and knew which birdsongs indicated food and which warned of danger.

A few brown leaves fell from trees and floated to the ground. Clouds of cream-colored insects fluttered in the morning sunlight. The breeze picked up, and I felt the fresh air touch my face. The wind swayed the leaves and branches and scattered the sunlight, creating flickering patterns of light and shadow that played across the forest floor. I inhaled the fragrances of morning mist, decaying leaves, and rich, dark earth.

My awareness had shifted to the senses of sight, smell, and touch. I was no longer listening. I willed my hearing back out to the full circle around me and gradually began to hear the familiar songs of a kingfisher chattering, a flicker chanting, and an eastern phoebe calling its name — *phoe-bee, phoe-bee.*

My hour was up. Curious about the strange quacking, oinking call, I stepped quietly over to the shoreline to investigate. Edging past yet another red-tinged maple, I peeked through the branches at the mist-covered lake and spotted two big birds perched on the branch of a flood-born snag. They were double-crested cormorants, large black birds, with their wings spread wide, drying their feathers in the morning sunlight.

I brought them into focus with my binoculars. They sat five feet apart, completely unaware of my presence, each engrossed in preening, long angular necks bending and twisting to comb through the shiny black, wet feathers of both wings, of both flanks. Wisps of mist floated around them, the filtered sunlight shone on their ebony feathers, their orange bills and throat. A moment of beauty, an image I would hold in memory, an image linked to a strange hoarse, grunting, quacking, oinking call.

Week 28 · August 29

## Forest Friends

Low gray clouds hung above, heavy humid air pressed down, an easy morning to feel lonely. I yanked the laces on my waterproof boots — waterproof in name only — realizing that soon I would be sitting with soaking, wet feet after walking through the rain-drenched woods to my sit spot. More significantly, I realized once again that I was on my own with my Prompton project. I had hinted to friends that they were welcome to join me for a session, had even asked several outright. But these invitations were met with an uneasy smile, followed by a brief and uncomfortable silence, and typically concluded with a quick change of topic.

Clearly, my enthusiasm for the "sit spot" experience wasn't contagious.

Thick, stagnant fog hung over the highway and veiled the houses as I drove to Prompton. Dark tree trunks loomed out of the fog and receded like specters in the mist. A big doe suddenly appeared in the middle of the road. I slammed on the brakes, slid on the wet pavement, and came to a stop five feet in front of her. She paused, looked at me as if I was rudely intruding her space, turned her head, continued across the road, and disappeared into the fog.

Near the boat ramp turnoff, three crows picked at a fresh roadkill rabbit, reluctantly flapping away as I approached and then settling back down to their scavenged meal as soon as I passed by. In the empty parking lot, the only living thing to be seen was a solitary blue heron wading in the shallows near the shoreline, but as soon as I opened the door it flew away into the fog.

I set up under the black cherry tree. Soon, the usual birds — the crows and blue jays, the robins and catbirds — began to call and sing, seemingly unaffected by the dreary weather or my gloomy mood. A chipmunk — small, brown, with tan and black stripes from head to tail — emerged from the base of a large ash tree ten feet away. I expected a typical short foray across the forest floor. But today, I was surprised. It moved slowly, purposefully across the leaf litter, foraging for food, packing tidbits into its cheek pouches, wandering further and further from its den until I lost sight of it. The chipmunk seemed particularly brave today or perhaps extra motivated, even driven to stay on the surface, to search for food, to begin preparing for winter.

Chipmunks stockpile nuts and seeds in expansive, underground burrows that can reach ten feet in length and typically have two well concealed entrances. The seed foraging and storage of chipmunks is important for the dispersal of tree seeds and helps to restock and diversify the forest that is their home. They also eat and distribute the fungi that live in symbiosis with tree roots; these fungi help the roots absorb needed minerals from the earth. This is another important way these little mammals contribute to the well-being of their forest home.

Chipmunks keep their sleeping quarters clean by removing nut and seed shells and their feces to adjacent refuse tunnels.

They usually spend about fifteen hours a day sleeping in their underground homes, which may be a good way to avoid the predatory hawks, foxes, and coyotes lurking above as well as a good way to conserve energy. Now, in late summer, the nuts and seeds were ripe and abundant, a good time to stay above ground and stock the pantry for winter.

I spotted a catbird in a blackberry bush near the shoreline, brought it into focus with my binoculars, and watched it deftly pluck a blackberry, swallow it, pluck and eat two more, mew to its flockmates, drop down to the ground, and pluck and eat the bright red berries of a poison ivy vine. Soon it would perch in other bushes, defecate, and spread blackberry and poison ivy seeds through the woods, another creature taking care of the forest that in turn takes care of it.

A burst of sunlight broke through the fog and illuminated the wet, brown earth, the gray and brown tree trunks, and the dense green canopy of leaves above. The burst of sunlight triggered a spontaneous inhalation and instantaneously lifted my mood and infused me with hope and optimism. Looking up, I noticed a thick branch of the black cherry angling toward an open patch in the canopy, seeking out and growing toward the sunlight. Into this patch of sunlight a trio of elegantly feathered cedar waxwings appeared, fluttering, feeding, and snatching insects in midair.

I heard a staccato chattering behind me, turned slowly, and spotted a red squirrel, climbing down a big ash tree, pausing to chatter again, jerking its head left and right and up and down, descending, chattering again, and jumping to the ground where it busily searched for food before skittering up another tree.

I knew these red squirrels, smaller than gray squirrels, to be feisty, quick, and determined. I have seen them bite their way into a squirrel-proof birdfeeder. Some years ago, a red squirrel became trapped in my basement, evaded all efforts at capture, dodged the curious cats, and eventually found an escape route through a tiny gap in the wall.

Red squirrels are expanding their range, moving out of the northern pine forests where they fed on the seeds of conifer cones, moving south into the hardwoods and adapting to new seeds and nuts. They are opportunistic feeders and will munch the leaves, buds, and catkins of willows and poplars, eat wild berries, graze on mushrooms, and even eat bird's eggs and baby rabbits. The females are sexually adventurous. Several days before estrous they leave their territory to advertise their impending availability. On the day of estrous they are chased through the trees by amorous males and may mate with anywhere from four to sixteen males. Litters usually consist of three to four pups. The mother moves the pups between two or more nests of grass built between branches.

Red squirrels are territorial. Juveniles need to find, establish, and defend a territory before the first winter arrives. They may search out a new territory, compete for a vacant territory, or be given a section of their mother's territory. I hadn't seen a red squirrel on the peninsula before and wondered if this chattering fellow was a youngster claiming a territory, an important job considering that only twenty-two percent of red squirrels make it through the first year of life.

A few minutes later I spotted a gray squirrel and watched as it climbed up a tree, ran to the end of a thin branch, jumped through the air to the thin branch of another tree, trapezed back and forth until it could climb onto a thicker branch, dashed down the thick branch to the trunk, and then descended the trunk to the ground. This gray squirrel was an impressive acrobat, a wild woodland squirrel.

It was also foraging and preparing for winter. Gray squirrels are scatter hoarders. When they locate a source of nuts and seeds, they store the food in a nearby cache — the hollow of a tree or a little hole in the ground that they cover with earth and leaves and twigs. During late summer and fall, a gray squirrel may construct a thousand or more of these food caches. Then during winter, they use their superb spatial memory and accurate sense of smell to locate the food caches. However, they don't remember the locations of all of their caches, and some seeds are left in the ground to sprout and grow into new trees. Another animal helping with the task of seed dispersal; another friend helping to care for its forest home.

The strange oinking-quacking call of cormorants sounded behind me. I slowly turned my chair 180-degrees around toward the lake, peered through the branches, and spotted two juvenile cormorants perched on a snag, each with a pale brown neck, a bright yellow-orange bill, each stretching and drying its wings in the emerging morning sunlight.

Six catbirds sat in a bush by the shoreline, mewing and flitting from branch to branch. I glimpsed another bird, scanned with my binoculars, and saw a small bird with a brown-gray back and pale yellow breast, a coloration pattern that describes many fall warblers, as these birds shed their colorful spring plumage for the fall migration, acquiring more generic patterns of gray, olive, or brown backs with faintly yellow breasts. I heard two unfamiliar songs and saw two different warbler-sized birds flit through the shoreline bushes. Ahead of me, a chickadee sang, a jay called, a robin whinnied. I was surrounded by birds, songs, calls, sightings, and flyovers.

Why had I never thought of turning my chair to look toward the tip of the peninsula, toward the lake? I had been sitting all of these weeks gazing into the woods, oblivious of all the life and activity behind me.

My feelings of loneliness had vanished, taken away by the sunlight piercing through the mist, by the images of the mutually supportive forest and its friends, by the experience of turning around and feeling surrounded by avian friends who had always been there, by the awareness that all of these experiences came from going alone to the woods where I was never alone.

## Week 29 · September 6

# Blue Surprise

Long, slender strands of pinkish purple clouds stretched across the predawn sky. Goldenrods bloomed in profusion along the highway, warm, butter-yellow plumes, wands, spikes, and clusters, all open to the coming sunshine, all attracting the first foraging bees of the morning. Five deer — two does and three fawns — browsed peacefully in a freshly mowed yard, their summer tan coats flecked with the first hints of winter gray-brown.

More freshly fallen leaves crunched under my boots along the West Shore Trail as I lugged my bulky equipment through the woods — a folding chair; a backpack loaded with bird, flower, and tree guides; a camera, binoculars, and a thermos of tea. Stepping onto the peninsula and heading toward my sit spot, I spotted a cluster of birds on the ground — cardinals, blue jays, and another larger bird.

This scene struck me as unusual. I froze in place, stared, tried to figure out what was going on, but I was too far away and the morning light was too dim. I stepped closer, but the birds all took flight and scattered. The blue jays and larger bird flew out over the lake and the cardinals up into the high canopy of leaves.

I was curious and frustrated. What were these different species of birds doing together on the ground? I realized that I needed to respond more quickly to these fleeting and mysterious events of nature. I resolved in the future to always string my binoculars around my neck as soon as I stepped out of the car. And I also needed to simplify my gear so that I could tread more lightly through the woods.

It was 6:50 by the time I set up under the big black cherry tree. The temperature was a brisk forty-two degrees, the sky was clearing, and a light breeze blew from the northwest. I heard the familiar birdsongs and calls, the jeering of blue jays, the cawing of crows, and the chattering of a kingfisher. Five bright yellow goldfinches lifted and dipped over the peninsula singing their sweet *per-chik-o-ree* flight song. Ah, I thought, another relaxed and peaceful morning chorus.

I heard a bumping sound ahead, perhaps a buck scraping his antlers against a tree to rub off the velvet. A deer snorted loudly, once, twice, three times. It must have seen, smelled, or heard me and now was snorting in alarm, trying to get me to move, to reveal myself. Its alarms were unsettling to the birds, and they all grew quiet. The deer continued its snorting for five minutes, challenging me, an intruder on its territory.

I realized during the past week that there was much life on this little peninsula that I didn't see, hear, or know about. Two days ago, while kayaking slowly around the peninsula, I discovered a tiny, partially hidden indention in the shoreline covered with lily pads. There I saw a green heron stilting across a piece of gray driftwood and spotted two young molting mallards slithering under the large leaves of shoreline plants. Near the tip of the peninsula, under a big dead branch was a spot whitened with bird droppings, possibly a perch for one of the bald eagles that lived on the lake, or one of the kingfishers that rattled up and down the shoreline.

The deer stopped snorting, and a few minutes later the birds resumed singing. Several unfamiliar songs and calls carried through the woods, most likely the songs of migrating birds from among the millions now working their way south from the arctic tundra and Canadian forests to the Caribbean islands, to the coasts and highlands of Central and South America, to the Amazon rainforests. The summer of abundance, of myriad insects and caterpillars, of plentiful wild berries, of mild temperatures and long sunny days was fading away. It was time to fly south.

Most of this migration took place at night when the air was still, the temperature cooler, the winds favorable, the predators stymied by darkness, and the stars and moon lit up the sky to guide avian navigation. The birds rested and fed during the day. I could hear their songs and calls around me now, brief, repeated several times, challenging to identify. During the week, I sat outside at night in a field and listened for the night flight calls (NFCs) of migrating birds, and from time to time heard a few cryptic chirps and chips high in the night sky, indicators of the massive migration occurring above me.

At 7:20 the sun finally cleared the eastern hills, illuminated the tree trunks, and brightened the green leaves. Sunlight touched my back and shoulders, and once again I spontaneously inhaled and felt my spirits rise. I contrasted these feelings with the experience of sitting in the darkness, listening for the night flight calls, vigilant, alert to the sounds of creatures moving through the grass, of predators prowling through the woods. This nighttime vigilance, this bracing for a fight or flight response seemed so instinctual in the dark, such a part of my human heritage as a creature once hunted at night. And now it seemed just as instinctual to feel comfort and security with the advent of sunlight and its accompanying warmth.

Soon my hour was up. I walked to the shoreline to search for clues that might explain the strange gathering of birds I had seen earlier. A patch of bright blue caught my eye. I turned and saw tight clusters of closed, purple-blue flowers atop two tall stems. I was stunned. I knew that woodland wildflowers raced to bloom early in the spring before the canopy of leaves filled in and grabbed the sunshine. But here, in the partial shade under the trees, were flowers, not the tiny and demure ground-hugging white and pink flowers of April, but big, bold, purple-blue flowers standing tall on thick stems ringed with whorls of dark green, spear-shaped leaves.

I pulled out my wildflower guide, paged through, and identified the flowers as closed gentian, a late-blooming native. These plants are also known as bottle gentian because the flowers resemble little closed bottles, like bottles of delicate, purple-blue, Venetian glass. The flowers do not open and only the biggest and strongest bees can force open the lips of the flower, enter its shaded recess, sip its nectar, and deposit pollen.

The flower's name comes from King Gentius of ancient Illyria who reportedly discovered the plant's medicinal properties some two thousand years ago. Both the North American gentian and its European cousins are renowned as a digestive aid. Gentian root has long been an ingredient of herbal bitters that effectively stimulate the function of the liver, gall bladder, and pancreas. The roots contain compounds so bitter they are used as a marker for measuring bitterness. Native Americans used the root as an antidote to snake bite.

When I returned home, I thought about looking through nursery catalogs to see if I could purchase blue gentian plants and try to get them to grow in a wooded, shady area of the yard. But then I reconsidered. For some reason I preferred that these flowers grow free and wild and unknown. I liked to picture these tall, late-blooming stems of bright, purple-blue flowers swaying gently in the wind, under the trees, along the shoreline of Prompton Lake.

# Tap, Tap, Tap

It was still dark when I started my early morning drive to Prompton, dark enough to turn on my headlights and for other drivers to have their headlights on as they headed to work, to school, or to take their children to daycare. I opened my mind to the mood of the morning. The word "comfort" popped into awareness, and I realized immediately that it felt comfortable in the car, even cozy, with the headlights lighting up the darkness, the warm air wafting around my feet, and the melodious piano tones of Mussorgsky's *Pictures at an Exhibition* resonating through the car.

The parking lot at Prompton was empty. I stepped into air that was in transition, air that still felt humid and heavy from a band of thunderstorms that had rumbled through overnight, but air that also held the first hints of a cooler, dryer, approaching Canadian high pressure front. Downhill near the lake, in a tall, thick pine tree, a trio of crows partially hidden by the drooping branches and long green needles cooed and gurgled back and forth.

Along the West Shore Trail a layer of wet fallen leaves cushioned and silenced my footsteps. Setting up under the big black cherry tree, I positioned my chair so I could see the brushy tip of the peninsula and look out to the lake beyond. After a few minutes, the peaceful, bird-business-as-usual morning chorus came to life — chickadees calling, blue jays jeering, a kingfisher chattering, cedar waxwings squeaking, catbirds mewing, geese honking, and the harsh *check, check, check* calls of red-winged blackbirds already assembling into restless, migration-ready flocks.

I heard a steady *tap, tap, tap* coming from the top of a nearby ash tree. I glanced up and spotted a medium-sized woodpecker clinging to the trunk of the tree. In the dim light, I couldn't see its plumage but thought it might be a hairy woodpecker, a common species in the Northeast. I watched it through the binoculars, marveling at how easily it clung to the trunk of the tree. This bird, like all woodpeckers, has two strong claws in front and one in back that allow it to grip the vertical surface of the bark, and it also employs its long, stiff, spiny tail to brace itself. Showing off its unique adaptation, the woodpecker scooted a few feet up the tree and then resumed its steady tapping. I would need brighter light to see its plumage and field marks and to confirm its identity.

The predawn light slowly increased. I watched the colors and textures come to life, the myriad shades of green and brown, the varied smooth, grooved, and rough bark of the various tree trunks. Puffs of wind rustled the leaves, swayed the blades of grass, and rippled the surface of the lake while the woodpecker continued to *tap, tap, tap.*

I saw movement from the corner of my eyes, turned, and spotted a chipmunk scooting along a dead log fifteen paces in front of me. It climbed ten feet up a tree, paused, skittered back down, ran to its hole, and slipped underground. A few minutes later it reemerged and then headed into the woods to forage for food. Later, I checked the entrance to its den and found a neat silver-dollar-sized hole cleverly placed between the roots of an ash tree, making an entrance that was virtually invisible.

I heard splashes on the lake, peered through the branches, and spotted four cormorants perched on a long black snag. These birds had become regulars at Prompton, and I studied them through my binoculars — two adults, larger birds with jet black plumage and bright yellow beaks; and two juveniles, smaller, slimmer, with brownish plumage and dull yellow beaks. They preened, stretched, and shook their wings, all engaging in the same activities, but each acting separately, each with its own sequence and timing — the scene reminiscent of toddlers engaged in parallel play.

I brought the woodpecker back into focus, hoping to see its plumage, but the light was still too dim, and I could only discern brownish feathers. The woodpecker suddenly flew away, lifting and dipping through the air in typical woodpecker flight, dodging through the trees, out over the lake, and across to the far shore. I checked my watch and my notes; the woodpecker had been tapping on the same tree for a full thirty minutes.

I watched the sun inch above the eastern hills and, as always, celebrated the return of light and warmth. Fifteen minutes later the woodpecker returned to the same spot in the same tree and resumed the same *tap, tap, tap*. The light was brighter now, and I studied the bird carefully through my binoculars, noted its medium size, stocky build, pointy beak, and brownish plumage. I saw where it had drilled neat, evenly spaced horizontal rows of holes into the trunk. I paged through my Sibley and found an illustration of a juvenile yellow-bellied sapsucker that looked just like my bird. And I read that sapsuckers drill neat horizontal rows of holes.

I had heard of this woodpecker and had always been faintly amused by its somewhat unusual and esoteric name. Now I saw it in action, drilling holes in the bark and using its brush-tipped tongue to lap up the leaking sap.

Curious about this bird, I later read that in the spring sapsuckers drill narrow circular wells into the xylem to sip the sugary rising sap. When the trees leaf out, they drill shallower, rectangular holes to tap into the phloem and lap up the sap flowing down to the roots. These rectangular wells need constant reopening to keep flowing, and that was what I was seeing and hearing. Sapsuckers prefer trees with the sweetest sap — sugar and red maples, paper and yellow birch, and hickory — but will drill into any tree. Their wells have been found on more than a thousand species.

Sapsuckers have additional feeding strategies and, like other woodpeckers, will pick ants and spiders from under the bark. Sometimes they perch on a branch, jump out, and snatch insects in mid-air like a flycatcher. And they frequent orchards and feed on fruit like an oriole.

Other birds take advantage of the sapsucker's handiwork. Hummingbirds rely on the sap during the high demand nesting season. Some bats and even porcupines find and feed at the sap wells. I marveled at this complex and mutually supportive web of nature. Every feeding strategy, no matter how successful, is best backed up by alternative strategies, an embodiment of the principle of redundancy and a demonstration of adaptability. And every feeding strategy creates opportunities for other birds and animals, almost as if the concentric rings of one bird's life touched the lives of other birds and animals.

I looked up at the sapsucker and listened to its *tap, tap, tap*. Although this was a young bird, it seemed to have found a good tree, a healthy tree with ready access to water, one that most likely provided a generous flow of sap. Soon this bird would continue its journey south to warmer climes in Central America where the sap still flowed. I hoped it might remember this little peninsula and return in the spring. And I hoped I might be there to see it cleverly clinging to the tree trunk and to hear its steady *tap, tap, tap*.

Autumn

## Week 31 · September 21

# Lunacy

It was a quiet morning, the only sounds the crunching of gravel under my boots as I walked to the car. Halfway there I stopped in my tracks, taken aback by the view of a pale, golden full moon floating above the western horizon and a blazing yellow disc of the sun pushing above the eastern horizon.

I drove to Prompton glancing again and again at the strange morning sky with a sinking moon to the left and a rising sun to the right — the cool reflected light of the moon and the warm direct light of the sun. The word lunacy sprang to mind, the nineteenth-century term for mental illness, a term based on the belief that the full moon triggered attacks of mania, paranoia, and mental instability. I wondered if this moment of double illuminating bodies might be an even more potent trigger for "lunacy."

Contemporary scientists conducting carefully designed studies with strict experimental controls have all but ruled out any link between the full moon and madness. But caregivers on the front lines — mental health workers, law enforcement personnel, emergency room staff, and midwives — all believe they see a spike in aberrant behaviors, criminal acts, acute illnesses, and the onset of labor and birth of babies around the time of the full moon.

Interestingly, science has verified that on the days preceding and following a full moon, people need an extra five minutes to fall asleep, sleep more restlessly, and get about twenty minutes less sleep than on other days. These effects occur even when subjects are isolated from both daylight and moonlight, suggesting that some human behaviors and biorhythms, typically involving restlessness and increased activity, are linked to the lunar cycle.

By the time I arrived at Prompton, the sky had morphed from a drab canopy of gray into a high dome of light blue. Diaphanous clouds of mist wafted across the surface of the lake. The sun had yet to top the dark green hills that rose across the lake, but a line of bright pink above the horizon heralded the approach of daylight. The air felt cool and fresh and smelled of earth and fallen leaves. This strange, double-orbed morning was also the last day of summer.

Wet leaves squished under my boots as I walked along the West Shore Trail. Drops of dew slid off the leaves and plopped onto the forest floor. The ash saplings had shed their leaves and stood slender, gray, and bare. A hard frost had wilted the succulent jewelweed. Summer's foliage was fading, and now I could see through trees downhill to the flat, blue-gray surface of the lake.

I had forgotten to pack my folding chair, but found a little green and yellow Green Bay Packers pillow on the back seat, a craft project made by my mother-in-law during her declining years. I stuffed the pillow into my backpack, and in a way it seemed suitable, as I wanted to sit closer to the ground, wanted to feel more connected to the earth, wanted to simplify the gear I carried. I placed the pillow between two large barked roots, sat down, and rested my back against the thick trunk of the big black cherry tree.

Soon I heard the morning bird chorus — blue jays queedling, chickadees chattering, kingfishers rattling, and a pair of catbirds mewing. I was surprised that the catbirds were still around after the hard frost, but surely they knew best what food was still available and when was the right time to head south. A flock of Canada geese, honking steadily, took off from the far end of the lake, gained altitude, and flew out to feed in nearby fields, also in no apparent hurry to begin their journey south.

I leaned back against the tree, looked at the ground, and spotted a cluster of tiny red berries clinging to the stem of a wild lily of the valley, the berries half-covered by brown, fading leaves. I looked at the moss and fungi growing on top of the tree roots, some patches dark green and flat against the bark, some light green and bushy, and some blue-green with a miniature forest of tentacle-like stems reaching into the air. Gazing at the different colors, textures, and heights of the moss and fungi, I realized that here was another complete world of competition and cooperation growing on the surface of the tree roots. I glanced back into the angled sunlight and saw spider webs, symmetric forms arcing from branch to branch, the threads damp and dewy, silky and shiny.

The world around my sit spot seemed pervaded with order, design, and coherence. The flowers, the trees, the birds, the squirrels, and now the moss, fungi, and spiders all seemed to live with purpose and grace. The world of lunacy, the world of dysfunctional thoughts, disconnected feelings, and bizarre behaviors seemed entirely out of synchrony with the harmonious world of nature.

I realized, of course, that in the forest, any traces of lunacy would be quickly culled. A delusional red squirrel would never survive its first winter. A paranoid goose would be cut off from the flock. A warbler with wandering biorhythms would fail to align with the tight schedule of migration, courting, breeding, disbursing, and migration. A disoriented oriole would never find the subtropical coffee plantations, would never be able to navigate by the stars and magnetic fields, and would never find the best nesting grounds. The ever-present predators kept a sharp eye out for any bird or animal that was different, slow, inattentive, or disoriented. In the life of birds and animals there is no margin for error, no tolerance for lunacy.

But in humans, mental illness is both present and persistent, a source of much suffering for the person affected and for his or her loved ones. Was mental illness the price we paid for a brain that seemed to stand outside of nature, for frontal lobes that conjured up myriad possibilities, for the complex emotional wiring required to regulate social interactions, for a motivational system that operated out of immediate time? Perhaps all of these human traits were just a small step away from madness, a madness that sometimes brought novel perceptions, new ideas, remarkable persistence, and even illumination to the human condition. Perhaps this is why we tolerate and care for those who live with lunacy.

I heard tapping high in a tree to my right. I looked up thinking I might see the sapsucker again, but these were intermittent taps, a burst from one tree and then another. The taps sounded above me in the black cherry tree. I rested my head against the trunk and felt the vibrations flow down and register against my skull. The bird flew on, a flicker, flying from tree to tree, feeding on insects and ants and caterpillars.

Quiet settled around me. I was near the end of my hour and considered leaving early, but then heard a *quack, quack, quack* from the lake — the call of a hen mallard. I leaned back for a few more minutes and pictured the mallards swimming smoothly and serenely on the water, imagined the hens with their warm, mottled brown plumage, their orange beak with a dark saddle across it, and their dark blue wing patches. I pictured the splendidly attired drakes with their iridescent green head, bright yellow bill, chestnut breast, white neck ring, white-gray body, and jaunty, black, curled tail feathers.

The ducks took off with a volley of splashes. I heard the quacking of the hens and the raspy veeping of the drakes as they flew up the lake to the shallow water where they could dabble and dip for seeds and stems and roots and tubers, where they could rest, refuel, and prepare for the journey ahead.

Quiet returned and now my hour was up. I stood, packed my gear and prepared to leave, but was startled by the loud *frahnk* of a blue heron flying right over me — a sleek and slender body, a long spear-like bill, a stunning six-foot wingspread. A bird called from the woods, a vaguely familiar *weedich* call. Another bird sang to my left, a lovely lilting musical song. A fall warbler flashing shades of olive and yellow plumage darted out of a bush, flew in front of me, and disappeared into another bush. It seemed as if the woods had come alive, as if nature was calling out to me, "Don't leave! Don't leave! We have more to show you, more to teach you about harmony and unity and coherence."

Week 32 · September 27

## September Surprise

Thick strands of whitish gray mist wafted down in the valleys where the morning chill transformed invisible humidity into visible mist. The mist floated up to the fields and drifted across the road. More maple trees had turned bright red, each tree luminous in the angled sunlight, each a bright red flag in the mist. Along the far crest of the Moosic Mountains, the white blades of the windmills protruded above the mist, catching the morning sunlight and looking like gleaming, white, floating propellers entirely detached from earth.

A single pickup truck with a boat trailer stood in the lot. Halfway up the lake, a solitary fisherman sat in a simple aluminum boat surrounded by shifting wisps of mist, casting patiently and repeatedly toward the shoreline. Two blue herons flew down the lake, their large wings flapping in a slow, powerful rhythm; long, sculpted bodies slicing through the mist; hoarse squawks piercing the stillness.

A thick layer of red, yellow, and brown wet fallen leaves muffled my footsteps along the West Shore Trail. When I turned off the trail into the woods, a small bird flew in front of me and landed in a bush fifteen feet away. I quickly brought up my binoculars, focused, and caught a clear view — an olive brown back, dull yellow breast, black beak — a warbler in fall plumage. I knew this view would be fleeting, so I burned the image into my visual memory. A few seconds later the little bird flitted away.

The minute I set up under the big black cherry tree, I pulled out my *Peterson Field Guide to Birds*, found the section on fall warblers, and carefully studied the page on warblers without streaks and wing bars. Holding the vivid image of the bird in my mind, I scanned the page and saw three likely candidates — a Canada warbler, an immature Nashville warbler, and a common yellowthroat. The first two are uncommon so I reasoned that my bird was a common yellowthroat, a conclusion made more likely by the fact that I had seen yellowthroats on the peninsula in June and that the wet thickets and marsh grasses along the shoreline were favored yellowthroat habitat.

How quickly all of this transpired. I was reminded how important it is to always be alert and ready; how crucial it is to focus quickly and fix an image in memory, an image that is visual and holistic and relies on previously learned categories of field marks. It felt as if I was developing a new kind of perception — quick and intuitive, yet simultaneously informed by the slower and more methodical categories of field marks, eye stripes, eye rings, wing bars, tail length and shape, posture, and behavior. It seemed like an interplay between flash perception and systematic observation, a way of looking that engaged more of my brain, an experience of seeing that felt more satisfying.

Pleased with my progress and glad to welcome a familiar friend back to the peninsula, I turned my attention to the familiar songs and calls around me — blue jays calling, crows cawing, a kingfisher rattling, chickadees chattering, a robin tutting, and from far across the lake, the *klee-yer, klee-yer* call of a flicker. A gray shadowy shape moved through a thick wild grapevine near the shoreline, and a few seconds later I heard the familiar nasal *mew, mew, mew* of a catbird, a call quickly answered by two other series of mews, each with a slightly different tone.

This peaceful morning chorus assured me once again that all was well and safe at Prompton Lake on this misty morning. Suddenly, I heard strange and unknown song snippets coming from a tree down the shoreline. I listened intently to the unknown song, a song that I represented phonetically as *deedala, deedala, deedala* followed by a *dit, dit, dit*, a song that seemed familiar. Straining to hear the song more clearly, I filtered out the noise of the cars whooshing along the highway and ignored all the familiar songs. As my focus on the mystery singer deepened, its song suddenly changed from *deedala* to *djzeep, djzeep, dzjeep*, then changed again to a sharp *chack, chack, chack,* and changed yet again to a melodious rising *wheeta, wheeta, wheeta.*

I began to count the repetitions of each new song — three, three, four, five, three, four, and three. The section on mimic thrushes from the *Birding by Ear* CD came to mind. Well sung repetitions in series of three or more are the hallmark of the northern mockingbird.

This was a surprise. I had seen mockingbirds in the Lackawanna Valley on the other side of the Moosic Mountains. Every spring and summer there was at least one pair living on the campus of the hospital where I had worked. I enjoyed hearing brief interludes of their clever, ever-changing, beautiful songs as I walked to and from my car. I appreciated their bold, confident, feisty presence, perched in plain sight on the small trees dotting the parking lot, jumping down and snatching insects from the ground, and feeding on tiny red crab apples with little regard for the comings and goings of people, arriving in early spring, lingering until late fall.

But the Lackawanna Valley, with its lower elevation and slightly warmer climate, seemed to be the very northern edge of their range. Only once had I seen a mockingbird on this side of the mountains — a visitor to my yard singing high in a tree. I wished him to stay, but he flew off.

A male mockingbird can learn as many as two hundred songs during its lifetime of eight or more years. This medium-sized, slender, gray bird with bright white wing patches is a persistent singer that may chant through the day and into the night. The male begins singing in February to establish territory and attract a mate. He continues singing through August. Then, after a brief pause, he resumes singing from September through November. He has a different repertoire of songs for spring and fall.

I closed my eyes and listened to his song, to the beautiful whistling tones, to the sudden and dramatic shifts to a new song, to the creative use of elements of other birds' songs, to the jazzy improvisation on these elements. I knew that this singing had a functional basis. It was an evolved behavior pattern related to males competing for females that selected the most talented, creative, and melodious singers. But as I sat and listened I heard an expression of beauty that seemed to exceed function.

This mockingbird's song simply seemed more beautiful than it needed to be and presented beauty as an independent element, a principle within the realm of nature. This thought was reinforced when I opened my eyes and looked straight ahead at a maple tree, its leaves a luminous deep red against a cobalt blue sky. Functionally, these leaves were just dying, drying, and dropping to the ground. They didn't need to be this beautiful, but they were.

I considered that my perception of beauty in song and color was subjective, a product of my experience and my human sensibilities that were crafted by evolution and had both cognitive and social functions. But this explanation didn't fully satisfy me, didn't ring completely true. Beyond function, I thought there must be a principle of beauty, a principle that expresses itself time and time again on this little wooded peninsula.

His morning performance concluded, the mockingbird moved on. The usual performers returned to center stage. At first the calls of the blue jays, the mews of the catbirds, and the tutting of a robin seemed plain in comparison. Yet as I listened, I began to hear a certain beauty, complexity, and resonance in all of these familiar calls. A soft tapping sounded above me. I looked up and spotted a male downy woodpecker, delicately latticed, black and white plumage with a brilliant red patch on the back of his head, tapping, flitting from tree to tree, singing his distinct descending whinny, displaying his unique take on the principle of beauty.

## Week 33 · October 5

# Cornucopia

Freshly fallen, yellow, spear-shaped black walnut leaves covered the yard and driveway, leaves knocked down by an overnight rain. The day before I had raked the whole yard clean. But it was full autumn now, leaves turning color, drying, dropping, being battered by the rain and blown by the wind, floating, fluttering, falling, and covering the ground.

I settled into my car, flicked on the headlights and twenty yards ahead of me in the yard saw a sleek, gray-brown doe browsing in the yard. She lifted her head, glanced briefly, and then resumed munching the sweet green grass, eating steadily, packing on pounds, on a timetable preparing for winter.

It was fifteen minutes before sunrise when I arrived at Prompton. Once again mist floated above the lake and shrouded the trees along the far shore. The parking lot was empty, the blacktop wet and shiny from last night's rain, the air calm, the sky partly cloudy, the temperature a mild sixty-one degrees. I stood and watched the mist shift and shape over the placid water and heard the start of the morning chorus, the first tentative calls of blue jays, crows, and cardinals.

I set up under the big black cherry tree again and settled in to look and listen. Immediately I sensed movement, glanced up, and spotted a large gray-brown bird weave and angle through the trees, set its wings, and land silently on the top of a broken-off tree. It had a streamlined physique, long squared-off tail, hooked beak, alert predatory posture. It was a sharp-shinned hawk looking for a quick kill in the dim morning light, flying stealthily through the trees, avoiding detection by the songbirds. I leaned forward for a better look, but the sharpie must have sensed my presence and lifted silently off the tree. With a few flaps of its slender wings, it glided through the branches and was gone.

The whole episode lasted only a few seconds. I was glad I was at my sit spot in the predawn light, glad I had seen the attack plan of this skilled hunter. Its furtive presence was a sobering reminder that the life of a songbird is hard and dangerous. Their bright plumage and enchanting songs can create an idyllic image, but in reality these little birds are engaged in a constant struggle to find food, claim and defend territory, hatch, protect, and fledge their young, and avoid the razor-sharp talons of sharp-shinned hawks.

As daylight increased, the landscape began to emerge — leaves of orange, red, yellow, tan, and brown, a few clinging to their branches, but most already blanketing the forest floor. The morning chorus was soon in full swing — robins tutting, blue jays calling, crows cawing, cardinals chipping, and a catbird mewing. A jetliner whooshed high overhead. Canada geese honked lazily from the far end of the lake.

I began to distinguish individual bird calls, the higher-pitched cawing of two crows up the shoreline — perhaps young birds — then down the shoreline, a more full bodied typical adult *caw, caw, caw*. A few minutes later from the woods ahead, two crows cawed back and forth with deep raspy voices sounding like old, salty pirates spinning yarns of travel and adventure, commenting on the day's prospects for foraging and pillaging.

I shifted my attention to the blue jays and began to hear different calls from different birds, some higher-pitched, some lower, some raspy, some short and direct, some longer and drawn out — each jay with a unique voice.

Crows and jays are members of the corvid family — intelligent, opportunistic, and social birds. Their distinct voices most likely allowed the birds to recognize their flockmates, to share information on food sources, and to warn of predators. If I could detect differences in their voices, then these clever birds must hear them even more clearly.

More songs and calls sounded through the morning air — the insistent *wicka, wicka* of a flicker, the melodious *cheerily, cheer-up, cheerily, cheer-up* of a robin, the tapping of a woodpecker, and the rattle of a kingfisher patrolling the shoreline. The wind picked up, rustling the leaves and sprinkling the last drops of rain down to the forest floor. A dog barked in the distance, a cow mooed plaintively. The sounds wove together into a harmonious and soothing composition.

I settled into a relaxed reverie, gazed ahead into the woods, and began to notice the angles formed by the living and fallen trees — young, straight ash trees at a precise ninety degrees from the ground; an older ash tilting at one hundred five degrees; a sapling broken off twenty feet above the ground, its top half forming a perfect forty-five-degree angle with the ground; other saplings broke closer to the ground forming a variety of acute angles. Straight ahead was a tall maple still covered in leaves, its branches bending through the air, describing a myriad of arcs and half-circles.

I thought of my young, personable, and enthusiastic tenth grade geometry teacher. If she had just once taken our class into the woods to see all of these angles in nature, to see geometry as an aspect of the living world instead of presenting boring black lines on the pages of a worn book, I might have done better in her class, better than the borderline and most likely charitable "C" I received.

Lost in a world of thoughts, I suddenly realized that I had been sitting and musing for ten minutes beyond my hour. I grabbed my camera, walked to the shoreline, edged through the bushes, climbed down to the water, and looked across the little bay and beyond to the high rocky dam. I saw a vista of angles and arcs of rocky coves and brightly colored trees reflected in deep blue, placid water — the shimmering geometry of nature, a vista that surely would have brought a smile to my teacher's face.

While taking pictures, I heard high-pitched calls from a nearby tree, looked up, and saw a flock of small, yellow-breasted birds flitting in and out of the branches. I pulled up my binoculars, but was distracted by movement to my right. I then turned and spotted a small bird with a short, sharp, black beak, white wing band, white eye ring, yellowish breast, white belly, and short tail.

As I was burning this image into memory, another bird darted into a nearby bush, a bird with a faded yellow breast, olive brown back, no wing bars, and no eye ring. The flock in the tree moved to the outer branches where I tried to bring them into focus, but found it challenging as they flitted from branch to branch. I heard high-pitched calls to my right, turned, and saw another pair of small birds, bright yellow, moving, calling, and dodging in and out of the bushes.

It was a cornucopia of fall warblers. The visual images, the field marks, and the behaviors tumbled around in my mind, producing sensory overload and completely overwhelmed my identification skills. These warblers, little birds that migrate to Central and South America — forty-plus confusing species — humbled me. My only consolation was that what I lost in individual identification was made up for by a collective warbler experience, a composite vision of their petite size and varied plumage; their tiny insect-snatching, fruit-eating, caterpillar-grabbing bills; and their active and determined demeanor.

It was, I reflected, a good outcome. As I was growing confident in my bird identification skills — perhaps a bit too confident — nature humbled me with its stunning richness, diversity, and complexity, yet also enriched me with a direct vision of warblers on the move, an incalculable swarm of tiny birds flying south from the Canadian woods, winging their way under the stars at night, and pausing during the day to rest and feed at Prompton Lake before resuming their epic journey.

Week 34 · October 11

# Darkness to Daylight

Above me the nighttime sky was a dark dome dotted with pinpoints of starlight. To the east, a thin pale line of light peeked above the horizon, the first hint of the coming sunrise, still a full forty-five minutes away. In my lap, the pages of my notebook looked like dim white rectangles. I couldn't see what I was writing and had to trust my fingers to form the letters and space the words. I listened to the sound of leaves falling to the forest floor, some touching softly, some with stems attached landing with a slightly louder scratchy sound.

Yesterday afternoon my neighbor asked me for an 8:00 AM ride to pick up a rental car. I flinched. I had wanted my Prompton morning to be free of any conflicting obligations or time pressure. However, desiring to be both a good neighbor and a friend, I agreed to pick him up. Meanwhile, I quickly devised a plan to make an extra early visit to my sit spot.

This morning my alarm chimed at 5:00 AM. Thirty minutes later I was on my way to Prompton under a nighttime sky, peering into the dual cones of headlight illumination and opening my mind for a word that might capture the mood of the day. "Busy" popped up and I immediately dismissed it. "Busy" had much more to do with my day than with nature.

As I slowed down to turn onto the boat ramp road, I saw an opossum, just struck by a car, lying on the highway, weakly lifting its head, its still-living eyes glowing in the headlights. I swerved around it, drove under the dark arch of pine trees, and pulled into the parking lot.

Complete darkness surrounded me as I stepped out of the car. I wished I had brought along a flashlight or, better yet, that headlamp resting in the top drawer in the mud room at home. I knew I could somehow shuffle across the paved parking lot and find the gap in the trees that marked the entrance to the West Shore Trail. But would I be able to stay on the trail as it wound through the woods? As my anxiety mounted, help arrived in the form of a memory.

Years ago I walked at night for exercise along a path that traversed fields and woods. Initially, I needed a flashlight to find my way. Then I observed my golden retriever finding her way unerringly along the paths, always turning at the right time, relying on some unique mammalian motor and spatial memory. I thought I might share at least a dormant fragment of this navigational sensibility and decided to try and trust my feet to feel the path, my legs to find the way. Soon, much to my surprise, my night-walking became almost as confident and fast paced as my day-walking.

Now I would have to apply this past learning to my current situation. After all, I had been walking the West Shore Trail for six months. My feet must have learned the feel of the path; my brain must have created an internal map of the route to the little peninsula. I exhaled, relaxed, and let my boots lead the way. Soon I was moving at an almost normal pace along the trail, anticipating its inclines and declines, its curves and turns. I saw a patch of greenish white luminescence near the trail, fungi glowing in the dark, a visual treat reserved for night-walkers. I turned off the trail, made my way through the trees and bushes, stepped over the rocks and fallen branches, and arrived at my sit spot beneath the big black cherry tree.

Now I sat in the darkness listening to the sounds, feeling sensations on my skin, and sniffing the air. Without visual input the other senses took over. The air, a mild fifty-five degrees, felt moist and humid against my cheek, maritime air circling in from the Atlantic Ocean. Puffs of wind skimmed across the lake, carrying the distinctive earthy, watery smell of a late algae bloom.

Cars and trucks whooshed along the nearby highway. A jetliner whispered through the sky high above, its lights blinking steadily in the darkness. I pictured the inside of the plane, a warm, well-lit silver tube filled with travelers settling in for their flight, pulling out books, magazines and newspapers, turning on laptops, anticipating arrival times and destination plans. The image stirred feelings of wanderlust, an itch and eagerness to travel, feelings that had been growing,

In the darkness, my mind meandered. I began to speculate on the nature of wanderlust. Is it a trait bred in by evolution, a genetic mutation in those early humans who fanned out from Africa, a mutation subsequently locked into our modern DNA? Or is the desire to travel and explore a byproduct of our complex frontal lobes and their capacity for knowing, categorizing, and planning? Maybe these cognitive capabilities are like a pack of cranial border collies craving a workout, longing for a session of trip planning and itinerary organizing. Or perhaps there is an addictive paradigm at play where the excitement of anticipation, the sensations of new pleasures, and the satisfaction of new learning creates such intoxicating rewards that inevitably the brain craves another fix.

As the light gradually lifted the darkness, my vision searched the world around me. I spotted a small opening in the trees ahead, an ideal campsite, a perfect spot to experience life on the little peninsula. I imagined myself setting up a tent in that spot, saw myself nestling into a thick sleeping bag, falling asleep to the night sounds, emerging in the morning, firing up a portable camp stove, and brewing a cup of steaming coffee while listening to the morning chorus of birdsongs. I wondered then if wanderlust might be linked to the visual imagery areas of the brain, a mental system faster than language and much more emotionally compelling.

At exactly 6:31 AM, I heard the first bird calls, quiet peeps and squeaks, random and intermittent, slowly picking up in intensity and frequency, reminding me of an orchestra before a performance. I pictured musicians plucking strings, checking tuning, moistening reeds, softly tooting trumpets and trombones. Then at 6:41, as if a conductor had raised a wand, the real morning chorus began — a trio of blue jays taking the lead with brassy loud calls, a duet of crows with deep cello caws, a family of cardinals with percussive chips, and a solo robin singing its cheerful piccolo melody.

I listened as the chorus grew louder . . . then quieter, heard the changing composition of songs and calls, watched the daylight brighten, saw the colors around me come alive — vivid shades of brown, red, orange, yellow, and tan in the leaves on the trees and the leaves blanketing the forest floor. Soon there was enough light to see my notebook, and I was relieved that my words were both legible and adequately spaced. Yet the handwriting looked different, almost as if another person, a night-walker perhaps, had written the words.

A gust of cold north wind whipped down the length of the lake, liberating more leaves, creating a fluttering multicolored shower all around me. The catbirds that I had seen and heard last week were gone, most likely on their way south to Florida and the Gulf Coast, responding to their own avian wanderlust. A flock of robins suddenly arrived on the peninsula, more birds migrating, roaming down from the north, from New York and Canada. I heard them clucking, tutting, and singing. Four darted by in front of me, adaptive birds, able to tolerate cold weather. If they can't stalk and snatch worms, they pluck fruit from trees and pick berries from bushes. They are one of the last birds to fly south, one of the first to return in the spring, and sometimes they even winter over in their northern breeding grounds.

Three red maples stood in the woods directly ahead of me, all about the same size, all seemingly in good health. The one to the left was covered with brilliant burgundy red leaves, the one in the middle was bare and leafless, the one on the right still wore its green mantle of leaves. I wondered if this was adaptability in action, three maples with three different timing strategies. One prudently dropping its leaves and shutting down its delicate internal plumbing to avoid frost damage, while another, a risk-taker, kept at it, kept pumping water up, kept photosynthesizing, kept sending sugar down to the roots, kept amassing nutrients for the next growing season while the third tree split the difference. Was the green leafy risk-taker the tree most ready to adapt to climate change and warmer temperatures? I paused by the three maples on my walk back, touched the smooth gray trunk of each, hoping for an answer to my inquiry.

A few minutes later, I pulled out of the parking lot in a hurry to pick up my neighbor. On the highway, two turkey vultures — big, black-feathered, bald-headed birds, the sacred cleansers of the earth — stood on the pavement, picking at the opossum. It died. They found it. Nature was busy.

Week 35 · October 18

# Clearing Skies

Outside my window the gusting wind ripped the last leaves from the trees and rattled the bare branches — the soundscape of a cold front bringing rain and chilly, stormy air. It all sounded too miserable. My watch read 5:00 AM. I flopped my head back on the pillow, pulled up the covers, and fell back asleep. An hour later when I woke up again, the wind had abated, quiet reigned, a more welcoming time to get up and head to Prompton.

Walking to the car, I paused and looked at the sky. To the southeast a thin line of pale pink, predawn light inched above the horizon. To the northeast thick clumps of black clouds scuttled off, the rear guard of a cold front retreating before an invading dome of Canadian high pressure. To the west the first hints of a high blue sky broke through the clouds. The temperature was forty-eight degrees and the air felt fresh and dry, a welcome respite from a week of warmth and humidity.

I reflected on the week's weather, the lingering humid, stagnant air that began to feel like emotional negativity spinning around, like a bad mood feeding on itself, a mood that intensified as low pressure built and approached. During the night, the crescendo of the cold front swept through along with turbulent wind and rain — a meteorological catharsis, a cyclonic therapy session — and now a brand new morning with an influx of fresh air. Altogether it felt like an emotional rebirth.

Along the highway, two big, gray-coated does greedily munched fallen apples from a fully laden tree and didn't flinch or glance as I drove by a mere ten feet away. Further along another doe stood — in the middle of the road. I slowed and flicked my headlights. She looked up with a confused expression. Only when I came to a complete stop did she continue across the road. Then, before I could push the accelerator down, her grown-up fawn bolted out of the woods and darted across the road to join her. Clearly, deer lack street smarts.

Pulling into the parking lot at Prompton, I noticed a dark object in the grass near the shoreline, but dismissed it as a thick clump of leaves. When I stepped out of the car and looked again, the object moved. It was a crow. I watched it stretch one wing, then the other, move its head around, shift its body back and forth. Performing crow calisthenics, I thought with a smile, loosening up after a long night of roosting in a tree. As I continued across the parking lot I heard the crow softly clucking and cooing, tuning up for a day of cawing and communicating.

A woodcock exploded into the air just ahead of me as I stepped onto the trail. I flinched in surprise and watched its stubby brown body and heard its whirring wings — the first woodcock I had seen since spring. Another bird pausing at Prompton on its southward journey.

From my sit spot under the big black cherry tree, I saw that the hardwoods — the ash, maple, and cherry trees — were now almost completely leafless, holding just a few lonely lingering yellow-orange leaves. But the poplars, birches, and Russian olives still held their leaves — yellow, gold, and green. Four crows flew over — strong wingbeats, black silent silhouettes — slicing through a cobalt-blue sky. A flock of migrating robins flitted around the peninsula tutting, clucking, and singing an occasional song. A downy woodpecker *tap, tap, tapped* above me. A soft *tsip, tsip, tsip* call sounded from a shoreline shrub, a call I couldn't identify.

Three loud gunshots pierced the morning stillness, followed by two more shots, duck hunters at the upper end of the lake, probably after puddle ducks this time of year — mallards, wood ducks, and teal. As a teenager I hunted ducks with my dad, shot them out of the autumn sky, plucked them, cleaned them, wrapped them in white freezer paper, wrote the date and type of duck on the paper. Later, during the winter, I ate them with pride and enjoyment when my mother prepared a wild duck dinner complete with wild rice and cranberry relish. Now, I just liked to watch ducks fly, to see their steady rhythmic wingbeats, to watch them swimming steadily through placid water, to see them bobbing up and down in windy, wavy water, and to enjoy their bright decorative plumage.

Across the lake I heard the clear whistled song of a white-throated sparrow, *Old Tom Peabody, Peabody, Peabody*, a song that brought a smile to my face and a pulse of warmth to my heart. This was my father's favorite birdsong. Although these sparrows seldom appeared near our family home in southeastern Wisconsin, in the spring, when we traveled "up north" to the family cabin in the woods, the song of the white-throated sparrow rang through the air. My dad called it "the song of the north woods."

Minutes later I spotted a small bird in a shrub near the shoreline, brought up my binoculars, and saw white and black stripes on its head, a bright white patch on its neck — a white-throated sparrow. It flew up and perched on a slender branch, then stretched up and plucked seeds from a goldenrod plume, a vignette of beauty, an image now indelibly linked to the white-throated sparrow, the singer of the north woods.

A squadron of blue jays flew onto the peninsula, singing, calling, perching, flying from branch to branch, and feeding on buds and seeds. A sharp-shinned hawk swooped in and landed on a dead limb. The blue jays cried out with such a loud and insistent chorus of warning calls that the sharpie gave up and flapped away.

I heard the soft *tsip, tsip, tsip* calls from the shoreline again and decided to walk over to investigate. On my way I noticed a little bird perched on a slender branch just five feet away. I froze, slowly brought up my binoculars, and had a perfect view of this bird — short tail, pointy beak, blue-gray head, white eye ring, two whitish wing bars, and a faintly yellowish breast — a ruby-crowned kinglet. It flitted from branch to branch, found a small berry, snatched it, swallowed it, and flew off.

I continued toward the shoreline still trying to find the source of the *tsip, tsip, tsip* calls. I brought up my binoculars, peered into the leaves and branches, and spotted a pair of birds — delicate brownish black stripes down the back, plain grayish breast, a brown head, a faint white eyebrow, and a faded black eye line — chipping sparrows. I counted a flock of seven flitting through the branches, picking at buds and seeds, staying in touch with their sweet *tsip, tsip, tsip* calls.

Returning to my sit spot, I felt satisfied with three close-up looks and three solid bird identifications that I confirmed when I later read about each bird's preferred habitat, each bird's niche in the world. White-throated sparrows like to frequent the edges of ponds and lakes and feed on the seeds of weeds and sing their distinctive song from time to time in the fall while migrating. The ruby-crowned kinglet is a common bird that winters in woodlands and thickets. Chipping sparrows travel in flocks, forage in bushes and on the ground, and communicate with soft flock calls.

A kingfisher flew down the shoreline, landed on a dead branch, bobbed its head up and down as if it was studying the water, and then flew away with a noisy rattle. Geese honked lazily from the far end of the lake. A gust of wind rattled the last leaves, tore a few more down, and carried the smell and feel of clean, fresh, dry air.

The birds all seemed active, flitting from tree to tree, perching on branches, searching the twigs, landing on the ground, foraging through the leaves, flying back up to a branch — all of it ceaseless, restless, tireless activity. I wondered how this worked out in terms of energy balance. The birds seemed to be moving more than eating, which meant they would burn more energy than they took in. But this must be an uninformed opinion. Survival pressures had finely tuned their ability to balance energy accounts. Obviously, the strategy to be on the move, scanning and searching for food, was the optimal strategy.

The geese took off from the far end of the lake and flew right over me. I looked up at their powerful wings stroking the air and heard their loud steady honking. They gained altitude, and then as if some invisible coach was directing them, they suddenly formed an organized V, cleared the tree-shrouded hills on the far side of the lake, and flew out to forage in nearby farm fields. I watched until they became tiny black specks in a clear blue sky, listened until their honking faded away.

My hour was up, and I began to pack up. I had seen, heard, learned, and experienced much during my sixty minutes under the big black cherry tree. And, I reflected, there were some deeper dimensions here, some feelings of renewal, of connection, of joy and awe that had permeated my being during the hour, feelings that now stayed with me as I walked back along the West Shore Trail.

## Week 36 · October 24

# Gleaning

During the night, light frost grazed the hilltops and ridges, but in the low areas, the valleys and river beds where the cold air settles, a killing frost hit hard. Now, as I drove to Prompton, I could see frosty icing covering the windows of passing cars. As the TV weatherman had said last night, "The growing season is over."

At Prompton, thick coils and swirls of mist floated over the still, warm waters. The West Shore Trail was bare, hard-packed, black-brown dirt, looking as if it had been swept clean, as if some dedicated wood gnome had broomed away the leafy, twiggy debris during the night.

I set up at my home sit spot under the black cherry tree. The leaves of the birches had turned golden yellow — small dry, serrated arrowhead leaves that shivered with each puff of wind. The shoreline shrubs, green last week, had turned bright red. With each exhalation, a tiny cloud of mist formed and then slowly dissipated in the frosty air. For the first time in months, I was again dressed in cold weather gear — wool socks, boots, turtleneck, heavy sweater, down jacket, hat, and gloves.

Around me I heard the familiar calls of crows, blue jays, cardinals, robins, and a flock of geese as they flew out to feed. It was another morning chorus informing me that all was well at Prompton Lake, telling me that another busy day for the birds and plants and animals and trees was beginning.

I heard a high-pitched *kleek-kik-ik-ik-ik* — a bald eagle — most likely the lake's resident eagle winging toward its favorite perch in a tall sycamore tree along the far shoreline. Then another call rang into the morning air, a loud, clear, familiar sound — *kee-ew, kee-ew, kee-ew*. I sorted through my memory files back to childhood. It was the call of a ring-billed gull; a sound often heard growing up along the shore of Lake Michigan. A hen mallard quacked, and a minute later five mallards flew directly over me, wings whistling.

Robins tutted and clucked nearby. I spotted a flock of six scattered among the bare, gray branches of a sugar maple. I watched them through my binoculars as they hopped along the branches, flitted up and down, picked at twigs, and chased each other around, each chase followed by a volley of whinnies. I wondered if this might be a migratory flock setting up a pecking order, bonding socially, creating ties needed for the arduous journey south?

The first beams of sunlight touched the treetops above me. Soft puffs of wind brought a fresh, clean, woodsy, earthy fragrance. A chickadee in a nearby bush called a high-pitched *chip, chip, chip*, a call immediately echoed by its mates. The chickadee flew over, landed a few feet away on the trunk of the black cherry, looked me over with its shiny black eyes, and called again. In response, another chickadee landed on the trunk, and yet another perched on a low branch. Two more landed in a nearby bush, a small flock clustered around me, investigating the human in their midst.

I listened to their squeaky calls and their cheerful *chick-a-dee-dee-dee* songs. I heard their tiny claws scratch the bark as they scuttled up and down the trunk, heard the flutter of wings as they flitted from branch to branch. Gradually they lost interest in me and resumed their feeding by picking in the crevices of the bark and snatching buds and seeds. Then they flew off, disappearing as quickly as they had arrived.

With their jet black cap and bib, pure white cheeks, gray wings, black tail, fluffy white breast, and disproportionately large, rounded head, chickadees present an endearing appearance. Smaller than a sparrow, only four and a half inches long, they weigh just a half-ounce. They are social birds that gather in small flocks during the winter, each flock with a distinct hierarchy and unique set of calls. In the winter woods, they serve the role of avian social facilitators while nuthatches, creepers, kinglets, warblers, and woodpeckers join their flocks. Accordingly, for a birder, the calls of chickadees often signal the presence of other birds. Chickadees are non-migratory and brave the winter cold with their dense feathers, fluffy down, and adaptable feeding habits. They spend subzero nights sheltered in tiny cavities in dead trees.

They communicate extensively and descriptively about events in their environment, are inquisitive, and will readily approach humans. Sometimes at home, they follow me when I bring sunflower seeds to the feeders. A woman who lives nearby in a cabin in the woods has taught chickadees to land on her shoulder and take seeds from her hand. She has given them names — Anna, Bella, and Karina.

I heard a high-pitched *zee-zee-zee* followed by a quick *ji-dit, ji-dit, ji-dit* coming from a thickly branched Russian olive near the shoreline. Curious, I got up and walked slowly over, scanned the branches with my binoculars, detected movement, and spotted a ruby-crowned kinglet, a bird I had first seen just a week ago.

I watched it hop from branch to branch, busily feeding on top of a leaf, on a twig, hanging upside down; small, pointy beak running across the underside of a leaf. It snatched a spider, swallowed it, and kept moving, picking, scanning, searching. Then it hovered over a leaf, picking at the surface with its sharp black beak. I watched the kinglet for five full minutes as it flitted through the bush, scouring the leaves, snatching insects.

The kinglet was gleaning, a feeding strategy by which birds catch insects, particularly spiders. Foliage gleaning occurs when birds carefully pick over leaves, twigs, bark, and even flowers to find insects. Hover gleaning occurs when birds hover above and under leaves to search for and snatch insects. Birds that use this gleaning strategy are typically small and compact with small, sharp-pointed bills, a description that fit the kinglet perfectly.

I had previously read the word "gleaning" in descriptions of bird's feeding strategies. Based on my understanding and use of the word — as in gleaning grain or gleaning information — I had a general sense of how the word might apply to birds. But now, after watching this little kinglet in action, I knew exactly what the word meant. I felt a sudden deep and satisfying appreciation for the value of direct experiential learning.

I thought back on those children I had tested who scored exceptionally high on measures of vocabulary. Curious, I would always ask how they knew the meaning of so many words. Usually they would tell me that it was from going places and doing things, from talking with family and friends, and not from studying vocabulary lessons. At this moment, as I could feel the meaning of the word gleaning settling firmly into my mind, I understood what these children had told me.

The wind picked up and swept the mist off of the lake. A lone goose flew overhead, high-pitched plaintive honks, trying to contact its flock. The robins continued to tut and whinny and chase each other through the sugar maple. Bright sunlight edged slowly down the tree trunks, illuminating the frosty woods, warming my neck and shoulders, and lifting my spirits. I packed up and headed home.

Week 37 · October 31

# Rachel Carson Reserve

With a strong push of the paddle, the kayak scraped away from the concrete boat ramp and floated freely into Taylor Creek. With several quick strokes, I surged to the middle of the channel and felt the tug of the ebbing tide, the moon-pulled water flowing toward Beaufort Inlet and out to the Atlantic Ocean. I paddled harder, pushed on the foot rests, and sliced through the current.

To my right, a long, loose line of moored sail boats of every size, shape, design, and color floated and swayed. Elegant shoreside homes lined the bank of Taylor Creek, and in the distance stood the waterfront buildings of historic Beaufort, North Carolina. To my left the creek opened into the wide North River, which opened into Back Sound, which in turn was bounded by the long, slender barrier island of Shackelford Banks. Ahead of me was my destination — Carrot Island — the biggest island in the Rachel Carson Reserve.

I beached my kayak on a patch of sand, dragged it above the high tide line, shed my life jacket, pulled out my backpack, stepped onto an elevated timber boardwalk that crossed the island, and set off to search for a good sit spot. Maritime shrubs surrounded the boardwalk — dark green live oaks; green, lacy-leaved red cedars; and scattered clumps of wax myrtle — all the shrubs short in stature, all bent by the sea winds, all bound together by vines of Virginia creeper, poison ivy, and pepper vine.

I followed the boardwalk across the island to an observation platform where the shrubs gave way to saltmeadow hay and sea oats, which in turn gave way to a vast marsh of tidal inlets edged with vast stands of green-brown cordgrass — slender, salt-resistant grass, stems stained gray by the tide. I set up in a corner of the observation platform and looked out across the tidal flats to the reedy middle marshes and in the distance to the dark green line of Shackelford Banks.

A friend helped me select this spot, a reminder that when on a quest friends can offer invaluable input and support. I had planned an early morning visit to a nature trail overlooking Bogue Sound. But the night before, while discussing these plans, he suggested that I go to the Rachel Carson Reserve. We had kayaked there a few days earlier, enjoyed the views of the island marshes, and wound our way through tidal channels where we spotted shorebirds wading and wild horses grazing.

I liked his idea. Access to the reserve was by boat only so my viewing time would be private and uninterrupted. The reserve provided the interface of water, marsh, and maritime thicket — the intersection of habitats that always attract the most wildlife. The plan also worked for both of my companions who could enjoy a cup of coffee at a nearby café while I did my hour-long observation. Afterward we would meet up for more kayaking. I also liked the connection with Rachel Carson, the author of *The Silent Spring*, a lover of nature and a matriarch of the environmental movement.

My hour began as the tide was noticeably ebbing. To my left, in a narrow inlet bordered by cordgrass, I spotted a great egret — three feet tall; statuesque; standing stock still on long, black legs; white feathers and plumes being ruffled by the breeze; long, yellow, spear-like bill poised to strike. Another egret flew in, landed gracefully, and assumed the same hunting pose. Many birds flew over the open water — seagulls stroking the air with a steady rhythm, terns weaving and angling, and a row of pelicans flapping their big wings and then gliding in a plumb-level line.

I listened to the soundscape. Some of the sounds were familiar — the rattle of a kingfisher, the *check, check, check* call of red-winged blackbirds, the steady chirping of crickets, and the plaintive *kil-deeah* of a wintering killdeer. But much of the soundscape was unfamiliar — the cries of the seagulls, the calls of the terns, the steady lapping of the water against the shoreline, and far across the bay the distant sound of Atlantic rollers hitting the beach, a steady rhythmic *shump, shump, shump.*

Gusts of sea wind carried the smell of fresh salt air. But when the wind subsided, I inhaled a rotten egg smell, the odor of decay on the tidal flats. The air felt moist and mild on my skin. The sky was cloudy, yet occasional bursts of sunlight broke through, creating a spotlight that moved across a vast stage of open water, marshes, dunes, and far barrier islands.

A solitary shorebird walked on long legs in the shallow water, probing beneath the surface with a long bill. I studied it through my binoculars, checked off its field marks — long, straight, blackish bill; long black legs; drab brownish plumage. I scanned my Sibley and identified it as a willet. Another willet flew in, flashing a bold black and white wing pattern, calling a clear *kyah-yah.* I watched the willets wading, probing, and picking through the water, employing their sensitive bills to find worms, crabs, clams, and invertebrates.

Willets are common now along the eastern shoreline, but during the nineteenth century they were esteemed as food and heavily hunted. The Migratory Bird Treaty Act of 1918 ended market hunting, and their numbers recovered. The pair of willets working the shallow water were most likely part of the western population that breeds in the high plains and winters along the east coast.

The wind picked up. The sky clouded over. Fine rain drops hit my face. The forecast had called for a partly sunny day, mild, dry, with light winds, so I didn't bring rain gear. Out on the bay a dark cloud of rain headed toward me. I would be getting wet, a reminder that near the ocean, the weather is always unpredictable.

Seagulls looped lazily over the marsh. I looked back at the willets and saw that a slick of black tidal mud had emerged. More birds flew in — an American oystercatcher, a large shorebird, eighteen inches long with a distinctive long reddish bill and a dramatic black back and white breast; a herring gull, a large bird with a gray back, a yellow bill with a red tip, a white head, and pink legs; two boat-tailed grackles, stark black, long-tailed, yellow-eyed. Two more willets flew in and began to walk and probe and pick in the shallow water.

The birds knew the rhythm of the tides and flew in at precisely the right time to take full advantage of the smorgasbord uncovered by low water. Each bird seemed to have its favorite location on the tidal flat — the willets in the shallow water, the oystercatchers at water's edge, the grackles on the mud — all of them sharing the splendid table set by the sea.

I wiped rain drops from my glasses and binoculars, covered my notebook with my backpack, and tried to ignore the wet chill. Five terns flew over the open water — snow white, delicately angled wings, agile flight — least terns. I watched them fly, scan, hover, dive down, splash into the water, snatch tiny silvery fish — such graceful white-winged hunters.

A brown pelican cruised over the open water, its wings flapping with strength and rhythm. I watched it glide then suddenly fold its wings, plummet into the water, snatch a fish, land on shore, tilt its head back, and swallow. I watched the terns and the pelican, their vision sharp, their timing finely tuned, arriving precisely when the tide drained water was shallow enough to force the fishes to the surface.

The egret flew away. A few minutes later another one landed in the same inlet. A crow perched in a nearby tree looked similar to the crows back home, yet seemed smaller, perhaps a young crow. When it called out a nasal high-pitched *ca-ah,* I realized it was a fish crow, a smaller cousin of the American crow that lives along the eastern seaboard.

Gazing at the birds, inhaling the salt air, and feeling the touch of windblown rain drops, I thought about Rachel Carson. She came to Beaufort in July of 1938 for a family vacation on the barrier islands and to visit the US Fisheries Station. According to Carson's biographer, Linda Lear, Rachel spent countless solitary hours observing the beach, the tidal pools, the marshes, the ebb and flow of the tide, the fish, the crustaceans, and the shorebirds. Lear wrote, "Rachel fell in love with the barren dunes of the outer banks that summer and with the mysterious relationship between shore and sea."

Inspired by her experiences, that in Lear's words brought tears of awe, and relying on the extensive notes from her observations, Rachel wrote her first book, *Under the Sea-Wind: A Naturalist's Picture of Ocean Life.* In this book she developed her unique writing style — a blend of poetry, nature description, and accurate science. Published in 1941, the book was not a commercial success, but was the first step in a writing career that culminated in *The Silent Spring,* one of the most influential books of the twentieth century, a book that successfully challenged the notion of "better living through chemistry," a book that brought into question the impact of humans on the web of nature.

I realized that my life span and Rachel's overlapped. I couldn't help but to compare our lives even though I didn't fare well in the comparison. While I struggled to eke out an hour of nature observation a week, she spent hours and hours of quiet, still, focused, and highly informed observation. She even went out at night with a flashlight to watch the comings and goings of the nocturnal shoreline creatures.

In September of 1962, I was a high school senior with only a casual interest in my studies and a strong interest in the consumption of beer and in spending as much time as possible with my girlfriend. During that same month, Rachel published *The Silent Spring* amid a firestorm of attacks from the chemical industry. Undaunted, she offered her ideas — ideas that would subsequently change the relationship of humans to nature.

My hour was up and I rejoined my friends. We kayaked up Taylor Creek through wind, rain, waves, and currents, wove through the moored sailboats and yachts and past the Beaufort waterfront. We paddled around the tip of Town Marsh Island and out to Bird Shoal where we beached the kayaks and walked onto the sand. We stood in silence and watched the waves roll across the sound, listened to the waves splashing on the sandy shore, and heard the timeless calls of the gulls and terns, the same sights and sounds that had touched Rachel Carson so many years ago.

## Week 38 · November 8

# Gang Blue Jay

Steam wafted from the thermos as the hearty Assam tea steeped. I gazed out the kitchen window at the long line of leafless forsythias edging the driveway. In the dim, predawn light the silhouette of a cardinal emerged with its jaunty head crest; short, nut cracking bill; and long, squared off tail. It was too dark to discern its colors, to determine if it was male or female, but its presence outside the window felt like a friendly morning greeting, like a welcoming to another day of nature observation.

Near the north end of Prompton Lake, a white pickup truck was parked along the highway. Nearby, a deer hunter, clad in a bright orange-red vest and cradling a rifle, waded through a field of belly-high, tan-brown, goldenrod stalks. I drove on, and a hundred yards further down the highway, well out of the hunter's sight, an eight point buck, dark gray-brown, heavily muscled, striding strongly, stepped across the road and vanished into the woods, safe for the day.

The trees and branches were bare and gray along the West Shore Trail. I searched for signs of life and finally spotted a few lingering pale green ferns, a hardy green stem of garlic mustard, a small patch of burgundy-leafed blackberry canes, a swatch of pale green moss on a rock, and a single dark green pine seedling.

Settling into my sit spot under the black cherry tree, I looked up into a cloudless, high blue sky. Cool fresh Canadian air had swept in overnight. Puffs of northwest wind swayed the dry, brown, dead stems of the grasses and goldenrods. The temperature hovered at the freezing point.

I sat and listened to a quiet morning chorus, dabs of sound on a canvas of silence. Canadian geese honked lazily, a crow cawed, and a chickadee sang. An interval of quiet arose and then a blue jay jeered, more quiet, and a robin tutted. Two shots rang out, a hunter after his quarry. The traffic along the highway sounded louder now that all the leaves were gone. A jetliner flew over, a shiny, silver, sun-illuminated tube tracing a path across the high blue sky. A ring-necked pheasant squawked across the lake, a call well learned during my childhood near the prairies and cornfields of southeastern Wisconsin.

The sun slowly lifted above the eastern hills and touched the trees, brightening the gray and brown tree trunks, and illuminating the forest floor, blanketed by a brilliant collage of fallen tan, red, yellow, orange, and brown leaves.

The arrival of full daylight seemed to spur the geese into action. Their soft intermittent honking grew louder and more insistent. Suddenly, they took flight, headed down the lake at tree-top height, at least fifty strong wings stroking the air, gaining altitude, sorting themselves into a V formation, and flying out to feed in nearby fields — all a familiar scene at Prompton in the fall, a scene that never failed to bring pleasure.

Five blue jays suddenly appeared, jeering loudly, weaving through the branches like jetfighters, landing directly above me in the top of the black cherry tree. Another jay joined them, followed by two and then three more, high in a tall ash tree to my right. I slowly leaned my head back, looked up, saw their white and gray breasts, feathers and down fluffed in the cold — fluffy puffs scattered through the branches like feathery, white ornaments on a Christmas tree.

I pulled up my binoculars and studied the flock of jays. What were they doing? Had they come to feed, to scan the branches for seeds, to pick at buds? But they weren't feeding. They were perched silently, hopping from twig to twig, flitting to nearby branches. I saw their jet black claws firmly grasping the wind-swayed branches and felt a flash of envy. How wonderful it must feel to perch securely in a tree and sway back and forth with each gust of wind, like sitting in the gently swinging gondola of a Ferris wheel when it pauses at the top of its circle, the moment when you can look all around and take in the full panorama.

The jays began to sing, slowly at first, a few familiar *jay jay* calls followed by pipe-like *queedle queedle* calls. Then they added rattling, clicking, and churring sounds I had never heard before. They introduced yet more calls — piping garbles, clear bells, a musical *twee dee*, and a *screek-squeek*, the calls and songs blending into a flowing soundscape, rising, falling, solos and harmonies intertwining and overlapping.

Head back, staring up at a web of gray branches and the scattered gray-white fluffs of the jays against the deep blue sky, I felt as if I was listening to music that seemed familiar yet unknown, music with elements of a New Age composition, of a medieval chant, of cool jazz, or something celestial, something heard in a dream.

I stared at the blue jays, transfixed. My stocking cap fell from my head. Above the trees, three white seagulls traced silently across the deep blue sky. Higher up, a small white cloud floated across the blue. A jay sang a loud *queedle queedle*, its body pumping up and down like a blue and white piston. Another jay answered and they *queedled* back and forth, both birds pumping up and down. I laughed out loud.

My hour was up, but I was reluctant to move. I felt like a privileged visitor to the blue jays' peninsula. I guessed that they gathered in these trees to sing on the days and during the hours I wasn't there. Gradually their calls and songs subsided. One flew away, then another, a pair, and then they were all gone. The performance was over.

I knew that blue jays are common birds often seen in backyards, but I later discovered that their lives are shrouded in mystery. Some migrate in large flocks down the Great Lakes and East Coast while others spend the winter in the forests of Canada. The next year, the birds that migrated might stay put while those that had previously wintered in the north head south.

Blue jays have complex social systems and communicate not only with their songs and calls but also with body language. In the comfortable company of their flock, they lower their spiky blue crest, but when threatened or displaying aggression, they extend the crest to its full height. The black bridle across the neck can be quite variable from bird to bird and may be another way jays recognize each other. Blue jays mate for life and live in a network of close family connections.

They feed on insects, nuts, and seeds and sometimes raid the nests of other birds for eggs and hatchlings. They have a preference for acorns and have developed elaborate strategies for hiding and later locating the nuts.

Their complex songfests are another mystery. Does this group singing strengthen social bonds? Does it serve as a kind of team-building exercise? Are they practicing for a time when they need to communicate about food and danger? Or, the most intriguing question of all, are they simply having fun, enjoying jamming, eagerly experimenting with new songs and calls? That thought made me wonder if fun, like beauty, was another quality inherent in nature.

Later I discovered a selection online called Blue Jay Magic Bells, posted by Lang Elliot, an expert in birdsong recording. I clicked on it and listened to a session of blue jay songs that Elliot had recorded in a stand of fir trees near Ithaca, New York. It sounded identical to what I had heard. Elliot wrote that the songs made him think of magic bells.

I walked back along the trail suffused with feelings of wonder and joy. In the parking lot a pickup truck parked by the boat ramp had a short, dark gray kayak sticking out the back. A man climbed out of the truck, and in my elevated mood I assumed he must be a kindred spirit, a fellow lover of nature. I walked over and saw that he was putting on waders and a camouflage coat — a hunter.

I greeted him and asked, "Going hunting in the kayak?"

He was a big fellow, dark hair, moustache, moving quickly and efficiently, a practiced outdoorsman. He answered in a friendly tone, "Yah, heading out for ducks."

I inquired, "In the kayak? What kind of ducks?"

He grinned broadly, "Diving ducks. Ruddy ducks and buffleheads are moving through." He added, "Some of the ducks are pretty dumb. I can paddle up close and shoot 'em. Last week I got a ruddy, and it was damn good eating, but them buffleheads taste like crap."

I began to sense that our purposes for being outside were divergent, yet I still felt a connection with him, an admiration for his willingness to venture out on a cold morning. And, I reminded myself, I had once hunted ducks and still enjoyed a dinner of roasted wild duck.

While zipping up his coat he added, "What I really like is hunting crows. I was out earlier this morning and shot three."

I thought about my friend the boat launch crow and realized I hadn't seen him in a while.

He continued, "Last year was my best year for crows. I shot 529. I'm not doing as good this year. With the three I got this morning I'm only up to 132."

I backed away. Whatever bond I imagined existed between us was now shattered. To me, this seemed like senseless, pointless slaughter.

He walked to his kayak, climbed in, and paddled up the lake. I walked to my car. He was probably in his fifties, hunting alone. I wondered if his approach to nature might fade away in the future. After all, at Hawk Mountain near Pottsville, PA, hunters had once gathered to slaughter hawks for sport, but now people travel from all over the world to watch and tally the eagles and hawks and vultures as they soar and float freely and unmolested on their journey south.


Week 39 · November 15

# Gray Birch Trees


Frozen ripples of mud crunched beneath my boots along the West Shore Trail. The faint smell of wood smoke wafted through the air. I pictured a morning fire crackling away in a nearby house bringing welcome warmth to a cozy kitchen. It was twenty-seven degrees out, motionless air, churning gray clouds far above, gray tree trunks in the woods, leaden gray water on the lake — a gray morning in a gray world. The only colors to be seen were a few long threads of fiery red and pink in the eastern sky, hints of the coming sunrise, and to the west a thin streak of pale blue.

The geese were on the move. A flock of thirty in a neat V-formation flew above the far shoreline and then in perfect synchrony angled off to the east, their usual direction. A smaller ragged flock winged along the near shoreline and headed west. Scattered groups of four and five geese flapped above the middle of the lake seemingly conflicted about which direction to go, which flock to join. Two of the groups headed east following the main flock, three turned to the west to join the non-conformists.

Perhaps the geese had a discussion last night about where to fly for the best foraging. I imagined a murmur of honks and calls, different geese advocating different directions, discussing distance, food abundance and quality, and safety issues. No consensus had been reached. A majority decided to stick with the standard eastward flight plan, a minority determined to venture west, a few geese made their decision at the last possible moment. An amusing scenario this congress of geese, but more likely I was seeing finely honed, avian intelligence in action; geese engaged in the relentless, ceaseless striving to find the best food in the most secure location while expending the least energy.

I set up at my usual spot under the big black cherry tree. It was quiet, no wind rattling the branches, no waves lapping against the rocky shoreline, and at first, no morning chorus. The noise of cars and trucks on the nearby highway seemed louder and more annoying than ever. I did my best to filter out this mechanical noise and gradually began to discern the winter woodland chorus — a nuthatch calling, chickadees chattering, crows cawing up and down the lake with differing voices and cadences, a blue jay jeering, and a pair of goldfinches singing their sweet lilting flight song as they looped overhead.

Weak sunlight filtered through the gray clouds, partially illuminating the woods but brought no warmth. The cold worked its way through my layers of clothing, and I began to feel numbness and stinging spreading down my fingers. I poured a thermos-top of hot, milky, sweet Assam tea, watched the steam rise, and sipped the hot beverage to fend off the cold.

A flock of ducks flew down the lake — small ducks, fast wingbeats, maybe ruddy ducks. They flared in unison over two fishermen in a canoe. I heard a high-pitched *kee-yer, kee-yer, kee-yer* call, a red-shouldered hawk on the hunt. A blue jay glided silently through the trees, landed on a thin, drooping branch of a birch tree, fed quietly and purposefully on the seeds, then slipped away as silently as it arrived.

More Canada geese flew above the shoreline, this time heading west. More birdsongs sounded — a flicker calling, a robin tutting. Then the woods fell silent. My mind turned back to the springtime when the little peninsula had teemed with life — buds opening, green leaves unfurling, wildflowers blooming, a symphony of singing birds, a chorus of humming insects and croaking frogs. That was exuberant life. Today seemed like the beginning of the season of death, a season of gray, a time of emptiness and quiet.

When my hour was up I walked to the shoreline to identify the birch tree where the blue jay had fed. It was a gray birch, distinguished by its multiple trunks, drooping slender branches, medium height, and prominent black chevrons at the base of the branches. I picked a yellow-brown leaf from the ground and saw the rounded triangular shape and serrated edge. I ran my fingers over the chalky white bark, bark that couldn't be peeled from the tree.

Curious about these trees, I discovered that gray birches are fast-growing, thin-trunked, short-lived trees reaching a maximum height of twenty to thirty feet, a pioneer species, quick to invade abandoned farm fields and disturbed land; their presence along man-made Prompton Lake fit their profile perfectly. The medium-hard wood can be used for furniture, high-grade plywood, and firewood. They grow from the Maritime Provinces of Canada down to northeast Pennsylvania.

Gray birches flower in the spring, producing slender, fluffy male catkins that hang at the end of the twigs along with upright female catkins. By fall the tree produces fruit, a heavy crop of slender, cylindrical cones, three quarters of an inch long and packed full of tiny two-winged nutlets that are eagerly eaten by a variety of birds, including goldfinches, pine siskins, juncos, chickadees, tree sparrows, kinglets, and blue jays.

I looked over at the adjacent little peninsula to a small hill covered with gray birches. The hill looked like a birthday cake festooned with chalky white tapers. I had always wanted to visit this little peninsula, but in summer the approach was wet and swampy and obstructed by tangles of brambles, spreading vines, and a dense thicket of red twig dogwood. Now, the water level was lower, the rocky shoreline exposed, so I walked over.

Climbing up the little hill, I heard a husky two toned *ji-dit, ji-dit* call, scanned the lacy branches, and spotted a ruby-crowned kinglet busily gleaning birch seeds. I watched it flip and turn and flutter, call *zee-zee-zee*, and fly away.

From the top of the little hill, I had a good view of the upper end of the lake. Seagulls swooped and swirled over the water. Six bright white ducks swam near the shoreline. The seagulls were ring-billed gulls, white with black wing tips, agile and graceful flyers. I watched them lifting, looping, swirling, hovering, dropping, and lifting again, like a fountain of white-feathered gliders, spraying up, and settling down.

I studied the ducks. They were buffleheads, males with bright white bodies, a striking white head set off above and below by a glossy green-purple band. They dove, popped to the surface, bobbed on the water, and dove again. I focused on one duck, counted the length of its dives — twenty seconds down, on the surface for fifteen, back under for eighteen, on the surface for thirteen, then down again.

The buffleheads looked so natural, and their life seemed so simple as they swam and dove and fed. But in fact these ducks are a North American success story as 500,000-year-old skeletal fossils have been discovered. Adaptability with food and habitat has served the buffleheads well over the centuries. This little flock was working its way south to winter on lakes and rivers and open ocean bays.

I was less than a hundred yards from my usual location under the big black cherry tree, yet was seeing a completely different view of nature. How quickly and dramatically habitats shift in the gallery of nature. I liked this little hill adorned with lacy-branched birch trees where I had a long open view of life on the lake. I planned to return to this spot the following week.

Week 40 · November 22

# The Beauty of Brown

My girlfriend during graduate school, an artist, told me about the beauty of brown. We were driving in compatible silence down a Wisconsin county road on a gray, rainy November afternoon through a landscape of shorn-off corn fields, reedy marshes, and ragged woodlots. I had already written the day off as dreary and resigned myself to wait for a sunny day. She broke the silence and said, "On a day like this when the sky is gray and the ground is wet, you can see all the shades of brown."

I looked again and felt as if a switch had been flipped in the color perception area of my brain. Suddenly, I also saw the rich palate of browns and tans — dark brown-black loamy earth, reddish brown fallen leaves, brown-tan grasses and weeds, pale brown frost-killed ferns, and yellow-brown cornstalk stubs.

She continued, "People think a sunny day is the best time to see fall colors, but on a day like this you can really appreciate all the hues of brown."

She paused, gazed out at the landscape and added, "Brown is the elemental color, the color of earth, the source of life, the color used by cavemen to record their impressions of nature."

Now, as I was driving down another county road on another gray, wet November day, her words came back to me. I looked around and saw the browns and tans around me — the tan grasses and weeds, the russet blanket of leaves under the trees, the reddish brown earth in the plowed fields.

At Prompton the parking lot pavement was wet, dark, and shiny. Light mist swirled over the lake. Soft mud squished under my boots along the West Shore Trail. Rain drops, like tiny baubles of blown glass, clung to the horizontal branches. The smell of earth and woods and water permeated the air.

Following up on my plan from last week, I walked over to the little nearby peninsula. At the top of the hill I set up a new stool, an upgrade, a camouflaged hunting stool — smaller, lighter, and lower with a triangular seat and a small back rest. Now I sat closer to the earth, feet firmly on the ground, and felt more alert, more prepared to stand or move if need arose.

The morning chorus of blue jays, crows, and goldfinches came to life. A chickadee flew so close that I heard the flutter of its wings. A kingfisher rattled as it patrolled the shoreline. Geese hidden at the far end of the lake honked softly. A high-flying red-tailed hawk screamed, and the ring-billed gulls circling over the lake called *kee-ew, kee-ew, kee-ew.* A female cardinal with subtle reddish tan plumage landed nearby and clicked companion calls to her flockmates.

I studied the area around me. Gray birches grew in profusion along the shoreline and around the top of the hill with a few red maple and ash trees interspersed. Ahead, the ground angled down to another band of birch trees beyond which sprouted an impenetrable thicket of red twig dogwood and blackberry brambles before the ground sloped gradually into the woods and up to the West Shore Trail.

All around me the wet leaves displayed many shades of brown — sepia, chocolate, coffee, and cocoa. I also saw shades of tan — beige, sand, buff, and wheat. I saw the reddish browns — chestnut, mahogany, burnt umber, and auburn. This multi-hued brownish blanket of leaves was dotted with fallen gray twigs and branches. I gazed at the nearest birch tree trunk — whitish bark, black chevrons, irregular blackish spots, gray-brown trunk at ground level, lacy reddish-tipped branches. I looked at a maple tree — gray trunk with flecks and patches and streaks of pale greenish moss, dark scars from fallen branches, light brown lines of split bark.

No swatches of a single color, everything an intermingling of colors and shades and textures. I flashed back to first grade, an introduction to color, a basic box of crayons, a mimeographed worksheet with big circles, the name of a color under each circle, one color for each circle. Had this template persisted in my mind? Was I predisposed to look for circles of a single color when all around me shades and hues melded and merged and mixed?

Movement on my right — ducks swimming silently, tracing graceful Vs on placid water. I turned slowly and spotted five whitish gray ducks with cinnamon heads and orange beaks. In my binoculars, even greater detail — blended white and gray feathers, bright white breast, crested rufous head, and a long orange saw-edged bill. They were common mergansers, a little flock of five hens.

They swam low in the water, dove down for fish, popped back to the surface, dove again, lunging forward with each dive, remaining underwater for fifteen to twenty seconds, surfacing, shedding drops of water from feathered backs. Then, simultaneously, as if responding to a message, they relaxed, floated higher in the water and began to preen, long orange beaks combing through wing and tail feathers. A few dull quacks, otherwise they swam in silence, slowly drifting closer to the shoreline.

One duck turned and swam toward the middle of the lake. The other four turned and followed the first duck. I marveled at their communication, their coordinated movement, like a well-rehearsed team of synchronous swimmers working from a shared mind. When they were fifty yards away, I cautiously reached for my bird guide, but these were wary ducks, and they noticed my movement. By the time I glanced up, they were already running across the water, wings pumping, feet splashing, lifting into the air, flying low and fast up the lake.

A little research later informed me that these mergansers were now heading south from their breeding grounds in the Canadian forests. In autumn, the males and females segregate into small flocks and linger on lakes, ponds, and rivers as they slowly work their way south. Mergansers are high enough on the food chain to be vulnerable to the effects of pesticides, toxic metals, and acid rain, all of which can degrade their habitat, reduce food supplies, and thin their egg shells. Common mergansers are a bellwether species, an indicator of the health of the environment. Fortunately, the ducks I saw looked healthy and fit.

My time was up. The gray clouds thinned, beams of light broke through and raced across the ground, brightening the myriad shades of brown and bronze and tan. I reflected how words can be gifts, how my girlfriend's words had given me the gift to enjoy the beauty of brown. I lingered and looked at a slender gray beech sapling that still held brown-tan leaves, dry leaves that rustled in each puff of wind.

## Week 41 · December 1

# The Brush Pile / Nyquist-Harcourt Wildlife Sanctuary

Strands of predawn red, purple, pink, and leaden gray intertwined above the eastern horizon. The temperature was a brisk twenty-eight degrees; the air felt and smelled fresh and clean. The condo parking lot was quiet except for the soft *stip, stip, stip* calls of a flock of dark-eyed juncos flitting in and out of a bayberry hedge, their white-gray tail feathers flashing as they flew. Most of the residents of the condo complex were still asleep. It would be several hours yet before they might emerge to pluck their blue, plastic-bagged Sunday newspapers off the sidewalk, before they might walk to a bakery for freshly baked bagels, or stroll to town for a farm-to-table breakfast.

In quiet solitude I walked down Huguenot Street toward the historic district of New Paltz, New York. To my left flowed the Wallkill River. Bands of freshly formed ice clung to the banks. In the middle of the river the open water flowed peacefully and steadily on its journey north to the Hudson River and then south to join the Atlantic Ocean.

A flock of thirty or more mallards swam in the ice-free, open water, edging cautiously away as I approached. The drakes were attired in their full fall splendor — iridescent green heads, yellow beaks, chestnut breasts, blue wing patches, jaunty upturned tail feathers. The hens presented a more subdued beauty — mottled brown breast, brown flecked orange beak, blue wing patches. The drakes called their quieter *kreep, kreep, kreep*, while the hens belted out long, loud descending volleys of quacks.

The street angled off to the right, but I continued along the river bank, past the sewage processing plant, and onto the community garden where behind a neat fence, garden patches presented a pleasingly ramshackle appearance. Some plots had been cleaned, tilled, and put to rest for the winter. Others still held a few neat rows of bright green, frost-wilted lettuce or clusters of tall, gangly Brussels sprout stalks. And a few plots looked abandoned, filled with weed stems, dead tomato vines, tossed-aside tools, and overturned buckets. Each plot seemed to tell a story, a story of the gardener's character and work style, or perhaps of the influence of life circumstances.

Continuing past the garden, I walked across an open meadow to the entrance of the Nyquist-Harcourt Wildlife Sanctuary. This fifty-six-acre preserve with 1,300 feet of river frontage contains a flood plain forest, open fields of grasses and weeds, patches of bushes, and a string of ponds formed when the river changed its course many years ago. According to its website, the sanctuary is a spot for all generations to enjoy a wild setting. The sanctuary is also a prime spot for birding; more than 140 species, including several rare ones, have been identified within its boundaries.

I had scouted the sanctuary the day before at dusk and found a promising location for a sit spot near the river by an intersection of woods and field. Now, returning in the early morning light, I found the spot again and set up under a tall ash tree, sat down, and settled in to listen and look.

At first the sounds seemed similar to Prompton. Cars and trucks whooshed along the distant highway, more vehicles than I would have expected for early Sunday morning. A police siren wailed, a jetliner whispered high above. Three rifle shots rang out in the distance. I heard familiar bird calls — juncos, a nuthatch, blue jays, crows, downy and red-bellied woodpeckers — calls I knew, easy to identify, comforting to hear.

Then, nearby, I heard an unfamiliar call, a soft *jimp, jimp, jimp*. I froze, listened intently, and tried to locate the calls, a task made difficult by their brief and intermittent nature. I continued to listen and scan. After a few minutes I spotted a small brown bird flitting from branch to branch inside a large loose brush pile only ten yards away. I slowly brought up my binoculars and waited for a clear view.

After a few minutes a bird flew up and perched on a branch at the top of the pile. Bringing it into focus, I mentally checked off the field marks — sparrow size and shape, short conical seed-cracking bill, russet and gray plumage, bold brown breast streaks, black chest spot, tan eye band. The bird ducked back down into the brush pile, then down to the ground where I heard it scratching through the leaves foraging for food.

The bird looked familiar, but was unexpected in this setting and at this time of year. I pulled out my bird guide, went to the sparrow section and realized that it was a song sparrow, one of my spring and summer friends from Prompton. I glanced back at the brush pile and spotted five more song sparrows, a little winter flock. They flitted through the brush pile, down to the ground, up to the branches, back down to the ground, feeding, foraging, softly calling, *jimp, jimp, jimp*.

I studied the brush pile. A large maple tree had broken off halfway up the trunk — probably during a storm — fallen across a walking path, and brought down a number of smaller trees. Someone had sawed up the tree and branches and thrown them into a loose pile big enough to create habitat for these sparrows. It was a place where they could feed and find shelter from the ever-present danger of marauding hawks. I had often read that brush piles provide good habitat for song birds, and now I saw it in action.

Song sparrows, like most brown-colored birds, spend their life near the ground. They perch in bushes and low tree branches and hop down to the ground to feed on ragweed, clover, and goldenrod seeds, on berries, and on any beetles, spiders, worms, or midges that might live under the leaves. They like forest edges and fields that are close to open water.

I was happy to see these song sparrows again. Their rollicking *maids, maids, maids put on your tea kettle-lettle-lettle* is one of my favorite birdsongs. But I had never seen them in fall and winter in the high terrain of northeast Pennsylvania. Here, in the Hudson Valley, a region with a more moderate climate, a climate temperate enough for apple orchards and vineyards, these song sparrows had found a winter home.

I have sometimes thought that the song sparrow might be a good national bird. While they aren't as majestic as the bald eagle and not as tuneful and well known as robins, they do inhabit all of the lower forty-eight states as well as Alaska. They are social birds with a lovely and distinctive song. They sing with a local accent and display regional variations in plumage and size; in other words, they are a bird that both unifies and allows for diversity.

A robin flew over, landed in a nearby tree, called, heard an answering call from across the river, and took off in that direction. Small flocks of Canada geese winged above the tree tops — loose flocks, flying slowly, setting their wings, descending, gliding, preparing to land in the open farm fields across the Wallkill River. These geese would remain in New Paltz for the winter, feeding in the fields during the day, sleeping on the river at night, forgoing the challenges and dangers of a southward migration.

I heard a loud chatter, turned, saw twigs moving, and spotted a gray squirrel swinging Tarzan style through slender branches; it jumped to a fallen maple, scuttled down the angled trunk, sprang to the ground, and scampered away. A few minutes later another squirrel followed the exact same route, paused when it hit the ground, looked at me with bright brown eyes, wiggled its whiskers, flounced its tail, and then ran off. I had heard that squirrels make precise highways through the trees; now I knew this to be true.

At 8:00 AM the church bells began to ring, a clear, sweet chiming carrying over the morning landscape. Chunks of ice cracked, broke off, and splashed into the river. Four mourning doves dodged and darted through the branches, pulled up, and landed at the top of a tree. A seagull flapped above the river. A flock of grackles called *kek, kek, kek.* A pair of geese flew over — a gander and a goose — honking in synchrony, the gander in a low tone, the goose in a higher tone, the tones seemingly emanating from a single source.

My hour was up. I started to pack up when a song sparrow fluttered out of the brush pile and landed on a tall weed stem a few feet in front of me. I watched it, clever claws clinging to the stalk, chestnut brown plumage, head and shiny black eyes alert and alive. It flew off. I finished packing and walked to the river to take pictures when another song sparrow flew in and landed on a branch five feet away.

Surely, it was a completely crazy and thoroughly unscientific thought, but it felt as if the song sparrows didn't want me to leave. They were putting themselves on display as if they had more to show me, more to teach me. Was this another example of synchronicity, the clustering together of observed and observer? Was this another instance of some curious quantum entanglement?

It was with both puzzlement and regret that I began my walk back to the condo, although these feelings were eased by the image of the warm condo kitchen and the thought of a hot breakfast of scrambled eggs, a freshly toasted bagel slathered with cream cheese, and a steaming cup of coffee. My body was chilled and my hands were numb after an hour of sitting in the cold morning air.

# Winter Weather Advisory

Changes in the weather — a low pressure front that had brought mild temperatures, stagnant humid air, and overnight rain was scuttling off to the east amid churning billows and roils of white-gray clouds. To the northwest, thick, dark, high, gray-black clouds bore down, an advancing winter storm with falling temperatures, rain, freezing rain, sleet, and eventually accumulating snow. The car thermometer ticked steadily down from forty to thirty-eight to thirty-six, an ominous confirmation of the forecast.

This dramatic shift in the weather, this battle of the meteorological fronts, looked and felt elemental, a transition tangible and physical, perhaps even emotional and intellectual, the cleansing and release of one state, the emergence of a new condition, a kind of climatological catharsis. I was glad to be heading out for my hour of observation in the middle of this turbulent "no man's land" between the two fronts, glad to encounter the approaching storm, wondering if I would feel some inner resonance with this meteorological purification, if I too might feel cleansed and renewed.

Prompton Lake was covered with a thin layer of new ice. The normally moving water was locked in place, the last vestiges of motion frozen into lines and ripples. Puddles from an overnight rain dotted the surface of the lake. Only a slender ribbon of water next to the shoreline remained open, cold water purified of algae, transparent water that provided a clear view of brown and gray rocks beneath.

Muddy spots on the West Shore Trail forced me to step to nearby firm ground and slowed my progress. My plan had been to return to the little peninsula, but surprisingly deep pools of rain water and soft slushy ice blocked the way. I turned back toward the main peninsula and found a high spot with a good view of the lake and woods, set up my camp chair, sat down, pulled out my notebook, binoculars, and bird guide, and opened my senses.

Gazing down, I studied the leaves covering the forest floor, wet leaves showing all the shades of brown and tan and orange and red that I had enjoyed during previous weeks, colors that were now fading and muted. I studied the wet bark of the tree trunks, the lighter gray of the maples, the gray-brown of the ash trees, and the mottled brown-black of the cherries. I inhaled the advancing air, colder air, plowing down from Canada, mixing with the smell of Pennsylvania earth and leaves.

Listening intently, the only sound I heard was a jetliner whispering high above the clouds. Then two dogs barked far down the highway, loud, deep barks. I heard no birdsongs and thought I might have erred by waiting until mid-morning. But as my hearing grew finer and reached out further, I detected the distant calls of blue jays, the far away cawing of crows, and nearby the sweet *stip, stip, stip* calls of a winter flock of juncos.

A loud, deep croaking *cr-r-ruck, cr-r-ruck* filled the air. I swiveled in my seat, looked up, and spotted a solitary common raven flying strong and steady over the hills across the lake, jet black against a turbulent gray sky. The raven, a lone traveler over the winter woods, evoked a sense of the vastness of nature, its call a voice of adaptability, resourcefulness, and resilience. This raven seemed a fitting companion on a stormy morning.

The northwest wind picked up in intensity. Strong gusts raced across the frozen lake, gusts that stung my face and roared by my ears. I listened to the wind sighing through the branches, heard the clacking of branch against branch, and in the strongest gusts heard the moaning of thick branches and slender trunks as they bent and swayed before the wind. Drops of freezing rain fell, a soft pitter-patter on the sleeves of my down coat, a brittle splatter on the wet leaves.

All of the sounds seemed to weave and blend into a kind of music. Perhaps, I thought, it was sounds like these that inspired prehistoric people to create music, chant-like music with a flowing pulse and rhythm, with a rising and falling volume, with changes in tone and texture, with solo sounds emerging and fading.

I reflected that this nature music was different from the music I grew up with, music that usually had structured chord progressions, crafted harmonies, and a progression toward resolution. Perhaps my hours of sitting in the woods and listening to the sounds of nature had changed my taste in music, had increased my appreciation for rhythm and texture over melody and structure, had enhanced my pleasure in music with ever-changing sounds, music with no distinct beginning or end.

Suddenly, a gap in the clouds, and bright sunlight burst through, beams of light raced across the frozen lake, illuminated the gray and brown hardwoods, the dark green pines and hemlocks. The sunlight warmed me a little, but couldn't overcome the cumulative effects of the relentless wind and the ever-falling temperatures knifing through my coat and gloves, chilling my body, and stinging my fingers.

I listened a while longer to the music of the wind through the trees, to the periodic calls of birds, to the occasional jetliner whispering overhead, to a car whooshing down the highway, the deep thumping of the bass sounding strangely out of place. A rapid high-pitched call sounded behind me. I turned and scanned, but whatever bird made the call was gone, a reminder that there are always new sounds to be heard in the woods, mysteries to appreciate and hopefully, one day, to sort and solve.

My hour was up. I walked to the shoreline and took pictures of the crystally new ice, of a multi-hued green and blueish moss covered rock, of a pale green fern splayed across brown leaves, of lacy tree branches against a blue-gray sky, all images of beauty seen on a stormy day. Then, feeling restored, refreshed, and rejuvenated by my hour in nature, I strode briskly back to the car. There were errands to run, storm provisions to buy, and perhaps a movie or two to select before the accumulating snow arrived.

Week 43 · December 13

## Companion Calls

The West Shore Trail was covered with snow that crunched under my boots and was deep enough to hide slippery patches of ice. I stepped carefully; the smallest inclines and declines demanded full attention. I grabbed onto branches and trunks of slender trees, yet still lost my footing three times and fell hard into the snow once.

I was the first person to tread the trail since heavy snow fell four days before, but many animals had preceded me. Canine paw prints ran down the middle, small- to medium-sized, maybe a fox trotting down the path before turning into the woods. Deer prints — deeply imprinted in the snow, large, medium, and small — joined the trail, then left. Rabbit tracks crossed, bigger prints for their powerful hind legs and smaller ones for their front paws. Between two sheltering rocks a maze of tiny mice tracks laced back and forth across the snow.

The temperature held steady at a cold seventeen degrees. A narrow streamlet that normally trickled under a little stone bridge along the trail was now frozen solid, the ice forming a translucent jacket over the rocks. I came to the seep that still flowed, spring water trickling and percolating downhill, sculpting a wedge of green down the snowy hill, a welcome sight on this quiet winter morning.

I set up under the big black cherry tree. The sun had risen ten minutes before, but it would be another quarter of an hour before it lifted above the dark hills to the east. Ahead in the open woods I could see the stone wall that coursed along the hill above the West Shore Trail — gray, flat, mossy stones topped by a layer of snow — the wall appearing much nearer than in the summer when it was shrouded in leaves and vines. I glanced out at the frozen lake, now a vast empty expanse of thick ice blanketed in fresh snow.

Clouds of condensation formed with each breath. Windy blasts of frigid air chilled my face. I pulled out two hand-warming packets, opened them, shook them vigorously, inserted one into each glove, hoping to keep my hands warm enough to write and adjust my binoculars.

Gradually, I heard the sounds of a winter morning, a pair of crows cawing, a woodpecker tapping, and the nasal *yank, yank, yank* of a white-breasted nuthatch.

A strong gust of wind ripped down from the north, swayed and rattled the frozen twigs and branches, creating a metallic clattering all around me. Cars whooshed along the highway. A distant gunshot rang out. Small snow pellets fell from low gray clouds overhead, pellets that clicked onto my coat sleeves.

It was the dead of winter, the time of short days and long nights, the time of strong winds and turbulent skies, the time of snow flurries and snow squalls. It wasn't unpleasant sitting in the woods and surprisingly, it wasn't boring. The ten-minute intervals passed quickly. Yet with each passing interval I felt a mounting sense of disappointment that I hadn't seen more wildlife, that I hadn't seen something interesting, something new and compelling. I took a few deep breaths and reminded myself to be patient, that whatever would happen would happen. This was nature's realm, nature's timetable, not mine.

As soon as I let go of my expectations, a blue jay flew in and landed on a branch thirty yards away. I brought up my binoculars and watched it, bright and blue and black and white against a snowy background. It perched on a slender twig, hopped left, then right, dipped its head, bobbed its tail and flew silently away. No feeding, no calling, no obvious purpose, just another blue jay being mysterious.

I heard familiar soft, steady, slightly metallic *tik, tik, tik* calls behind me. I knew these were companion calls from a winter flock, social calls that let the birds stay in touch, calls that communicate location. I also knew that the relaxed back and forth rhythm of the calls meant the flock was at peace, that all was well.

I had heard these calls before, but suddenly was unsure which bird was making them. I looked, but couldn't spot any birds. Companion calls are notoriously hard to locate, each call a short burst of sound on one frequency, no difference in tone, no song-like pattern for the auditory system to grab onto and to locate. This was, most likely, by design; these calls were perceived and recognized by the flock, but cryptic enough to avoid detection by predators.

I wanted to learn this companion call, to match the sound to an image of a bird, and then lock it permanently into my memory. I decided to risk standing up even if it created a disturbance and scared the birds away. I stood slowly, turned gradually, searched the trees and shrubs along the shoreline, but saw nothing. I kept scanning and finally detected movement in a thicket of red twig dogwood where I spotted one cardinal and then a few seconds later another. I brought them into focus with my binoculars — two females perched on reddish branches, buff brown bodies; red-tinged wings and tail; jaunty crest; strong, conical orange beaks edged with a swatch of black. They shifted and moved on the branch and called *tik, tik, tik.*

A male cardinal flew in and landed on the branch, the same distinctive crest and strong orange bill, but with brilliant, red plumage, plumage that complimented the red bark of the dogwood and stood in stirring contrast to the snowy white expanse of the lake beyond. He edged along the branch, found a creamy-white berry, reached up, artfully plucked the berry, and swallowed it. I inhaled, struck by the beauty of the moment, a scene seared into my mind — red bird, reddish branches, snowy background, creamy white berry.

The male flitted to another branch. I looked at the bushes and counted six cardinals all together — three females and three males — a winter flock, traveling together for security, foraging for food. They continued to call softly back and forth, sweet sounding social calls that Jon Young describes as part of the baseline sounds of nature, sounds that evoke a sense of harmony and feelings of well-being.

Suddenly, a loud, resonant *kik-kik-kik-kik* filled the air. I looked up and saw a pileated woodpecker winging over the frozen lake. It flew in strong and steady, landed high on a dead maple, called again, and then began to hack at the trunk with its long sharp bill. I watched its bright-red, top-notched head move back and forth like a feathered piston, heard the smack of its bill drilling into the tree, saw splinters of wood falling to the ground. It paused, called again, then flew back across the lake. I couldn't help but think that it was showing off, pointing out that while the cardinals were pretty, it was spectacular.

One by one the cardinals drifted away. A blue jay called, crows cawed, another shower of snow pellets rattled against my coat. My hour was up. On the way back I heard, then saw a small flock of chickadees — high-pitched, squeaky calls, another flock communicating, coordinating, connecting, working their way through the winter woods.

# Winter ... again

# The Cave Dweller

Red and orange strands streaked the sky above the horizon and brought to mind the old saying, "red sky by morning, sailor take warning." Not surprisingly, the weather forecast called for foul conditions with strong winds, heavy rain, eventually turning into freezing rain. I stepped cautiously around the patches of ice scattered across the recently plowed driveway, tossed my gear into the car, started up the engine, and drove off.

On the corner, a young boy bundled up in a thick parka, snow pants, stocking cap, gloves, overstuffed backpack — looking like a miniature SWAT team trooper — stood in the dim light waiting for his school bus. Unconcerned by the early hour, the darkness, the layers of garments imposed by a protective mother, and oblivious to my presence, he gazed at the ground, energetically kicked chunks of snow and ice, lost in his world of little boy thoughts.

I peered into the cones of headlight illumination, appreciated the sonorous piano tones of Mussorgsky's *Pictures* and felt good about getting an early start. Driving past a friend's house, I saw him climbing in his car, heading to work, and felt fortunate that I was on my way to my "work" in the woods. I drove past the empty snow-covered fields of an organic farm, down the long slope of Bowen's Hill and over the Lackawaxen River where I saw sharp shards of ice sticking out of the frozen water.

The dam tender was plowing the fresh snow from the parking lot as I pulled in. He drove over, rolled down his window, and after a few minutes of conversation told me how much he enjoyed Prompton;

John Harvey

how in summer he rowed the boat up to the far end of the lake where he always saw something interesting, something beautiful. He remembered seeing tall white birds along the shoreline. I told him that these were great egrets. He said the ice was now at least three inches thick and the ice fishermen would be showing up soon. We exchanged holiday wishes and said farewell. I sensed that he might have preferred to abandon his plowing tasks and join me in the woods.

The new snow was deep and heavy and wet on the West Shore Trail, hard stuff to trudge through, untouched by humans, but already crisscrossed by a web of rabbit, deer, and mouse tracks. I labored down the trail. Soon I felt my heart thumping and heard my breath growing loud and labored. I had to stop and rest. As my body settled down, I heard the morning chorus of winter birds start up — the sharp descending rattle of a downy woodpecker, the nasal *yank* of a nuthatch, the strident *jeer* of a blue jay, and high above, the wild *key-yeer* of a red-shouldered hawk.

Plodding on through the snow, I came to the seep where a sudden blur of movement to the right caught my eye. I froze in place, turned slowly, scanned, and spotted a tiny brown bird creeping over the wet rocks and fallen branches. It disappeared behind a rotted stump. I brought my binoculars up, evened my breathing, and waited patiently for the little bird to reappear.

There it was, stepping busily over the moist green moss. I quickly noted the field marks — dark reddish brown back; finely mottled reddish brown breast; dark brown wing bars; short, sharp beak; and a stubby upturned tail. It walked undaunted through the thin sheet of icy water, picked for morsels of food, climbed over fallen branches, flitted up to a low branch, then darted back to the ground.

It looked like a wren, but was smaller, had a curious upturned tail, and appeared acclimated to the shallow, wet environment of the seep. I knew about house wrens, feisty little birds that sing loudly and chatter busily in my backyard. But they are warm weather birds, arriving in May, nesting in a birdhouse, voraciously consuming insects, raising their brood, and departing in August. This bird seemed thoroughly at home in the winter woods.

A high-pitched *jip, jip* call sounded from the woods past the seep, perhaps its partner voicing a companion call. The little bird

184

scooted behind a log, reappeared, flew up to a low branch, bobbed its tail, flicked its wings, and flew off in the direction of the call.

A brief encounter, I realized, like so many nature encounters. Our paths had intersected for a mere thirty seconds. Now, as I slogged on through the thick snow, I reviewed all my visual and behavioral impressions of this tiny bird. I was determined, as soon as I reached my sit spot, to comb through my Sibley and identify this new arrival.

My plan was to head to the little adjacent gray birch peninsula. I thought the firmly frozen lake would create an access route and, as planned, I was able to step across the ice, walk up to the crest of a small hill, set up my chair, and settle in.

I paged through the wren section of my Sibley and found my bird — a winter wren — an uncommon, secretive bird that breeds in the coniferous forests of Canada and winters in Pennsylvania. I later learned that this bird is only three to four inches long, weighs a mere three to four ounces, and is the smallest member of the wren family. Its taxonomic name, *Troglodytes heimalis*, is taken from the Greek *trogle* — a hole — and *dyein* — to creep. The name means cave dweller and refers to the bird's unique behavior of disappearing into cavities and crevices while feeding on insects, larvae, millipedes, and spiders.

Although I heard its quiet companion call, unfortunately I didn't hear its full song — a long, complex, exuberant series of high, tinkling trills that blend half-tones and overtones and is one of the most complex and musical birdsongs. Winter wrens build tiny nests of grass, moss, lichen, or leaves hidden in a hole, in a stone wall, in upturned tree roots, or on a low branch. Their domelike nest has a side entrance and is so well concealed that even from a few feet away it can be difficult to detect. On cold nights, they roost in hidden holes, dark retreats, or in their nests where small groups may congregate to keep warm.

I marveled at how this tiny bird had flown down from Canada on its stubby little wings, discovered Prompton Lake, and found the seep, the one spot along the ten-mile shoreline that provided its preferred habitat of moving water, wet rocks, rotting tree stumps, nooks and crannies — a spot where it could find food and shelter in the dead of winter.

Savoring my encounter with the winter wren, I began to study the terrain around my new sit spot on the little peninsula. I was sitting on a small man-made hill of dirt piled up during the construction of Prompton Dam. Now, sixty years later, the hill offered an unplanned but harmonious diversity of trees and shrubs. All around me grew gray birches, red maples, black locusts, blueberry bushes, clumps of red twig dogwood, and a single, small, smooth-barked, multi-trunked ironwood tree with slender, brown leaves still clinging to the branches, leaves that quivered in each puff of wind. I reflected that all of these various plants and bushes and trees had grown from seeds deposited by birds or carried by the wind.

I heard soft *stip, stip, stip* calls nearby, scanned the area, and in a nearby birch tree spotted a small flock of dark-eyed juncos. I focused the binoculars on one bird, watched it hang on a thin branch and pick seeds from a birch catkin with its short blunt bill. The flock added a few bright trills to their back-and-forth companion calls. They flitted through the lacy birch branches, feeding, calling, trilling, and suddenly took off in unison, flew across the lake to a stand of hemlocks where they continued their search for food. This was another bird that bred in Canada and was thoroughly at home in the winter woods of northeast Pennsylvania.

When my hour was up, I decided to take a shortcut back across the frozen lake. Stepping tentatively out on the lake, I heard the ice crack beneath my feet. I slowed down, stepped lightly, and cautiously edged onto the frozen lake. Soon the ice grew quiet beneath my footsteps and felt as solid as concrete. I tramped across the lake, paused, turned, and looked back at the little gray birch peninsula, at the blend of trees and bushes, at the nature-landscaped hill. The scene looked like a postcard picture framed by white snow below and gray sky above.

As I approached the boat ramp, a white pickup truck pulled in. A young bearded man wearing a worn green parka and a faded ball cap climbed out — an outdoors type. He stepped onto the ice, looked down, tapped his foot, and glanced up and down the lake.

He greeted me with an easy camaraderie and told me that he had been searching for a hard frozen lake, that he had a "big itch" to go ice fishing. He tapped his foot on the ice again and said, "The ice is thick enough and it's perfect weather for ice fishing. Not too cold, not too much wind."

Pointing toward the north end of the lake, he added, "I've been out here when the wind is ripping down from the north, and you can see the snow squalls bearing down on you. That's really cold."

He turned back to his truck, pulled out a sled, and began to quickly unload and pack his gear on the sled. I wished him good luck and continued to my car. I was eager to feel the warmth of the car heater and to return home for a hot breakfast at the kitchen table where I could watch the moving flames and feel the radiant warmth of the gas fireplace. It had been another day of seasonal changes and new arrivals at Prompton Lake. I realized how instructive, how important, how inspiring it was to see the changes from week to week.

Week 45 · December 28

# Caw, Caw, Caw

I lingered in the car looking into the predawn light at the blueish white, snow-covered lake. A pair of ice fishermen trudged onto the frozen lake, pulling their sleds packed with gear. Soon they would arrive at their chosen spots, drill holes through the thick ice with their power augers, bait their hooks, set their tip-ups, and sit and watch and wait for a bite.

The temperature was a mild thirty-three degrees, and the soft southwest breeze promised even warmer air. On the southern horizon, billowing gray clouds stained with streaks of purple, orange, yellow, pink, and red created a rapidly shifting canvas of colors and patterns, fleeting impressions impossible to capture with a camera, although I tried.

Over the Christmas holiday many had visited Prompton. The West Shore Trail was a maze of boot prints, snowshoe impressions, and even the continuous roll of mountain bike snow tires. My boots crunched through a thin, crusty layer of snow. In the distance, crows cawed; nearby a nuthatch called. I stopped at the seep, hoping to catch another glimpse of the winter wren, but today saw only wet mossy rocks, heard only water trickling down the hillside.

I planned to return to the little gray birch peninsula, but for some reason felt uneasy with that decision, stopped, checked my intuition, and received a clear message to go to my regular spot under the black cherry tree. Later, I would understand the wisdom of this guidance.

I sat down, looked, listened, and immediately noticed a different winter soundscape. Water gurgled down a rocky streambed that had been silent since spring. The warmer temperatures, recent rainfall, and snow melt of the past few days had recharged the water supply of this seasonal stream. Sharp cracks and crunches from the shoreline sounded like someone or something walking on and breaking through the ice. Reflexively, I turned and looked, but no one was there. It was just the shifting, splintering, and cracking of the icy crust covering Prompton Lake.

A crow with a deep hoarse voice cawed loudly from across the lake. Another crow answered with a loudly emphatic *caw, caw, caw,* equally deep toned, but without the husky quality. A third crow chimed in with a higher-pitched *caw.* Once again I reflected on the differences in the voices of the crows.

A bird moved in a tree down the shoreline to my left. I pulled up my binoculars, and using a nearby dead tree as a reference point, located a blue jay working its way from branch to branch, snatching buds and seeds, flapping down to the ground, then back to the tree. A second blue jay foraged in a nearby tree, both birds feeding in silence, bright blue swatches against a backdrop of white snow and gray tree trunks. Then they flew away.

Jetliners whooshed high above the blanket of gray clouds — 7:48, 7:55, 8:01, 8:08 — one plane every five to ten minutes, a parade of silver sky tubes soaring and circling, heading to the New York area airports.

Loud tapping came from a tree along the shoreline, slow, intermittent taps, a burst of quick taps, a pause, then more slow taps. I scanned with binoculars, spotted movement, waited, and was rewarded with a clear view of a pileated woodpecker with its bright red topnotch. It flapped its large wings, flew to a nearby tree, grabbed the trunk with its strong claws, steadied itself with its strong tail, and hacked away with its chisel-like beak. Then it scooted up the trunk, paused, chopped, climbed higher, chopped, worked its way up the tree, drilling for food, hacking out holes. Then with a loud *kik-kik-kik-kik*, it flew away into the woods.

The patch of trees along the shoreline appeared to be today's birding hot spot. For reasons unknown to me, different species of birds were landing and feeding in the same spot. I was glad I had listened to my intuition and come to this location. Although the hot spot was almost a hundred yards away, I had a clear view and could watch all the action.

As I mused upon the mystery of birding "hot spots," a jet black crow winged silently over the white frozen lake and landed at the top of a tree right in the middle of the hot spot. I studied it through my binoculars, watched it silently move from branch to branch, flap its wings to steady its position, search for buds and seeds, pick delicately, quickly, precisely.

Then, seemingly satisfied with its interval of feeding, it hopped out to the tip of a high branch and cawed loudly three times; its beak open wide; its sleek, shiny, black body rocking with each caw. It cawed again, and suddenly two more crows flew in, landed in adjacent trees, and both of them answered with loud caws. The first crow cawed again; the other two answered. This, I thought, must be a *caw*nversation.

The first crow took off, flew up the shoreline toward me, landed on the tip of a soft, green pine branch that bounced up and down with its weight, and cawed again. The other two crows, along with a newly arrived fourth crow, flew over, joined the leader in the pine tree, and they all launched into a boisterous chorus of caws. The first crow took off again and flew another hundred yards up the shoreline. The other three crows followed, and they resumed their chorus of caws. The quartet of crows flapped another hundred yards up the shoreline, stopped and cawed again. I watched as they worked their way stepwise up the shoreline, gradually becoming tiny black specks against a gray sky. Gradually the sounds of their caws faded away.

I felt as if I had seen a brief documentary on the behavior of crows. At the beginning, the first crow had been alone in the tree, hopping, jumping, flapping, focused on finding food. Then it switched to a social mode and called in its family members. I was surprised how quickly they appeared, how completely they joined the social interaction, perching at the end of branches, rocking back and forth, cawing lustily in a lead and response pattern.

The feeding and coming together seemed both functional and understandable. The mysterious part was the game of follow the leader. If it was play, I wished them full enjoyment. I also felt a pang of envy wishing that I could join in, that I could fly freely through the woods from tree to tree, and that I could sing in a chorus that carried for miles.

I glanced up at the sky, still gray and cloudy, no real sunrise, no real increase in illumination, just a brief tease of sunlight on the tree tops before the clouds took over. I listened to the gurgling of the water, the cracking of the ice, and the voices of ice fishermen carrying over the frozen lake.

I packed up my gear and walked back to my car. Like the crows I saw that morning, I switched to social mode, drove downtown to a local café and met friends for breakfast — latte and a croissant — and for back and forth conversation. And then a thought popped into my mind. Perhaps I could persuade my friends to join me in renting a plane from the local airport. We could fly over to Prompton, soar above the shoreline, above the trees, over the hills and ridges, and enjoy a crow's eye view of Prompton Lake.

Week 46 · January 4

# Ten Below

I peered at the outside thermometer through the thick sheen of frost coating the kitchen window. Ten below zero, exactly as forecast. I considered heading back to bed, slipping under the warm comforter, falling back asleep, and waiting for a milder day.

After all, I didn't need to suffer unduly, and I didn't need to take chances in dangerously cold temperatures.

The TV, radio, newspapers, and news websites had been filled with reports dramatizing the dangers of the subzero temperatures — video clips of people rubbing frost-bitten fingers and toes, reminders to carry an emergency kit in your car, warnings to keep your pets inside, and most importantly, directives to only go outside if absolutely necessary.

But I had made my decision the previous night. I wanted, even needed, to experience nature in conditions of extreme cold. I wanted to set my eyes upon the deeply frozen forest and observe the reactions of the birds and animals. And there was some risk in going out to face the challenge, to try and outsmart the cold, to test myself against the elements.

I had a plan. I would leave home right after sunrise so that when I arrived at my sit spot the first rays of warming sunshine would greet me. I would wear heavy, insulated boots and layer up with long underwear, thick corduroys, turtleneck, wool sweater, scarf, stocking cap, and a bulky winter coat that reached to my thighs. I would activate my glove warmers before I left home. A safety plan was essential. I would write down the location of my sit spot, text home when I arrived and text again when I left. I didn't relish the prospect, however remote, of slipping on the ice, breaking a leg, and slowly freezing to death in the woods.

Just as the sun peeked above the southeastern horizon, I stepped out of the house and instantly felt the frigid air nipping at my exposed face and stinging my nostrils. Fortunately, the tree branches were motionless. There would be no added wind to drive the temperature even lower.

A light layer of fresh snow coated the highway, yet traffic proceeded normally for a Saturday morning. One car ahead of me and five or six passing by in the other lane were on their way to town. A golden retriever, old and white-muzzled, sat on the front step of a house, staring at the door, waiting to be let in. Plumes of smoke floated up from house chimneys — bright white, thick, fluffy plumes, the way smoke always looks and rises in deep cold. A milk truck backed down to a dairy barn to make the morning pickup. A herd of cattle with thick brown and black coats, breath steaming, milled around a barnyard munching hay. A black crow was perched on a dead branch by the highway. A flock of house sparrows flew across a field. The car thermometer ticked steadily down to minus ten degrees.

The parking lot at Prompton had already been plowed after the previous day's snowfall. A single pickup truck stood near the lake. A few yards off shore an ice fisherman was drilling a hole with a hand auger. At least I wasn't the only crazy person out in the cold. Shouldering my backpack and camp chair, I walked across the plowed pavement to the West Shore Trail and stepped onto the snow-covered trail. It was completely quiet in the woods, the only sound the squeaking of my boots on the cold, dry snow.

Setting up under the black cherry tree, I settled in and began to listen and look. Soon the first bird calls sounded from the bushes along the shoreline — soft metallic chips, the companion calls of cardinals. A female flitted up through the branches, then back to the ground. Her calls expressed no sense of alarm or distress.

Ahead, in the woods, chickadees squeaked, chuckled, and sang. Goldfinches flew overhead piping their musical flight song. A nuthatch whinnied, busily, cheerfully. A pileated woodpecker tapped, drilled, and called. A flock of juncos drifted through the trees, calling and trilling back and forth. I listened to the morning chorus of bird calls and was struck by the realization that the birds were behaving normally. They seemed unfazed by the severe cold, going about business as usual.

A blue jay flew in and landed on the branch of a maple tree twenty feet away. I sat motionless and watched it feed, hopping along the branch, turning, reaching up, adroitly plucking buds and seeds. It fed quietly, purposefully for three minutes, then perched absolutely still like a blue and white sculpture — dignified, contemplative, feathers and down puffed out for extra insulation its only adjustment to the cold.

Another blue jay flew in and landed in the same tree. They sat silently, one at the top of the tree, the other at the middle. The first blue jay called out and flapped down to a bush. The second jay followed. They began to *jay* and *jeer* loudly back and forth and then suddenly took flight and winged across the lake.

I gazed at the blanket of fresh white snow that coated and smoothed and leveled the forest floor, hiding every blemish and irregularity. I looked at the long blue-black tree shadows stretching and angling across the glistening white snow. I glanced up at the cobalt blue sky, an infinite dome of blue, the kind of pure blue usually best seen from a high mountain top.

I tried to open my thermos, but drops of tea had frozen underneath the cap. I twisted hard and the outside metal cover separated from the inner plastic cup. The adhesive joining the two pieces had splintered and failed in the cold. I grabbed harder and twisted carefully, finally managing to free the cup and pour hot steamy tea. I sipped the hot beverage and thought how hard extreme cold is on human equipment; metal and plastic freeze, crack, and break.

After a few minutes of exposure to the cold air, my bare fingers began to sting. I burrowed my hands back in the gloves and closed my fingers around the hand-warming packets. My toes felt cold and numb inside my boots, my face frozen and brittle. I kept the gloves on to pour and sip the rest of the tea. I took extra care not to drop anything in the snow, not to get snow on my hands or in my gloves.

The birdsongs faded. The woods fell quiet. I didn't hear a single jetliner, and then I remembered there had been substantial snowfall in the New York City area, the airports had closed, and hundreds of flights had been canceled. A few minutes later I heard the soft, distant whoosh of a jet, looked up, and spotted a shiny silver tube winging westward. The flights were resuming; life was returning to normal.

My hour was up. With a stiff, clumsy, gloved hand I inscribed "Made It!" in my notebook. I set off across the frozen lake, heard my boots crunch and squeak on the snow. I looked at miniature, sinuous, snow dunes carved by the wind, fields of snow ripples like a little white desert stretching across the surface of the lake. I came upon a bare spot of ice, a spot swept clean by the wind, and gazed down at the deep crystalline ice that looked like a five-inch-thick diamond coolly refracting and reflecting the morning sunlight. This cold winter day seemed to offer its own version of beauty.

# Lake Effect Snow

Lake effect snowflakes drifted down, white parade confetti falling in the illumination of my headlights. Overnight an Alberta Clipper, a pocket of moist Pacific air chilled and churned into a storm in the lee of the Canadian Rocky Mountains, had passed overhead, dropping a quick two inches of snow. Now the trailing northwest wind skimmed moisture from Lake Erie and Lake Ontario, carried it south, crystallized it into snow, and sprinkled it over northeast Pennsylvania.

The nighttime snow had coated the highway, melted, refroze, and the new flurries coated the road again — a perfect recipe for an icy, slippery road. Not surprisingly, the car began to lose traction on the very first hill. The tires spun, the RPMs shot up. I carefully angled the steering wheel to the right, edging the passenger side tires onto the shoulder. Gradually the tires gripped the gravel and regained traction. With a sigh of relief I made it up the little hill.

I drove carefully then, winter driving, both hands clutching the steering wheel, maintaining steady speed uphill, down-shifting downhill. The little front-wheel drive Corolla held the road, and gradually, I relaxed my grip and took in the view — a blue-gray sky, a fresh blanket of snow covering the fields, a fluffy topping of snow on the branches, puffy crowns of snow on the fence posts and mailboxes. I listened to the piano notes of Mussorgsky's *Pictures* resonating through the car and wondered if he had looked out his window on a similar Russian winter landscape, felt inspired, and then the melodies, notes, and harmonies flowed from his mind and heart.

It seemed appropriate to be driving through snow on my birthday. According to family legend, on the night of my birth, my grandmother drove my mother to the hospital through a raging blizzard. A dramatic story — my father on a warship in the Pacific, my mother going into labor, the snowstorm bearing down, the drifts edging across the road, the wind ripping over the frozen prairie, the urgent journey to town. I loved this story as a child and imagined that these circumstances gave me a unique connection to snowfall. But I also wondered if with each retelling, the snow grew deeper, the wind stronger, and the blizzard more ferocious.

I walked cautiously along the West Shore Trail, pushing my boots down into the fresh snow, feeling for icy patches, grabbing tree trunks for support, slipping, almost falling. In two spots I saw a few fresh webs of mouse tracks, already signs of life in the new snow. I turned off the trail, trudged through the woods, and set up under the big black cherry tree. The temperature was a fresh but comfortable twenty-two degrees. A light breeze blew from the northwest. The snowfall tapered off and ended.

A cathedral-like quiet fell upon the woods, sounds softened and muffled by the new layer of snow. My hearing searched further and further into the distance and eventually picked up distant sounds, crows cawing far to the north beyond the lake, the faint gurgling of flowing water somewhere down the shoreline.

Prompton Lake looked vast, white, and empty. Thick clouds hid all traces of the rising sun. Snow began to fall again. I heard it first, tiny icy crystals clicking on my jacket sleeve. Then I saw the flakes, bigger now, drifting down, angling, pushed by the strengthening wind, exotic large complex snow crystals plopping on my notebook, melting, spotting the paper with tiny watermarks.

A flock of juncos appeared in the woods and worked their way through the gray, bare trees, the synchronous rhythm of their soft flock calls sounding through the morning air. Watching these winter birds flying peacefully through the falling snow, I felt my shoulders and neck and face relax, felt a blurring of the boundaries between self and surroundings, between observer and observed.

Suddenly, I turned and looked up and at that moment spotted a little black and white downy woodpecker looping through the trees toward me. Why had I glanced up? Had I sensed its approach? Was I beginning to develop the proverbial eyes in the back of my head?

A jetliner flew over, a hushed whisper far above the clouds. The snow picked up in intensity, more and more flakes fell, landed on my coat, more white celebratory confetti drifted down through the branches and dropped to the ground.

Two blue jays landed in a tall maple tree, hopped from branch to branch, busily picked at buds, finished feeding, perched in stillness, and then flew off — bright blue and white birds flying into white falling snow, into blue-gray light, harmonious colors, a sublime composition.

I gazed at the tree trunks, silent and gray like a legion of frozen gray tombstones. But death was an illusion in the woods. Under the blanket of snow, under the decomposing leaves, under the layer of hard frozen ground, the roots were alive, welcoming the newly fallen snow that would in time melt into nourishing water. The trees sensed the increasing length of the day, registered the rising angle of the sun, waited in silence, circulating sap, preparing for rebirth.

Across the lake, a raven called, an earthy, guttural *cr-r-ruck, cr-r-ruck*. I pictured it, a big black solitary bird, flying more like a hawk, flapping and sailing. I heard a red-tailed hawk, a high-pitched, raspy, descending *keeer-r-r*. I heard a red-shouldered hawk, a clear repeated *key-yeer*. The big predator birds were active. Perhaps the gray cloudy sky and fresh falling snow made for good hunting conditions. Perhaps last week's cold snap had pushed them south to search for food

The woods grew quiet. I watched the snow falling through the branches, uncountable crystals, each adding its weight and volume to the white blanket that already lay upon the earth. More silence and then more sounds — a blue jay calling, a nuthatch whinnying, a woodpecker tapping, the ice cracking and crunching, then silence again.

My hour was up. I walked back to the parking lot and saw that the snow had covered my footprints and tire tracks. I warmed up the car, brushed off the windows, pulled out, picked up speed, but lost traction halfway up the hill. I backed all the way down slowly and carefully, tried again, made it a few feet further, stalled, and had to back down again. I was stuck.

I sat in my car, listened to Mussorgsky, looked across the frozen lake to the stands of snow-covered, dark green pines and hemlocks. After a while, the dam tender arrived, plowed the road, scraped the snow from the parking lot, and spread salt on the hill. I tried again. This time I made it up the hill, and with a feeling of deliverance I turned onto the highway and headed home. Yet my feelings were mixed. A part of me liked those moments stuck in the parking lot while I savored my interlude of snowy solitude and honored my birthday reconnection with the falling snow.

# The Bird Whisperer

It was dark when I arrived at Prompton, too dark to walk safely through the snowy, icy woods. I lingered in the warm car and gazed out through a frame of dark pine boughs at the dim emptiness of the lake. A thin line of illumination slowly edged above the eastern horizon. Gradually, the shapes and forms of the bushes and trees along the far shoreline emerged. Listening to the piano tones of Mussorgsky's *Pictures*, I imagined I heard the chiming of balalaikas and the deliberate footsteps of a person walking through an art exhibition, pausing here and there to take in the colors, composition, and beauty of each painting. It was too pleasant sitting in the cozy car, sipping tea, listening to music, and watching the day begin. I forced myself to set a deadline; when the car clock flashed 7:00, I would step out into the cold predawn air.

The West Shore Trail was a mess. In the high spots, a thin coating of fresh snow hid slick icy patches. In the low spots, brown muddy spikes of frost-heaved ice jutted up from the ground. I walked carefully down the trail, across the seep, and angled through the woods to my home sit spot under the big black cherry tree.

The temperature was in the low twenties. Purple-streaked clouds now clustered over the eastern horizon while a blanket of thick gray clouds covered the sky above. A light, steady breeze blew down from the north. I settled in, sat still, and soon heard the welcoming winter morning chorus — the cawing of crows, the calls of juncos, the clicks of cardinals, and the chatter of chickadees.

Loud crunches and cracks sounded behind me. In the dim light my imagination took over. I pictured a bear or a buck struggling and smashing its way across the ice. I assured myself that it was just the ice shifting, but my imagination kept conjuring up images of an increasingly large, unknown, and potentially dangerous creature approaching. Finally, I had to stand up, turn around, look at the lake, and confirm that nothing was there; just the ice, twisting, heaving, adjusting, and then falling silent again.

Suddenly, I heard a very special song, one I had been waiting and hoping to hear, a simple, clear, whistled, descending *fee-bee, fee-bee,* the spring song of a male chickadee. And then a minute later another spring song carried through the woods, the *peter, peter, peter* of a tufted titmouse. Remarkably, a few minutes later a male cardinal launched into his spring song, a clear whistled *whoit-whoit-whoit* followed by a string of *purty, purty, purty, purty* calls.

These songs were welcome, uplifting musical hints of spring on a cold, gray, winter morning. I listened again and again to these spring songs carrying through the wintry woods and felt my spirits spontaneously rise, felt a smile of hope spread across my face. Here, amid the persisting cold and darkness of winter were the first tangible harbingers of spring.

For the birds, however, these songs signaled the beginning of a crucial and demanding chapter in their life. The males would begin to drift away from their winter flocks and start to search out and claim the best nesting spots. Their plumage would grow brighter and more colorful. Their songs would become more practiced, frequent, and insistent, songs designed to exude vitality and impress and attract the ever-choosy females, songs that would hopefully one day come to mark the boundaries of a breeding territory.

The trigger for the onset of these songs was the advancing daylight, which by mid-January was noticeable and gaining momentum. In the case of the chickadee, once the daylight reached a specific length, a gene on the surface of the male's brain switched on and released a thyroid-stimulating hormone. This hormone in turn stimulated the pituitary gland to secrete hormones that caused the male's testes to grow, which then inspired his territorial singing.

With my boots wedged under the snow for added insulation and my gloved fingers stinging with cold, I could hardly contain my happiness at hearing these spring songs. And who knows? Perhaps my brain was subliminally registering these lengthening days, causing some similar cascade of hormonal and neuronal changes that in modern terms might bring more energy, initiative, and optimism, but in prehistoric times may have triggered the desire to look beyond the horizon to seek out new hunting grounds and search for new mating opportunities.

A solitary crow flew over, stark black against the high gray sky, the first bird I saw. I had been sitting still for forty minutes, relying entirely on my hearing to understand the day's nature story.

Jetliners flew above me, whooshing whispers above the clouds. The voices of ice fishermen carried across the lake. Suddenly, the morning soundscape was shattered by the loud jarring, sputtering, coughing, roaring racket of a power ice auger. Once again a whiff of combusted gasoline quickly invaded my nostrils. Quiet returned a few minutes and five new ice holes later, but it took five minutes more for my ears to fully recover, for the roar of the ice auger to fade, for my hearing to once again reach out through the full circle of sound.

Soon my allotted hour was up. I packed up my gear, walked to the tip of the peninsula, and stepped tentatively onto the ice, ice that cracked and crunched at first, but as usual felt solid once I stepped further onto the lake. Pausing, I turned and looked back at the peninsula, the home of my weekly sit spot, then started my trek across the ice to the boat ramp.

Halfway back an ice fisherman stood in the middle of an array of ten or more tip-ups. He glanced at me, and something about his posture told me he wanted to talk. I walked over. We exchanged greetings. I knew that with my chair, backpack, and binoculars, I didn't fit into any typical and expected categories such as ice fisherman or hunter. However, I had learned that if I said birdwatcher, people were quickly put at ease. He asked what birds I had seen. No need to go into too much detail. I said blue jays, chickadees, and juncos.

He answered, "We have 'em at home. My wife feeds the birds and we see 'em at the feeder every day. She calls the chickadees in. They fly over, land on her shoulder, hop down, and eat sunflower seeds from her hand."

He continued, "In the summer my wife whistles and the bluebirds come. They sit on the gutter and fly down to eat the mealworms that she sets out. Last summer she even fed a catbird."

He reached in his pocket, pulled out a little container, opened it, showed me a bunch of tan mealworms and said, "Just like these worms. The birds come right around and eat 'em when she calls."

He closed the container, stuffed it back in his pocket, looked off in the distance, and said, "You know, my wife, she's kind of like a bird whisperer."

He was in an appreciative mood, and I wondered if the increasing daylight contributed to his positive outlook. We said our goodbyes, and I resumed my trek across the ice. The sun broke through the clouds. I turned toward the sun and saw glints of blue, pink, red, and yellow, the sparkly rainbow play of sunlight on fresh snow crystals.

Resuming my walk, I spotted an eagle standing on the ice near the far shoreline. I focused my binoculars and saw it clearly — bright white head, sharply curved yellow beak, bright yellow eyes. It stood over a deer that had become trapped in the ice and froze to death. The eagle bent down, ripped out a chunk of frozen flesh, swallowed it, looked around warily, possessively, bent down again and ripped off another chunk. I watched it feed for five minutes. Then it paused, looked around, flapped its long powerful wings, lifted off the ice, settled into a rhythmic flight, and flew up the lake where it landed at the end of a long dead limb, slowly folded its wings, and gazed regally around its realm.

I continued my walk across the ice toward the boat ramp. Crunching through the snow, I reflected that this had been another morning filled with impressions of nature. Now images of winter and spring, of people and birds, of interactions and connections, of diversity and unity swirled around in my mind. Back in the car, I turned on the engine, waited for and welcomed the warmth of the heater, and listened again to Mussorgsky's chiming balalaikas, and once again heard the slow, purposeful footsteps of an engaged and appreciative art observer, the footsteps of a kindred spirit.

# The Roost

It was another cold morning, zero degrees with northerly gusts driving the wind chill down to ten below. Overhead, an endless dome of cobalt blue stretched high into the blue-blackness of space. To the east, the bright yellow sun-orb peeked above the dark forested hills. A dusting of fresh snow coated the West Shore Trail, already crisscrossed with animal tracks, including a web of rabbit tracks under a bush where they had hungrily nibbled twigs and buds and debarked branches. Crows, many crows, cawed from the woods across the lake.

I set up under the black cherry tree, faced west, and instantly felt the cold sting of the wind on my face. All around me the branches swayed and clicked and clacked, the percussive metallic sounds of frozen wood blown by a cold wind. Morning sunlight streamed onto the snow, illuminating the myriad crystals, catching and refracting sunlight, creating a layer of diamond dust. I leaned forward, saw my blue-black shadow appear next to the long shadow of the cherry tree, leaned back and saw our shadows merge.

A faint half-moon lingered in the western sky. A white, puffy cloud drifted toward the moon, a canary-shaped cloud, a hungry canary ready to gobble up the moon as if it were a floating white berry — a video game scenario playing out in the sky.

A flock of chickadees flew onto the peninsula. A male sang its clear spring *fee-bee* song. I counted the repetitions — one, two, three . . . lost track after twelve, the song more insistent and more frequent this week, an increase possibly driven by the lengthening days. Another male chimed in with a slightly different song, three distinct descending notes, *fee-bid-it, fee-bid-it, fee-bid-it,* an innovative song, one that might appeal to a female, that might provide an evolutionary advantage to that male.

Crows cawed raucously from the far hills. Four flew over the lake heading west. Then, groups of crows flew over me, jet black against the high cobalt blue sky, cruising twenty feet above the trees, wingbeats strong and steady. I counted groups of four, five, three, five, four, five . . . more than fifty crows altogether, flying west, a river of crows flowing through a clear blue sky. Out over the lake another flock of twenty or more also winged to the west, flying quietly, steadily, purposefully.

I reasoned that all of these crows must have departed from a roost. I later learned that starting in the fall and peaking in winter, crows gather in nocturnal roosts. During the late afternoon, individuals, families, and flocks work their way to these roosts, assembling in nearby congregating spots where they noisily caw and squawk. Then, as dusk falls they flap silently to the roost area, perch in trees, and with quiet caws, croaks, and gurgles, settle down to sleep. They awaken in the predawn light, stretch their wings, shift around, caw back and forth, and then fly off to forage.

Ornithologists are unsure of the exact functions of these roosts. One purpose may be mutual security. Great horned owls kill and eat crows with considerable efficiency. Big flocks can watch for these predators, cry out warnings, and band together to mob the owls and chase them away. The location of the roost may also be chosen for its proximity to food sources. Another purpose may be information sharing. Crows returning from a day of futile foraging may hear news of a field filled with corn or grain or other food and on the next day pursue these better possibilities.

I wondered if crows might also enjoy the learning opportunities a roost provides, might enjoy stimulating and exercising their brains, might enjoy learning new calls, adding to the more than two hundred they already know. Perhaps they even draw a kind of strength, a sense of belonging and social well-being from the roost.

Crows are known to be intelligent. Experiments have documented that they can learn multiple steps to obtain a food reward. In the wild they drop shells and nuts on hard surfaces to open them. They have been known to linger by fresh road kill, waiting for a vehicle to run over the animal again to split it open so they can feed on it. Crows also learn and remember the faces of both helpful and harmful humans.

A group of crows is called a murder, and my first thought was to title this chapter "A Murder of Crows," but I reconsidered. A murder of crows is an overly poetic label in the same silly league as an ostentation of peacocks, an exaltation of larks, and a skulk of foxes. But the term "murder" isn't just silly, it carries and reinforces negative stereotypes of crows, including their association with death, based on popular beliefs that crows gather outside a house before a person dies, that they congregate before battlefield slaughter, that their raucous calls sound like a person calling "bloody murder." In addition, crows are typically regarded as avian vandals snatching and eating the chicks of song birds and as troublesome pests that eat and damage crops.

But in fact, crows may be the birds that are most like humans — social, intelligent, persistent, playful, and opportunistic. Their consumption of insect pests, small rodents, and weed seeds, along with their behavior of cleaning up road kill, far outweighs any harm they do. They have no more association with death than a seagull. Ornithologists simply refer to a group of crows as a flock and admire and continue to research their many unique qualities and traits. Native Americans honored crows as clever, resourceful, even inspiring companions.

Our negative view of crows may, in a Jungian sense, represent a suppression of the shadow, a rejection of our own primal power. Releasing negative beliefs and embracing the spirit of the crow may be one way for us to reconnect with nature, to integrate primal power into our conscious life.

I saw more crows on the move — groups of three, four, or five, some heading west, some heading east, some working up and down the shoreline. And then they were gone, the morning flight from the roost was over.

I huddled in my coat, clutched my hand warmers, and heard the flight song of goldfinches, a sweet musical whistle, a descending, *per-chik-o-ree*. I spotted a flock in a nearby tree, brought up my binoculars, focused on a single bird perched on a thin twig, a puff of pale yellow against a vast blue sky.

The wind abated. I felt sunlight on my neck and back. I had, with almost no effort or discomfort, been sitting motionless in the cold for sixty minutes. I stood, turned to the sun, took in the light and warmth, packed up, and walked back through the woods, picturing flocks of flying crows, thinking about the mysteries of the roost, realizing that I had heard and seen crows almost every week. Crows were, in fact, among my most constant companions, my most present and persistent teachers during my year at Prompton Lake.

## Week 50 · January 31
# A Flock of Finches

Another early departure on another dark winter morning. The illumination from the headlights revealed gray pavement, gray tree trunks, gray branches, and on the periphery, pale snow-covered fields. I welcomed the warm air from the heater, enjoyed the orchestral sounds of Mussorgsky's *Pictures*, and opened my mind for a word that might describe the essence of my upcoming observation session. "Relief" flashed into awareness. I asked myself, "Relief from what?"

Possibilities paraded through my mind. Relief that the temperature was a relatively mild twenty degrees and there was no wind to drive down the chill? Relief that I had finally arrived at week fifty of my yearlong commitment? (This did feel significant as I was now heading into the home stretch and was growing increasingly confident that I would achieve my goal.) Or, perhaps I was sensing nature's deep relief to have once again survived the coldest and darkest months of the year.

I slowed down, extended the duration of the drive in the warm car, and thought about the word relief. Curious about the precise meaning, I looked it up on a dictionary app as soon as I parked and read, "the pleasant and relaxed feeling that arises when something unpleasant stops." I found myself wondering what today's session might reveal about "relief."

Old grayish snow littered with wind-fallen twigs and crisscrossed with animal tracks covered the West Shore Trial. I plodded along through the dirty snow, made my way to the peninsula, and set up at my home sit spot site under the big black cherry tree. Thin gray clouds floated overhead; a light listless wind blew from the north. A single crow, stark black against the gray sky, flew overhead, set its wings, and glided gracefully toward the stand of hemlocks across the lake.

I settled in and soon heard the morning chorus. Chickadees called, including a male singing its *fee-bee* spring song. A blue jay piped, and a crow with a raspy voice cawed and was answered by one with a smooth caw. A pileated woodpecker called a loud *kik-kik-kik-kik* and was answered by another deep in the woods ahead. A downy woodpecker landed above me in the black cherry tree, scuttled up the rough bark, tapped a rapid drum roll against the trunk, called its tinny-toned descending whinny, and then looped away through the woods. More voices joined the morning chorus — the nasal whinny of a white-breasted nuthatch, the scream of a red-tailed hawk, and more crows cawing in the distance.

I was happy to be present for another morning chorus, pleased to hear the variety of musical songs and calls, to recognize the different voices, and to sense the affirmation that in the woods at Prompton Lake, all was peaceful, all was safe, and nature was in full operation on this winter morning. Certainly, this harmonious morning chorus could offer soothing relief to a worried mind or a troubled soul.

Cardinals clicked softly back and forth ahead in the woods. I spotted a pair perched in a red twig dogwood and studied them through the binoculars — the male with his bright red breeding plumage, crisp black face patch, conical red bill, gray-tan claws gripping a dull red branch above white snowy ground. The cardinals flitted up to another branch and flew from tree to tree, calling, picking at seeds, constantly in motion, a scene of beauty that filled my heart with happiness.

I heard plaintive musical calls, soft delicate notes nearby, notes that sounded vaguely familiar. I looked to the right, to the left, and into the woods ahead, but couldn't locate the birds singing these sweet notes. I felt a tinge of frustration. I thought I knew all the winter birdsongs.

Slowly, all the birdsongs and calls diminished and the woods grew silent. I gazed down at the snow-covered ground and thought about the world of life beneath the snow, the subnivean world of scuttling mice and voles, hunting weasels, bacteria and fungi and mosses. I looked out at the lake, blue-white snow covering the thick ice, a scene of apparent emptiness, yet beneath the frozen surface, water plants grew, tiny crustaceans swam and multiplied, minnows fed on the plant life and dodged predatory pan fish — bass, walleyes, and muskies. I felt surrounded, supported, even nourished by this dynamic, vibrant yet hidden web of life.

The morning chorus gradually resumed. Crows cawed in the distance with various voices and cadences. A blue jay flew through the branches, perched on a slender twig, picked at buds, bobbed its tail, and fluffed its feathers. A second jay flew in and landed in an adjacent tree. The two jays foraged for food and flapped from branch to branch in synchronous silence. Then, still in synchrony, they bolted out of the trees, broke into a peal of loud *jay, jay, jay* calls, and flew across the lake.

A few minutes later I heard the sweet, soft notes again; so near, yet so elusive. I looked and scanned, but couldn't locate the birds making these calls. This mystery was growing. I was becoming more and more frustrated.

I glanced down at my watch and was surprised to see that my hour was up. For the second week I sat motionless for a full sixty minutes. I seemed to have developed some new capacity to sit down, shift my body into park, and turn my attention to listening, looking, sniffing the air, and feeling the temperature, humidity, and wind. I no longer sought out nor needed any distractions — no tea breaks, no pee breaks, no stretches, shifting, or fidgeting.

I wondered how this skill of still-sitting had evolved. Was it the result of fifty weeks of training, of sitting in the woods, downplaying the restless needs of the body and mind, while up-training my capacity to look and listen? Or had the intense enjoyment of experiencing nature taken precedent over physical and mental restlessness?

I walked over to the shoreline to snap a few pictures. Glancing up at the top of two gray birch trees where I expected to view bare branches, I was surprised to see what looked like lingering leaves or little chunks of fruit. I looked again and suddenly felt as if an obscuring film had been peeled from my eyes. The scene was transformed. What had been inanimate was now fully animate; leaves and fruit were actually little yellow birds flitting through the branches, a flock of fifty goldfinches perching and feeding in the gray birch branches.

Through my binoculars I studied a single bird in its pale yellow winter plumage, saw it clinging with tiny clever claws to a thin drooping birch branch, observed it deftly picking seeds from the tiny cone-shaped catkins with its strong, skilled, conical beak. The flock members called softly back and forth. I learned later that these soft calls were typical goldfinch feeding and contact sounds.

Occasionally, a few finches would fly to the other birch tree, singing the more familiar *per-chik-o-ree*, the flight song I knew and recognized. I watched them feeding, flitting, and flying from tree to tree, branch to branch. Then, as if responding to some internal flock communication, they departed from the trees in front of me and flew in small groups over to the little peninsula, alighted in the gray birch trees there, and resumed their feeding and their sweet calls.

The mystery was solved and I breathed a sigh of relief. I packed up my gear and trudged contentedly back through the snowy woods, picturing a hot breakfast of scrambled farm fresh eggs, toasted whole grain bread from a local bakery, and rich, steaming, home-roasted coffee, the perfect way to relieve my growing hunger. With a smile, I reflected that my hour in the woods had provided relief on many levels, relief for my mind, heart, and spirit, and soon for my body.

Week 51 · February 7

## Endurance

The morning forecast called for ten degrees with no wind, conditions I could easily manage by layering up with a turtleneck and wool sweater, my puffy down coat and insulated boots; if necessary, I could insert warming packs into my gloves. I had learned to cope with the cold and felt a sense of confidence, even control, as I drove to Prompton. But when I opened my mind for a word to capture the mood of the morning, "endurance" arose, a word that surprised me.

A fresh dusting of overnight snow coated the highway. High banks of plowed snow flanked the highway, creating a tunnel effect. In my friend's yard I saw a flock of twenty turkeys milling around under a bird feeder, scratching the frozen ground, searching for fallen seeds. Silver-white hoar frost glistened on the branches and twigs; layer upon layer upon layer of tiny shimmering ice crystals formed from the moisture in the air by the super cooled night temperatures. Ahead, the snow-capped Moosic Mountains stretched along the horizon. Crossing the bridge, I saw that the Lackawaxen River was choked with clusters and chunks of jagged ice and only a few slender, dark threads of cold water still flowed downstream.

I looked at the car thermometer, saw it jerk from minus seven to minus eight, and was sure I had misread it. I looked up, studied the road ahead, took another peek, and now it read minus nine. I thought something must be wrong with the thermometer or with my vision. Again I looked up, blinked, cleared my vision, looked again, and saw the temperature drop to minus ten, a full twenty degrees colder at Prompton than at my house, a mere three and a half miles away. I realized that with no wind, the heavy cold air must have flowed downhill and pooled in the valley surrounding the lake, the very conditions that had created the thick hoarfrost.

Suddenly, what had seemed like a cold, but manageable morning, had turned into another challenge. When I arrived at Prompton, I procrastinated in the car, sipped the last of my hot tea, braced myself, climbed out, and instantly felt the sting of cold air on my exposed skin.

The West Shore Trail was buried beneath a foot of recent snow topped with a brittle icy crust that shattered with each step. I trudged slowly down the trail, each step laborious, lifting my boot up high, stepping straight down, breaking through the crust, pushing down deep to solid ground, lifting my other foot up for the next step, repeating the process over and over. Once again I heard my heart thumping, saw clouds of mist forming with each exhalation, and felt my leg muscles growing fatigued and shaky. All the while the frigid air nipped my face and numbed my fingers. After what seemed like a very long walk punctuated with numerous pauses to catch my breath, I finally arrived at my sit spot under the black cherry tree.

Pushing the legs of my camp chair down into the snow, I sat down and wedged my boots deep into the snow, searching for extra insulation. I pulled out my notebook, grabbed a pencil in my gloved hand, and settled in to listen and look. It was 7:23. The sun had risen at 7:06, but it would be a few more minutes before it peeked over the hills and offered any warmth. The sky above was a high pale blue dome.

A white-breasted nuthatch whinnied. A blue jay cried a strident *jay, jay, jay*. Crows cawed. The soft *stip, stip, stip* companion calls of juncos sounded in the background. A male cardinal launched into his spring song, a series of resonant musical *cheer, cheer, cheer* tones. This peaceful morning chorus told me that once again, for the birds this was simply another day for foraging and feeding, for staking out a territory, for attracting a mate. The realization that the birds were unfazed by the deep cold made my shivering and suffering seem small and insignificant.

I glanced down at my notebook, at the page I was writing on, and saw that it was filled with marks, arrows, lines, and abbreviations denoting the presence, location, movement, songs, and calls of the birds. I looked back at several pages from last February, from the first weeks of my observations, and saw that the pages were mostly empty. I was sure that the same birds were calling and singing last year, but last year I didn't hear them or see them, and more importantly, didn't understand the story they were telling.

I reflected once again on the idea of fitting in. Last year it took thirty or forty minutes before I heard or saw birds. Now, I heard them right away. Had the birds grown accustomed to my weekly visits, concluded that I wasn't a threat, and decided to go about their normal business? Or had something inside me changed? Was I emitting a more peaceful, harmonious vibe? Had something in my posture, in my stride, in my mind, or in my heart evolved? Whatever the cause, I felt thankful to be accepted, to blend in, to be connected to nature, to hear, to see, and hopefully to understand.

The sun finally ascended above the hills, illuminated the tree tops, and spread steadily down the trunks, revealing a world of colors — brown and gray bark, bright white snow, vivid green pine boughs, and long stark blue-gray shadows. The highest tree branches, still covered by the hoar frost, sparkled and shimmered like diamonds in the sunlight with flashes of red and pink and blue and yellow. I took pictures, but the multihued icing on the branches didn't show up. Some moments of beauty simply can't be captured by a camera and must be committed to memory.

As the sunlight reached my back and shoulders, I tried to tell myself that I could feel the warmth, but in fact I felt cold. My toes stung, my fingers were numb, and my face felt frozen and brittle. My ears tingled with cold, but I was reluctant to pull my wool hat down as it would interfere with my hearing, my primary avenue for experiencing life at my sit spot. The minutes ticked by. A half-hour elapsed. I hoped I would be able to endure the full hour.

More birdsongs sounded through the morning air — the clear whistles of a tufted titmouse; the lilting flight song of goldfinches; the loud *kik-kik-kik-kik* of a pileated woodpecker; the steady drumming of a downy woodpecker, perhaps a male proclaiming his prowess, inviting females to visit his territory. The tree branches, stiff and frozen in the subzero cold, swayed and clacked in the wind.

A crow, jet black against the pale blue sky, landed at the top of a nearby tree, perched for a few minutes, then took off and flew away with crow-like flight, strong but irregular wingbeats. It flew purposefully toward the far shore, yet something in its flight suggested flexibility and adaptability, a readiness to dip down if an opportunity for food or exploration presented itself.

Two blue jays flew in and landed in a gray birch tree on the nearby little peninsula and began to sing a few rounds of a resonant *boick, boick;* an interval of quiet; then a high-pitched *cheeeek, cheeeek;* silence; a three noted *boy-de-dit, boy-de-dit;* more silence; and then a long imitation of a red-shouldered hawk, *kee-yer, kee-yer, kee-yer;* more silence; and a loud *jeer, jeer, jeer* chorus. Seemingly satisfied with their performance, the jays took off and winged silently across the lake. I was glad they had come by to entertain and distract me.

The morning chorus faded into stillness. The freezing air penetrated deeper and deeper into my being. I continued to sit motionless, listening and watching. I glanced at my watch and tracked the final thirty seconds as they ticked by. I had endured.

Week 52 · February 14

# Final Challenges

I chose Friday as the day for my final observation session and then kept a wary eye on the forecast. On Tuesday a big low pressure front formed along the Gulf Coast. The radar sweeps showed ominous, long fingers of precipitation reaching far out into the Gulf of Mexico, pulling in warm moist air and strengthening the system. By late Wednesday the rapidly moving front started its relentless track up the Atlantic coast. On Thursday afternoon the storm had exploded into a full blown Nor'easter that dumped nine inches of snow as it swirled over northeast Pennsylvania. When the snowfall stopped, I charged out to the garage, fired up my snow blower, blew the driveway clean, confident that I would be ready to go in the morning.

But when I woke up, eager to complete my yearlong commitment, a glance out the window told me I wouldn't be leaving any time soon. Overnight the big storm had spun out over the North Atlantic, pulled cold ocean air into its counterclockwise circulation, and dropped another six inches of wet, heavy snow on my driveway. Feeling frustrated, I got up, headed out to the garage, fired up the snow blower yet again, and in the dim predawn light guided it slowly up and down the driveway. The engine strained and whined to throw the heavy wet snow; the high decibel roar of the engine blitzed my sense of hearing. This was not the way to prepare for my last session of listening to nature!

Forty-five minutes later, I pulled onto the state highway, recently plowed, salted, and already showing streaks of gray pavement between furrows of gray-brown slush. However, when I turned onto the still unplowed county highway, I encountered deep, white, rutted snow. I immediately switched into winter driving mode, eased off the gas to hold traction uphill, carefully downshifted heading downhill, and held the steering wheel lightly while my foot barely touched the brake. All around me the houses, yards, and driveways were buried in snow. People were starting to dig out, some plowing with trucks, some spraying plumes with blowers, and some shoveling the old-fashioned way.

At Prompton the road to the boat ramp hadn't been plowed from either snowfall. I had no choice but to pull as far as possible onto the shoulder, park my car, load up my gear, and hope the car would be safe. I walked down the boat ramp road through the fresh snow to the West Shore Trail where I encountered an even greater walking challenge than last week. Fifteen inches of fresh snow lay on top of a foot or more of old snow. I took my first step onto the trail and saw that the snow reached up to my thigh. Once again I had to lift my boot high for each step, ram it down through the deep snow, feel for the ground, and grab onto branches to keep my balance. I labored forward for a hundred yards, heard my heart thumping wildly, felt myself gasping for air, and had to stop to catch my breath and let my shaky legs recover.

I should have worn snowshoes! Even after a year of weekly visits to the woods, a year of making thoughtful decisions about the right clothing and the right equipment, I hadn't evaluated today correctly, hadn't anticipated the challenge of the deep snow. I had made an error, the kind of error that can lead to accidents and injury. A lesson relearned — always think through possible equipment needs the night before; always reevaluate in the morning; and always remember that conditions in nature can be dangerous.

I trudged forward another hundred yards, paused, heard agitated calls of cardinals from thick shrubs by the shoreline — four or more birds *tik, tik, tik*-ing loudly, quickly, insistently. I wondered what was causing their agitation. Was a hawk on the hunt?

I continued my slog out to the peninsula and finally arrived at the big black cherry tree where I pushed my stool deep into the snow, sat down, settled my breath, and commenced the now familiar process of sitting still, opening up my senses, looking, listening, feeling, and sniffing. It was five after eight, an hour after sunrise, but the light was still dim, the cloud cover heavy, the existence of the sun only to be assumed. The temperature was twenty-five degrees, mild enough to write notes without wearing gloves. A light northerly breeze puffed across the empty lake.

On the little peninsula, deep quiet reigned, a cathedral-like quiet created by the sound-absorbing effect of the thick blanket of new snow. No cars buzzed along the highway, no jetliners whispered overhead, and surprisingly no birds sang. The silence was soothing yet disappointing as I had grown accustomed to hearing birds and had enjoyed listening to the spring birdsongs over the previous few weeks. Perhaps I had arrived too late and missed the morning chorus. Perhaps the snowfall created a survival challenge for the birds and left little energy for singing.

But soon the familiar and welcoming songs and calls began — a blue jay jeering; goldfinches flying over, dipping, rising, singing sweetly; crows cawing, other crows answering; and a second blue jay. It was another morning chorus proclaiming that all was well in the woods, that life went on. Then I heard a clear, descending two-toned whistle, *here, here, here*, a song I had heard last February. I searched through my memory and remembered that this was another spring song of a tufted titmouse; at least one bird was still thinking about spring.

Suddenly, strong gusts blew across the lake, kicking up swirls of snow, creating miniature white funnel clouds that raced over an empty white surface. The wind peeled the fresh snow from the long limbs of big pine trees, and I watched the plumes of snow drift down to the ground. The gusts whipped through tree branches, swaying, then wildly, creating the familiar clacking and cracking chorus of frozen wood. The wind wafted the scent of pine needles to my nose. The wind, I realized, had become my good friend during the year, a friend that informed, entertained, even enchanted. As suddenly as it arose, the wind abated and quiet returned.

The silence was broken a few minutes later by the loud calls of a common raven — deep, throaty, gurgling croaks, richer and deeper than a crow's caws. A minute later another raven answered with a series of *cuk, cuk, cuk* calls followed by a series of resonant *cr-r-uck, cr-r-uck, cr-r-uck* calls. This was the third week

I had heard ravens. If my one hour of observation out of the 168 hours in a week represented the data collection procedure known as time sampling, then ravens must be more prevalent in the area than I had imagined.

Ravens have expanded south from their home in the forests of Alaska, Canada and the northern US. They are adapting to human habitation, spreading into urban areas, and moving into the regenerating forests of the Northeast. Bigger, longer, and narrower than crows, they are strong, smooth, even acrobatic flyers. Intelligent and opportunistic, they follow humans to track down food scraps. In winter they travel alone, in pairs, or small groups. In spring they employ teamwork to rob nests; one raven distracts the parents while the other swoops in to snatch an egg or chick. They have even been known to lurk in a tree above a birthing ewe and then pounce on the newborn lamb.

Many years ago I learned to recognize the calls of ravens in the north woods of Wisconsin and had always associated their calls with deep wilderness. I listened now to their deep, wild calls as they flew above the far shore, searching for food in the snowy woods. Somehow, it felt right to hear ravens on this day of deep snow. Gradually their guttural, primal calls faded into the distance. Another interval of quiet, and then, once again, blue jays, goldfinches, and crows began to call, joined by a downy woodpecker's sharp descending whinny.

I glanced at my watch and noted the last minute of the day's observation, the last minute of the year's commitment ticked by. I stood up slowly, feeling deeply satisfied to have completed the year, but also sad to end my adventure, sad to leave behind what had turned out to be the best hour of the week. I took pictures of the snow-covered lake, of my camp chair stuck deep in the snow, of the various views from my sit spot.

On the way back I tried to step in my previous foot prints to ease the effort. Looking down at my boot prints, I thought of all the times over the last year I had walked along the West Shore Trail. For a moment I felt the "vibes" of my many journeys along this path, all the sensory impressions from the seasons, all the myriad feelings of expectation, curiosity, and discovery.

Glancing up I saw the clouds beginning to break apart; patches of bright blue sky appeared. Beams of sunlight burst through and illuminated the white snow, spotlighted the red twig dogwood, highlighted the drooping gray birch branches.

A blue jay flew in and perched in a tree near the trail, called out a friendly *jay, jay, jay*, fluttered ahead, sounded different calls, and seemed to be accompanying me. A pair of downy woodpeckers landed above me, scrambled up the tree, paused, and seemed to tap the trunk in a beat to accompany my march through the snow. Cardinals appeared around me and called soft rhythmic *tiks* as if they were asking me to join their flock. A chickadee fluttered in, perched on a thin branch three feet away, gazed at me with its shiny black eyes, squeaked, gurgled, and sang *chick-a-dee-dee-dee, chick-a-dee-dee-dee*, a song that for a moment sounded like *don't leave, don't leave, you must come back, you must come back*.

I laughed. Of course chickadees can't talk. But then, I thought, maybe they can communicate. I smiled, looked down, found my footprints in the snow, continued my walk back to the car, and thought, "Yes, I would come back."

# Epilogue

Commitment fulfilled — one year, fifty-two hours of nature observation in six states and on two continents. How did I change? What did I learn? And was any learning that occurred due to my efforts or due to the inherent transformational potential of nature? Were my experiences solely personal, or was there some wider relevance and resonance, some universal applicability to the health, well-being, and development of all. And finally, were there any elements in my experiences that might inspire and guide others?

Reflecting back on the year, the most dramatic changes occurred with my senses. Simply stated, I now see, hear, feel, and smell much more. The hours spent gazing at forests, fields, flora and fauna; hearing the sounds of wind, water, and birdsong; feeling the sensations of temperature and humidity on my skin; and inhaling the fragrances of nature forever changed how I experience the world around me. This heightened sensory acuity now purrs along in the background of my consciousness and often breaks through in surprising and spontaneous ways. Part of my mind is always registering sensory input, always reading the state of my surroundings, and always longing for the solitude, harmony, and nature connection of the sit spot experience.

I developed the ability to truly see colors — the various browns and grays of earth, rocks, trees, and decaying leaves. I came to discern the full spectrum of green — the yellow minty greens of spring, the rich greens of summer, the dark green of pine boughs, the pale green of ferns. I observed the plumage of the birds — the orange and red and yellow and black and white woven into myriad patterns from simple to kaleidoscope. And there were the views of the water, the color moods of Prompton Lake — deep blue, light blue, green-blue, and gray-blue, shifting and shimmering, placid and wavy, changing from day to day, hour to hour, minute to minute.

Arriving at my sit spot before daybreak, I watched the last darkness of night turn to the first light of day and saw the colors of sunrise — twisting, twining strands and streaks of yellow, pink, purple, red, and blue. Sometimes the colors were muted and fleeting, sometimes brilliant and spectacular. Yet every morning nature staged a celebratory light and color show, a spectacle I now seek and appreciate, a show repeated every sunset.

Scanning the trees and bushes to spot birds and mammals, I learned to look assiduously and persistently, to notice the slightest movement of leaves, to spot the briefest flutter of wings, to glimpse the shortest flash of color. My peripheral vision improved. Sometimes I'd know when and where to look, as if I had developed some a kind of anticipatory vision.

Sitting still allowed me to become more aware of tactile sensations — the touch of the wind against my face, the warm soft breezes of summer, the crisp invigorating gusts of fall, the cold biting winds of winter. I learned to feel the humidity — the dry air of a Canadian high, the moist atmosphere of a low pressure front flowing up from the Gulf of Mexico.

I came to recognize and appreciate the smells and fragrances of nature — the watery-weedy lake, the sun-warmed earth, the decomposing leaves, the sweet ferns, the fragrant Russian olive blossoms, and even the pungent smell of combusted gasoline — smells that came to be a key for understanding each hour's experience. Now, when I step outside, I unconsciously pause to sniff the air and register the background smells.

The most profound changes came with my hearing. Sitting on the little peninsula surrounded by the vision-limiting dense canopy of leaves, I soon discovered that hearing was my most valuable sense. It provided me with information from near and far, from concentric circles of sound. Up close I heard insects buzzing and whining around my face. Nearby the waves softly and rhythmically lapped the shoreline. Overhead and all around the birds sang and called, leaves whispered and whooshed, and branches rattled. Further out on the circles of sound I heard crows cawing down the shoreline, blue jays calling from deep in the woods, motor boats puttering down the lake, voices carrying across the water. Far in the distance, I could discern dogs barking, trucks rumbling over pavement, a cow mooing, a gunshot. And five miles above me jetliners whispered through the sky. I instantly noticed any novel sounds — the crunch of deer hooves on leaves and twigs, the rustling of squirrels through leafy litter, the cracks and crunches of shifting ice.

In line with Jon Young's explanation, I learned to recognize the different types of bird vocalizations — the territorial songs of spring, the sweet synchrony of companion calls, the strident and urgent alarm calls. I committed a number of new songs and calls to memory, and gradually they became as familiar to me as the voices of family and friends. Most remarkably, I learned how bird language communicates the condition of the woods, telling me all was safe or informing me that there were dangers or disruptions present, a hawk on patrol, or a hiker striding through the woods.

Over the course of the year, I became increasingly sensitive to anything that affected my hearing. The wind was crucial — carrying sounds from upwind, obscuring sounds from downwind. When the wind blew strong, my circle of sound contracted. I noticed, sometimes with irritation, how man-made sounds drowned out the sounds of nature. I felt the disruption caused by the whining of tires on asphalt, the roaring of an ice auger, or the buzzing of a chain saw.

Gradually, over the months, fundamental changes occurred with my hearing and permanently sensitized me to always monitor the sounds around. If I step outside, even for mundane tasks like taking out the garbage or getting the mail, my hearing does an immediate 360-degree scan. I pick up on the songs and calls of birds in my yard, the familiar ones — cardinals, robins, and house sparrows — and the less common ones — a Carolina wren or a visiting warbler. Most importantly and enjoyably, I register, resonate with, and respond to the state of the environment around me.

Enhanced sensory awareness opened the door to new learning.

Every week I encountered some previously unknown bird, animal, plant, or tree that demanded careful inspection, descriptive notes, rough sketches, and multiple photographs. Once home, I would begin the research process, pouring through guide books and conducting online searches. Through this process I learned, for example, the full story of the late- and brief-blooming bottle gentian, the coy courting behaviors of cedar waxwings, the mysterious life of the winter wren, and the mutually beneficial seed-spreading behaviors of the gray squirrel.

I learned to see meaningful patterns in nature — formations of ferns, patches of wildflowers, colonies of bushes, and stands of trees. I began to perceive distinct niches of nature formed from unique combinations of earth, plants, trees, and water — niches that interface and blend; niches that offer sustenance, support and shelter; and niches that are, with unerring precision, found by the insects, birds and animals that can prosper there.

A surprise came with this learning process. I had pictured myself as an intrepid amateur naturalist who, armed with binoculars, magnifying glass, and guidebooks, would sleuth out hidden facts; a nature detective who through effort and intellect would pry loose the esoteric secrets of nature. In fact, it slowly dawned on me during the year that nature was a better equipped and more determined teacher than I was a student. Every time I went to my sit spot it seemed as if nature showed me something new, taught me something previously unknown, revealed hidden patterns and processes. My tiny offering of an hour of time and a portion of my attention was richly rewarded with instruction.

I learned about the skunk cabbage piercing the frozen ground, the early arriving woodcock crouched in the snow, the uncountable red maple flowers falling to the forest floor, and the parade of wildflowers blooming in sequence through spring, summer, and fall.

At first I thought it was all coincidence; I was simply fortunate to be in the right place at the right time. But then, each week, as something new was revealed, I began to realize that nature is the most open, the most generous teacher, a teacher waiting for a learner who takes the time to sit and stay present, persistent, and patient.

The weekly learning seemed to set the stage for flashes of insight.

For example, I understood intellectually the concept of the seasons, the progression of the months of the year, the idea that each animal and each plant has its own unique timetable. But by returning to the same spot each week, I began to grasp a more nuanced and vivid understanding of seasons within seasons within seasons. I saw the woodland wildflowers bloom and bolt before the branches above them leafed out. I heard and glimpsed the warblers flood in during late April and early May, some pausing before flying further north, others claiming a small plot of territory to nest and raise chicks, all of the journeying timed to take full advantage of the explosion of insect life. And then as quickly as they arrived, the warblers and other migrant birds stopped singing, disbursed into the forest, and soon were preparing for their return to the tropics, always on a timetable.

Nature's relentless adaptability revealed itself. After the surprise deluge of late June flooded the lake and jammed mats of debris against the shoreline, an ovenbird immediately ventured out onto the debris to hunt for food, quick to take advantage of this new dining opportunity. I saw the goldenrod growing and blooming and young saplings sprouting in the few open spots in the woods, reaching out into the patches of sunlight just as the tree branches above stretched into the same gaps between trees. And the family of catbirds that lived on the peninsula lingered surprisingly late into fall, perhaps taking advantage of milder temperatures due to climate change.

I came to understand interdependence. In spring I witnessed the emerging hordes of insects and caterpillars that feed on the abundance of leaves and at the same time nourish the flocks of migratory birds whose prolific nestlings in turn feed the hungry nest robbers — crows and blue jays — that in turn are hunted by the hawks and owls. Sitting in the midst of this interplay of interdependence, it seemed that giving from abundance is the nature of nature, the bond that binds all living beings.

As the weeks went by and the hours of observation accumulated, I became more decisive. For example, I initially had difficulty choosing a sit spot. I would walk onto the peninsula, using a linear, logical, and analytic approach, but find my mind flooded with conflicting ideas and thoughts and end up in a state of mental paralysis. This indecision was even more pronounced when I traveled and had to find a spot in a new locale.

I made mistakes. Once I sat in a hollow where I couldn't see the lake. Another time I tried so hard to hide myself from nearby ice fishermen that my field of sight was restricted. Once I chose a mountain meadow — lovely to look at, but empty of bird life.

Along with these failures were successes. At Prompton I found my way to a spot under a black cherry tree where I had a full view of the woods and the lake, a location that became my "home sit spot." In Colorado I sat on the ground under a Ponderosa pine with a view down into a thickly vegetated creek bed and across an open meadow. In Germany I found a spot with a view of a coastal moor to one side, a tidal mud flat to the other, and a patch of thick forest behind me — ideal terrain for viewing wildlife diversity.

With these successes something shifted. Choosing a spot grew easier. I could quickly analyze terrain, see where environments intersected, and immediately locate the places that naturally attracted the greatest abundance and variety of wild life. I began to sense when a spot felt right — right for the weather, right for the time of day. Now when I walk in a park or hike on a trail, some part of my mind scans for and recognizes good sit spots, and there I stand for a minute to observe and enjoy nature.

This decisiveness — a blend of analysis and intuition — felt quicker and more thorough than my previous thinking and seemed to spread to other realms of life. Decisions regarding money, work, social interactions, and leadership came easier as I was able to size up a situation, see the best course of action, and move forward.

I observed instinct in the animals around me and, in turn, felt like I became more instinctive, quicker, and more primal in my responses. When the shadow of a crow coursed across the ground, I flinched and was immediately alert. When the ice shifted, producing loud crunches, I became instantly vigilant. And on cold dark mornings when the sun would finally lift above the hills along the eastern shore of Prompton Lake, I welcomed the warming rays with the same feelings of relief, gratitude, and renewed hope as did my ancestors, the hunters who waited for daylight on the plains of Africa and in the forests of Europe. This elemental alertness to both danger and safety has stayed with me, like an app running in the background, enlivening and sharpening my experience of life.

Intuition, an invaluable self-protection process, emerged on the day of my encounter with the big black bear. After this incident, which taught me the importance of listening to the voice of intuition, there were more instances of guidance from within. I remember following a hunch and moving over to the adjacent little peninsula where I discovered the beautiful world of the gray birch trees and the finches, juncos, and chickadees that feed on them. Other times I would hear an unfamiliar birdsong and have an immediate idea as to its identity. Sometimes, for no conscious or known reason, I would suddenly turn and look, and a bird would fly into sight, almost as if I had anticipated its arrival.

Most remarkably, I learned to open my mind for a word to capture the mood of the day. Often the word that emerged was surprising and made no logical sense; yet later its meaning would be revealed. Upon reflection, I don't think I acquired intuition; I believe I became still enough to hear its voice, detached enough to let go of normal preoccupations, and open enough to follow its guidance.

Perhaps the greatest gift gained during my year at Prompton was a deeper connection to nature. I recall driving to Prompton for my first observation, worried I would be bored, imagining that I would feel lonely. The boredom never occurred; the loneliness faded away. My very first one-hour sit spot session, one I had prepared for by bringing a book for something to do, was, to my surprise, filled with sensory impressions, birds on the move, a chorus of nature sounds, and the ever-shifting sensations of wind and sunlight. At the end of the first hour, I wrote in my notebook, "Time flew by!" Each subsequent observation provided more moments of interest, more episodes of learning, and more surprising secrets of nature. My hour at Prompton became the most interesting and most satisfying hour of my week.

There was no room for loneliness. I felt relaxed, comfortable, and safe during my sessions of solitary sitting. I felt surrounded by newly found friends — the birds that lived on and visited the peninsula; the animals that revealed their presence; the wildflowers and trees that showed me their life cycle; the never-ending variety of wind and weather; elements of nature that felt like close, supportive, affirming, teaching, sharing friends. In time I came to feel more alone when surrounded by people who engaged in too much talking and too many senseless activities. I began to long for the company of nature, a longing that continues and is now fulfilled when I take time — even a few minutes, even in my backyard or a city park — to sit quietly, watch, listen, feel, and enjoy my surroundings.

During the first weeks and months of my project, I struggled with the yearlong commitment. The self-imposed weekly obligation weighed on my shoulders like a backpack full of rocks. I struggled to find a free day each week, and then when that day arrived, I couldn't get out the door until late morning. But strangely, almost effortlessly, as the weeks and months proceeded, this all changed. My commitment, perhaps rewarded by the deep enjoyment of each hour in the woods, took on a life and a will of its own. A positive routine developed. I would return from my hour of observation, pore over and annotate my field notes, conduct research on new things seen, reflect on the essence and meaning of the hour, write up my experiences, and then begin to eagerly anticipate my next session. Over the course of the year I found myself spontaneously waking up before first light, leaving before sunrise, and lingering in the woods at the end of my hour.

All of this made me wonder if there might be something inherently developmental, something intrinsically transformational about nature observation, something enhanced by returning to the same spot every week, actively and openly focusing my senses, and then recording, reviewing, and reflecting upon my observations. Perhaps these are the fundamental steps in a most natural learning process. Maybe our brains, minds, and hearts are designed to learn directly through the senses and in the world of nature. By tapping into this process, I found the energy and strength to fulfill my commitment.

My year at Prompton Lake was an extraordinary year for me, a transformational year, a year of change that continues to unfold. I am profoundly grateful for this experience. And as the first humans who gathered around nighttime fires seem to have discovered, the best experiences are made richer and deeper through sharing. The opportunity to describe my year of adventures in these pages has deepened and illuminated my understanding of the natural world, of myself, and of the processes of learning and growing. It is my hope that a few of the words in this book might inspire readers to seek out their own unique and comfortable experiences in nature. Thankfully, the opportunity to engage in nature observation is available to everyone, in every setting, during every stage of life.

# Selected Bibliography

Carson, Rachel. *Under the Sea-Wind: A Naturalist's Picture of Ocean Life*. New York: Simon and Schuster, 1941.

Carson, Rachel. The Silent Spring. Boston: Mariner Books, HoughtonMifflin Harcourt, 1962.

Collins, Billy, ed. *Bright Wings: An Illustrated Anthology of Poems about Birds*. New York: Columbia University Press, 2017.

Haskell, David G. *The Forest Unseen: A Year's Watch in Nature*. New York: Penguin, 2012.

Macfarlane, Robert. *The Old Ways: A Journey on Foot*. New York: Penguin, 2012.

Macfarlane, Robert. *The Wild Places*. New York: Penguin, 2008.

Maclear, Kyo. *Birds Art Life: A Year of Observation*. New York: Scribner, 2017.

Young, Jon. *What the Robin Knows*. New York: Houghton Mifflin Harcourt, 2012.

Williams, Florence. *The Nature Fix: Why Nature Makes Us Happier, Healthier and More Creative*. New York: Norton, 2017.

Wulf, Andrea. *The Invention of Nature: Alexander Humboldt's New World*. New York: Vintage, 2017.

# Author's Notes

### Prologue
The inspiration to set aside an hour a week to sit in the woods and observe nature came from my reading of Jon Young's *What the Robin Knows* (New York: Houghton Mifflin Harcourt, 2012).

### Week 1 · Obstacles and Discoveries
In Chapter 4 of *What the Robin Knows*, entitled "The Sit Spot," Jon Young describes how to select and conduct a sit spot. I followed many of his guidelines and made some modifications that worked for me.

### Week 2 · A Stiff Breeze from the Northwest
A great source of information about the birds I saw during my year is the Cornell Lab of Ornithology's website *All about Birds* (www.allaboutbirds.org).

### Week 3 · Wind and Snow
Information on Prompton Dam and Prompton State Park can be found online. Here is one article that touches on its history and present: www.wayneindependent.com/article/20150519/NEWS/150519768.

### Week 5 · Pictures at an Exhibition
I found good information about Modest Mussorgsky's *Pictures at an Exhibition* at en.wikipedia.org/wiki/Modest_Mussorgsky.

### Week 6 · A Constant Chorus
Jon Young (*What the Robin Knows*) notes on page 68 that sunrise is a special time to observe nature. Over the course of the year I found this to be very true.

### Week 8 · Changes
I often found a need and felt a strong desire to learn more about what I had seen and heard during my hour of sitting. Usually I

was able to quickly find relevant information online. Here are a few of my sources on the trout lily and peeper:
(1) wildwoodsurvival.com/survival/food/edibleplants/troutlily;
(2) en.wikipedia.org/wiki/Erythronium_americanum;
(3) en.wikipedia.org/wiki/Spring_peeper; and
(4) animals.nationalgeographic.com/animals/amphibians/spring-peeper.

## Week 9 · Red Maple Flowers

I loved learning more about this common tree at:
(1) www.arborday.org/trees/treeguide/treedetail.cfm?itemID=867; and
(2) en.wikipedia.org/wiki/Acer_rubrum.

## Week 10 · Skunk Cabbage

The information I discovered about Craig Holdrege and the Goethean or whole nature approach opened my eyes to a different way of viewing the natural world, an approach that looks at dynamic living systems. Here are a few references:
(1) natureinstitute.org/pub/ic/ic4/skunkcabbage.htm;
(2) "Seeing Nature Whole — A Goethean Approach" at natureinstitute.org/nature; and
(3) "About Craig Holdrege" at natureinstitute.org/about/staff/choldrege.htm.

## Week 11 · New Arrivals

The bird guide I used in the field was David Allen Sibley's *The Sibley Field Guide to Birds of Eastern North America* (New York: Knopf, 2003). Another excellent guide is Roger Torey Peterson's *Field Guide to Birds of Eastern and Central North America* (New York: Houghton-Mifflin-Harcourt, 2010). I subsequently discovered two very useful smartphone apps that help with field identification of birds: Merlin Bird ID and iBird PRO.

## Week 13 · Am Finkenmoor, In der Duhner Heide

Information about this area of Germany can be found at these sites:
(1) "Wernerwald" at www.cuxhaven.de/staticsite/staticsite.php?menuid=114&topmenu=13;

(2) "Wernerwald" at de.wikipedia.org/wiki/Wernerwald;
(3) "Wadden Sea"at www.waddensea-worldheritage.org; and
(4) "Wadden Sea" at en.wikipedia.org/wiki/Wadden_Sea.

Jon Young (*What the Robin Knows*) describes the "bird plow" effect on pages 119–121 of his book My understanding was solidified when I saw it occur right in front of me, reinforcing the importance of experiential learning.

### Week 16 · The Colorado Hummingbird
This was another time when the *All About Birds* website (www. allaboutbirds.org) provided an abundance of information on a bird I had never seen before.

### Week 20 · Easy Living
Audio guides are a great way to learn bird songs and calls. I found the following guide to be an excellent resource, and I continue to listen to it: Richard K. Walton and Robert W. Lawson, *Birding By Ear: Eastern and Central North America (Peterson Field Guides)*. Audio CD. (New York: HoughtonMifflin Harcourt, 1999). There is also a second CD entitled *More Birding by Ear*.

### Week 22 · Cherokee Marsh
Information on Cherokee Marsh can be found at the following sites:
(1) dnr.wi.gov/topic/Lands/naturalareas/index.asp?SNA=130, made available by the state of Wisconsin; and
(2) cherokeemarsh.org, maintained by the Friends of Cherokee Marsh.

### Week 23 · Wild Cherries
I enjoyed learning about wild cherries at these two websites:
(1) en.wikipedia.org/wiki/Prunus_virginiana; and
(2) plants.usda.gov/factsheet/pdf/fs_prvi.pdf.

### Week 24 · Calm and Still
During my year of sitting I would often run across books that described projects similar to or related to mine. David Haskell's

*The Forest Unseen* (New York: Penguin Books, 2013) was one of my favorites and taught me to look much more closely at the square yard around me.

### Week 26 · Affinity
An excellent explanation of synchronicity can be found on page 211 of Carl Jung's classic book on depth psychology, *Man and His Symbols* (New York: Doubleday, 1964).

### Week 28 · Forest Friends
Although I often see gray squirrels, chipmunks, and red squirrels, studying them in action in the forest and reading about the life history of each helped me to better understand and appreciate these mammals. Here are a few useful resources:
(1) en.wikipedia.org/wiki/Chipmunk;
(2) en.wikipedia.org/wiki/Eastern_gray_squirrel; and
(3) en.wikipedia.org/wiki/American_red_squirrel.

### Week 29 · Bottle Blue
At the end of August and during the first week of September, I keep my eyes open for another view of the beautiful and unique blue gentian. The following websites offer more information on this flower:
(1) en.wikipedia.org/wiki/Gentiana_andrewsii; and
(2) www.wildflower.org/plants/result.php?id_plant=GEAN.

### Week 31 · Lunacy
These are a few of the sources I examined on the controversial topic of the effects of the full moon:
(1) www.accuweather.com/en/weather-news/do-full-moons-and-supermoons-really-affect-human-animal-behavior/61402994;
(2) www.ncbi.nlm.nih.gov/pubmed/16407788;
(3) en.wikipedia.org/wiki/Lunar_effect; and
(4) www.health.com/mind-body.

### Week 32 · September Surprise
Mockingbirds and their amazing mimicry abilities are so fascinating that I just had to read more. Here is a helpful resource: en.wikipedia.org/wiki/Northern_mockingbird.

## Week 33 · Cornucopia

The fall warbler migration is both an amazing feat and an exciting identification challenge for serious birders. The following website gives a hint about the complexities of fall warblers: www.migrationresearch.org/mbo/id/fall_warblers.html. Tom Stephenson and Scott Whittle wrote the best book available on warblers, *The Warbler Guide* (Princeton, NJ: Princeton University Press, 2013).

## Week 36 · Gleaning

Here is a source for interesting information on gleaning: en.wikipedia.org/wiki/Gleaning_(birds).

## Week 37 · The Rachel Carson Reserve

This is one of my favorite places on the planet, and Ms. Carson is a constant source of inspiration. Here is a resource on the reserve: www.beaufort-nc.com/rachel-carson-reserve.html. Also in this chapter, I referenced Linda Lear's moving biography of Rachel Carson, *Rachel Carson: Witness for Nature* (Boston: Mariner Books HoughtonMifflin Harcourt, 2009).

## Week 38 · Gang Blue Jay

Here is a short introduction to the language of blue jays: www.birdwatching.com/tips/jaytalk.html. The Lang Elliott recording of *Blue Jay Magic Bells* was no longer online when this book was completed. The interested reader might check his website, musicofnature.com, to see if he has reposted it. While there listen to some of his other terrific nature recordings.

## Week 39 · Gray Birch Trees

Gray birch trees are not mentioned in many poems, but I have come to see them as lovely, adaptable, and dynamic in their environmental niche. Here are two informative sites: (1) en.wikipedia.org/wiki/Betula_populifolia; and (2) macphailwoods.org/nature-guides/trees/grey-birch.

## Week 41 · The Brush Pile

The Nyquist-Harcourt Wildlife Sanctuary is a beautiful natural area nestled right against the Wallkill River in New Paltz, New York. This site provides useful information: www.nyquistfdtn.org/nyquist-harcourt-wildlife.html.

## Week 43 · Companion Calls

I have learned to appreciate and enjoy the companion or contact calls of birds as much as their songs. Jon Young's *What the Robin Knows* is an excellent source for more information, as are the following websites:
(1) en.wikipedia.org/wiki/Contact_call; and
(2) academy.allaboutbirds.org/the-language-of-birds.

## Week 44 · The Cave Dweller

Seeing a winter wren in the midst of winter scenery is one of my favorite memories from the year. Here is more information on this remarkable little bird:
(1) www.allaboutbirds.org/guide/Winter_Wren/lifehistory; and
(2) thewebsiteofeverything.com/animals/birds/Passeriformes/ Troglodytidae/Troglodytes-troglodytes.

## Week 47 · Light Snow

Weather events had a significant effect on my sitting sessions. Being out in the midst of a snow squall is a powerful experience. These sites describe events known as the Alberta Clipper and Lake Effect Snow:
(1) en.wikipedia.org/wiki/Alberta_clipper; and
(2) en.wikipedia.org/wiki/Lake-effect_snow

## Week 48 · The Bird Whisperer

Hearing the first bird songs of spring on a cold winter day is unforgettable. Here are two hard science sources on a heart-softening experience:
(1) channels.isp.netscape.com/whatsnew/package.jsp?name=fte/ birdssing/birdssing; and
(2) www.independent.co.uk/environment/nature/light-fantastic-why-birds-burst-into-song-at-dawn-as-spring-arrives-798380.html.

## Week 49 · The Roost

Crows are possibly the most misunderstood and under-appreciated birds in the forest. Here are some sources of truth about crows.
(1) www.allaboutbirds.org/guide/American_Crow/lifehistory;
(2) www.pbs.org/wnet/nature/a-murder-of-crows-crow-facts/5965; and
(3) corvidresearch.blog/faqs-about-crows.

## Week 51 · Endurance

Hoar frost can turn the woods into a panorama of sparkling ice diamonds. Here are some sources of information on this weather phenomenon:
(1) www.weatheronline.co.uk/reports/wxfacts/Hoar-Frost.htm;
(2) en.wikipedia.org/wiki/Frost; and
(3) weather.com/science/weather-explainers/news/hoarfrost-explained.

## Week 52 · Final Challenges

The calls and presence of ravens became an integral part of my winter experience. Information on this fascinating and hardy bird can be found at the *All About Birds* website:
www.allaboutbirds.org/guide/Common_Raven/lifehistory.

# About the Author

John R. Harvey, Ph.D. is a naturalist and consulting psychologist who resides in the Pocono Mountains of northeast Pennsylvania. John grew up in rural Wisconsin where, with the encouragement and example of his parents, he developed a lifelong interest in the outdoors, conservation, and understanding the natural world.

As a psychologist Harvey works with children and adults with developmental and acquired challenges of learning and memory. He has an abiding interest in relaxation training, stress management, and personal development. He is the author of *Total Relaxation: Healing Practices for Body, Mind and Spirit*; *Deep Sleep: Complete Rest for Health, Longevity and Vitality*; and a contributing editor for *The Quiet Mind: Techniques for Transforming Stress*.

Obtaining his doctorate from the University of Wisconsin-Madison, Harvey served for many years as Director of Psychology at Allied Services in Scranton, Pennsylvania, and was an adjunct faculty member at the University of Scranton. His years of experience as a clinical psychologist help him to appreciate the healing potential of a nature connection.

Keep up with John's latest sit spot adventures at www.foreststillness.com.

# SHANTI ARTS
## nature · art · spirit

Please visit us on online

to browse our entire book catalog,

including additional poetry collections and fiction,

books on travel, nature, healing, art,

photography, and more.

www.shantiarts.com

CPSIA information can be obtained
at www.ICGtesting.com
Printed in the USA
BVHW092023101121
621196BV00003B/70

9 781947 067592